Beyond the Biological Limits

Today I speak to some 15,000 people a year, and I find a universal, unsung lament that summarizes most people's lives: "Something was supposed to happen but it didn't." We read the psychological studies concerning the post-coital blues, depression following intercourse, and post-partum blues following childbirth, where as usual, something was supposed to happen but didn't. There are no studies of the post-adolescent blues because this ailment is generally our permanent state and accepted as our natural human condition.

Ten years ago, through working on my book *Magical Child*, I found a portion, at least, of what was supposed to happen as a child but had not . . . *Magical Child* hinted at the great power inherent in our beings. What I have learned since the writing of that book is that such power is a post-biological affair; the development of these powers beings after we have completed our physical maturation.

—FROM THE INTRODUCTION OF *MMAGICAL CHILD MATURES*

"Continually fascinating, highly readable and refreshingly positive . . . I felt a bit luckier to be a human being after reading his book."
—Allison McCracken, *Rochester Post Bulletin*

BANTAM NEW AGE BOOKS

This important imprint includes books in a variety of fields and disciplines and deals with the search for meaning, growth and change. They are books that circumscribe our times and our future.

Ask your bookseller for the books you have missed.

MAGICAL CHILD MATURES

Joseph Chilton Pearce

BANTAM BOOKS

TORONTO · NEW YORK · LONDON · SYDNEY · AUCKLAND

For Chidvilasananda—
teacher, model, guide, and friend

This low-priced Bantam Book
has been completely reset in a type face
designed for easy reading, and was printed
from new plates. It contains the complete
text of the original hard-cover edition.
NOT ONE WORD HAS BEEN OMITTED.

MAGICAL CHILD MATURES

A Bantam Book / published by arrangement with
E.P. Dutton

PRINTING HISTORY
E.P. Dutton edition published June 1985
Bantam edition / August 1986

Bantam Books are published by Bantam Books, Inc. Its trademark, consisting
of the words "Bantam Books" and the portrayal of a rooster, is Registered in
U.S. Patent and Trademark Office and in other countries. Marca Registrada.
Bantam Books, Inc., 666 Fifth Avenue, New York, New York 10103.

PRINTED IN THE UNITED STATES OF AMERICA

O   0 9 8 7 6 5 4 3 2 1

If I could only live at the pitch that is near madness
When everything is as it was in my childhood
Violent, vivid, and of infinite possibility:
That the sun and moon broke over my head.

Then I cast time out of the trees and fields,
Then I stood immaculate in the Ego;
Then I eyed the world with all delight,
Reality was the perfection of my sight.

And time has big handles on the hands,
Fields and trees a way of being themselves.
I saw battalions of the race of mankind
Standing stolid, demanding a moral answer.

I gave the moral answer and I died
And into a realm of complexity came
Where nothing is possible but necessity
And the truth wailing there like a red babe.

RICHARD EBERHART
Collected Poems 1930–1976
New York, Oxford University Press, 1976

Contents

Acknowledgments

Thanks to Marilyn Ferguson's *Brain/Mind Bulletin* for its endless flow of information. Thanks to the many people who have sent research papers in response to my lectures and workshops. Thanks to Minas Kafatos for his criticism and help with the section on physics. Thanks to Laurence Becker for his interest and for sending me the poem by Richard Eberhart, and to Oxford University Press for permission to use that poem here. Thanks to Bill Whitehead for his enormous help in editing this manuscript. Thanks to copy editor Raymond Van Over for his helpful suggestions. My greatest thanks to my meditation teacher, to whom I have dedicated this book, and to the worldwide Siddha Yoga foundation for all the kindness extended me. For interested readers, the U.S. address for this organization, devoted to teaching meditation, is:

The Siddha Yoga Foundation
P. O. Box 600
South Fallsburg, New York 12779
914/434-2000

Introduction

In the summer of my sixth year a great expectation arose within me; something overwhelming was pending. I was up each morning at dawn, rushed to the top of Dorchester Hill, a treeless knoll of grass and boulders, to await the sun, my heart pounding. A kind of numinous expectancy loomed everywhere about and within me. A precise shift of brain function was afoot; my biological system was preparing to shift my awareness from the pre-logical operations of the child to the operational logic of later childhood, and an awesome new dimension of life was ready to unfold. Instead, I was put in school that fall. (There was no kindergarten in my day and we went straight into first grade if we turned seven with the first semester.) All year I sat at that desk, stunned, wondering at such a fate, thinking over and over: Something was supposed to happen, and it wasn't this.

A similar sequence unfolded in my fourteenth year. A huge expectancy arose, more poignant and powerful than the earlier force. This was localized within my chest and what Thomas Wolfe spoke of as the "grape bursting in the throat." Again I was engulfed in the momentous feeling that something universal and awesome was pending. Puberty had unfolded at the same time, of course, and I found on every hand that this explosive longing of the heart was attributed to sexuality. Sex certainly exploded at that time, too, but it was not at all the same as that affair of the heart. This grape bursting in the throat was far more persistent than the earlier expectancy at age seven, but, as it turned out, not as persistent as sexuality. By my early twenties whatever was supposed to have happened long since had not, the feeling of expectancy slowly waned, and I was left with a sense of loss and despondency that sexual exploration did nothing to abate. The issue within had not been misplaced libido.

Today I speak to some 15,000 people a year, giving workshops and lectures, and I find a universal, unsung lament that summarizes most people's lives: "Something was supposed to happen but it didn't." We read the psychological studies concerning post-coital blues, depression following intercourse, and post-partum blues following childbirth, where as usual, something was supposed to happen but didn't. There are no studies of the post-adolescent blues because this ailment is generally our permanent state and accepted as our natural human condition.

Ten years ago, through working on my book *Magical Child*, I found a portion, at least, of what was supposed to happen as a child but had not. I felt relief, as long years of searching seemed to move toward culmination; outrage, for I found that we were vastly more than the behavioristic ideologists had taught us to believe about ourselves; and a renewed sense of expectancy, as though new chapters lay in store for my own life. As I was finishing the work, I had an encounter with a spiritual teacher, which I later described in my book *The Bond of Power*, and underwent such a dramatic, shaking experience that I felt impelled to withdraw from the world of book-writing and lecturing; disappeared, in effect, and left no address. Something enormous *had* happened, more seemed pending, and my whole life centered on getting to the core of this event. After three years of this retreat and search, I fell fully into what I now call the post-biological stage of development, that which should have happened, or been initiated, in adolescence. A lifetime of bewildering questions began to be answered (though a new set arose) and I began to understand the self-pitying despondency of our early twenties, when we sense the gross shortchange of our lives and begin that incessant casting about to lay blame anywhere and everywhere. I understood why at about age twenty, even as I attempted to cover my sense of loss by knuckling down to play the game, get those degrees and credit cards, and take my place in the machine, such deep anger festered within me. Something was supposed to happen, and my sense of outrage was justifiable, for, as I found in my fifty-third year, what should have happened earlier is an astonishingly magnificent process.

Magical Child hinted at the great power inherent in our beings. What I have learned since the writing of that book is that such power is a post-biological affair; the development of these powers begins after we have completed our physical maturation. When I wrote *Magical Child* I knew nothing of a post-biological development; I tried in that book to squeeze everything into the biological period of development of those first fifteen years, which I now realize was a limitation of that book. Because there is a serious discontinuity between the logic of our biological lives and that of our post-biological development, I look for analogies, for metaphors to help bridge the gap. Many of our activities and ideas offer analogies to our own internal states, however, since anything we produce is in some way a reflection of us.

For instance, the wave-particle dilemma in physics is analogous to the difference between the biological and post-biological states of mind. Physicists say both wave and particle states of energy are needed to explain a phenomenon, yet the two—wave and particle—are mutually exclusive. You can observe one or the other but not both at the same time. Physicists speak of wave energy as non-localized; it has no time or space characteristics and so doesn't exist in the same sense that physical matter exists. The particle, or physical matter, is localized energy; it has a location in time and space. Yet this localized, fixed energy is a restricted way of looking at the non-localized or unrestricted energy. Non-localized energy is an unrestricted field of possibility from which the particle of matter manifests. For the particle to manifest, the field's open potential "collapses" to that single expression of the particle; and no field is then manifest. For the field to manifest, the particle must respond in its wave form, at which point it cannot exist in its localized way.

In the same way, biological development, of which we are quite aware, is the localized and restricted form of the creative energy of life. Localized energy is restricted or limited to a specific set of relational necessities. Post-biological development is the wave-form corollary of this, in that it leads us to a non-localized awareness, a state of awareness that is unrestricted and fluid, not subject to the rules of relational necessity. In physics this principle of complementarity rules out our viewing both states at the same time, and we must assume the states are mutually exclusive though mutually interdependent. This is a paradox, but paradox is the threshold of truth, for at paradox we must drop the logic applicable to one state and adapt to a new set of rules concerning the new state. Our failure today to meet our problem lies in our inability or unwillingness to shift logical sets. The logic of a particle world will not fit the logic of a wave-form state, and we can operate in only one logical set at a time, at least in our preliminary, biological stage. This is not the case, however, with the mature mind, for full maturation gives us the capacity to leap the logical gap of paradox, allows us access to the excluded middle of logic, allows us to enter into the play of dynamics between reality and possibility. (We find random and rather haphazard forms of this in paranormal phenomena, as, for instance, when we walk on beds of white-hot charcoal without injury or pain, a practice now spreading rapidly in the United States through what is called neuro-linguistic programming.)

Our awareness can only unfold from a localized and restricted set of necessary relationships, but once established in this localized reality we can develop a non-localized, unrestricted operation. This is what I call post-biological development. Our first stage of development gives us our awareness of being physical creatures in physical bodies, and opens for us a wonderful physical world for exploration. But physical things are restricted and subject to necessary relationships. All matter decays, and such fragile and complex bits of matter as bodies and brains decay quickly and easily. So as soon as our physical systems are stabilized, a second form unfolds for development, through which we can move beyond this transient physical system. (Whether or not such a development takes place is another matter.) Non-localized reality is a continuum of possibility only; however, to enter into it we must construct a perceptual vehicle (Piaget would say a construction of knowledge) for that kind of awareness.

I cannot deny or eliminate from my discussion the esoteric nature of post-biological development, even though anything esoteric seems foreign to our culture. The complementarity of quantum mechanics is quite esoteric, even to many physicists (who turn their backs on it, preferring to stick with the good commonsense logic of particles). And since our

Western culture drove all traces of post-biological development underground centuries ago, I have to risk credibility in discussing it. Post-biological development survived in the East, rather underground, too, perhaps, but in a strong, substantial way, in what is called yoga. The word means yoke or union, and the union is between local and non-local states (at least for now). To shift from locality to non-locality is to shift logic and perceptual sets. Our physical bodies are the perceptual set and logic of local reality. Nature devotes some fifteen years of each human life to establishing this system, and we take this extraordinary creative process for granted. At its completion she opens the developmental means to create a corresponding logical and perceptual set, or vehicle, for exploring non-local possibility. It is as simple, as logical as that.

Two short quotations may indicate the direction of this esoterica: one is from the East, given by Mircea Eliade in his book *Yoga: Immortality and Freedom* (N.Y.: Pantheon, 1958). The other is from the recently discovered Nag Hammid library, a set of codices concerning the sayings and actions of Jesus according to the very early Gnostic "followers of the Way." (In a fierce struggle lasting some two centuries, the Gnostics were driven underground and largely destroyed by the bishops of the early Christian church. These Gnostic codices, some of which may be older than the oldest of the Gospels of the Christian New Testament, touch on the sublime among much that is ridiculous. A few pearls are buried in a field of—at times—unintelligible gibberish.)

Eliade quotes from *Further Dialogues of the Buddha*: "I have shown my disciples the way whereby they call into being out of this body of four elements another body of the mind's creation, complete in all its limbs and members, and with transcendental faculties." And in the Gnostic *Gospel of Thomas* we find: ". . . when you fashion an eye in place of an eye, and a hand in place of a hand, and a foot in place of a foot, and a likeness in place of a likeness, then you will enter the kingdom. . . ."

Nothing in our popular concept of yoga (the healthy, poised, and sexy body) or in Christianity suggests anything about a mental body we must create to enter the kingdom within. We had to create our physical bodies and their perceptual systems, however, as Piaget makes clear, so why should it be any different with a non-physical system? Non-local possibility has no reality except as we create a reality out of it; it has no existence until we give it existence by our attention and energy. To learn of an open-ended nature we must create an open-ended perceptual system. All developmental researchers agree that growth of intelligence is a movement from early concrete thinking to abstract thinking. They recognize that genuine abstract thought unfolds around adolescence, but they have no inkling, apparently, of the real dimensions of this non-localized, or abstract, realm.

Since post-biological movement is based squarely on the biological, nature has arranged that this second stage unfold at puberty, when we move into the final stage of physical growth and general biological orientation. A neat overlap is thus provided, since the only way into the non-localized state is through the conceptual patterns achieved in our biological development. This second stage of life is the real subject of this book, but since it is based on the first stage, I must, of necessity, outline the earlier, biological development to some extent. I have found that the first stage, the biological, unfolds correctly only when in the service of the second stage, only when it leads toward and prepares for the mature unfolding. A rule of development is that each stage, while perfect to itself, is fulfilled only as it is integrated into the next higher structure of knowing.

In the same way, life achieves its perfection when it fully prepares us for death. Near-death experience has recently been a topic for best-selling books, but the implications of the death-and-dying movement are misleading. There is a tendency to heave a sigh of relief and, thinking all is well, just wait for the ending that is also a beginning. The idea of a post-biological development thus becomes superfluous since all is well with no effort on our part. The truth we need lies in post-biological development and always has, but in this age of contrasts, the cosmology of the death-and-dying people, available to all, stands at a neat polarity with the equally popular but unavailable rigors and terrors of Carlos Castaneda's taking of the kingdom by storm.

Meanwhile, we face a very real possibility of global extinction by our own hands. This threat, I think, throws the psyche of the globe into what might be thought of as a healthy crisis. It confronts us with an imminent death we would otherwise deny, which just might be the shock needed to wake us up. Scientific people, particularly the medicine men, have been covertly hinting at the ultimate magic for several decades now: the subtle suggestion that given enough money, prestige, fame, Nobels, and adulation, they just might not only extend our lives but even outwit death indefinitely or entirely. Even to entertain such a notion (and we have been actively seduced by it) is to lose the meaning of life, which brings on the necessity of the threat of mass death. For life and death are the perfect complementaries: mutually exclusive yet interdependent. Without death life loses meaning, for this earth is not a permanent home, by design or nature. It is our kindergarten.

Actually, the bomb offers nothing new at all, in one sense: None of us can—or has ever been able to—guarantee himself one extra heartbeat. The issue of the bomb simply presents to us culturally what we have tried to deny individually. Each stage of our development is meaningful and perfect only as it leads naturally into the next stage. The perfect pregnancy prepares for and leads to childbirth, the termination of pregnancy. Leaving the womb provides entry into a far less restricted world and the opening of a new development. The perfect life prepares for the termination of life. We leave our biological womb to move into non-biological realms. Everything that happens in the womb prepares the infant for the new life outside it, and everything in our lives, while complete and rich in itself, prepares us for life beyond it, or is supposed to. As preparation for birth can only take place in pregnancy, so preparation for the non-biological state must be made while in the biological.

I travel around the globe giving workshops on development some eight months of the year. (The other four I spend in Ganeshpuri, India, concentrating on my own post-biological development.) I am struck continually by an apathetic anxiety that has spread abroad, in parallel with an excited optimism in that segment of people involved in or following the explosive developments in brain research. The brain/mind has finally been sensed as the key to things, and people from all walks of life and every branch of science are getting into the act. Marilyn Ferguson, in her *Brain/Mind Bulletin*, reports that some 500,000 published research papers are now appearing yearly on the brain/mind issue. An effort of such magnitude, of course, produces varying results; and though the percentage of significant discovery might be small, it grows in keeping with the magnitude of the labor. Research strikes me as valid when it contributes to a functional, meaningful self-portrait. The human is not just the measure of the human; any and every view of the universe we make is anthropomorphic and autobiographical. The portrait of ourselves that is emerging from brain research is awesome, but one must keep collecting the bits and pieces and "look for the pattern which connects," as Gregory Bateson urged. From the portrait I have found emerging, I am as optimistic about the survival and triumph of human society as I am pessimistic about the survival of a technological culture. For everything points toward something the yogis and sages of all ages have recognized: We are the vehicles of creation itself, the physical embodiment of the Creator. Though this expressive body seems at the point of death from self-inflicted wounds, we have within us a recovery capacity equal to our folly.

The following sketch of development is offered in this spirit of optimism and pessimism, in fair measure. We must all walk in a tightrope venture between ecstasy and terror—things can go either way. For me the balancing act involved takes place squarely within the frame of yoga, which admittedly tips the balance toward ecstasy without denying the terror. Yoga, which means yoke or union, is the path to the union of our human and divine natures. This is the only path to the truth of our being, the way out of our current impasse. It is what the post-biological plan is all about. Within this yogic frame of reference I find the "triune nature of brain" offered by Paul MacLean easily the most important item in current brain research. And I use the equally important theories of formative causation offered by biologist Rupert Sheldrake; physicist David Bohm's holonomic movement; the general principle of complementarity given by physicists Minas Kafatos and Robert Nadeau; and, of course, the developmental stages outlined by Jean Piaget. All these contribute fresh vitality to our yogic "skeleton," and, as good bones should, they support the work to follow without becoming obtrusive. That is, we should not notice their presence at all times, though at intervals we may need to lay them bare to make a point.

This book presents a cosmology, an outline of creativity

that embraces our experience. We are the measure of ourselves and in taking our measurement we find that we have measured our universe and its creation. I think this gives us a functional outline of who we really are, and by functional I mean one that works toward our well-being. Our current behavioristic models have led us to death and despair since they have left out everything that truly makes us tick. They left out the juice, the meaning and purpose, and left us with knee-jerk reflexes. One example, fire-walking, calls the lie to this monstrous error of behaviorism. The model of ourselves that leads us to freedom is one that encompasses anything and everything within our experience, an open-ended yet structured model. Our self-portrait must have room for the precursory modes of intuitive, non-verbal awareness; must give a means for explaining such diversities as that 40,000-year heritage of the Australian Aborigine called Dream Time; the symbolic, make-believe world of my three-year-old; the ecstatic experience of the Kalahari ¡Kung, dancing about their fire and raising their Kundalini; Kekule's Eureka! experience of a ring of snakes that translates to the language of chemistry as the benzene ring, the basis of all modern chemistry; and must make room for a workable notion of the relation between consciousness and reality.

Any outline of intelligence is meaningless and sterile unless it deals immediately with *spirit,* for spirit is the central nexus of human experience. Nor can spirit be added as an afterthought, like salt thrown in to flavor the stew, or a sweet postscript added for the spiritually inclined, like a politician throwing in a reference to The Lord with tremorous, pious voice. Spirit must be foremost in our considerations from the beginning if development is to be seen in its full scope, and if we are to avoid the common pitfall of a self-encapsulated intellectual trap. Spirit is the spine and skull of our developmental skeleton, and the spark of the intelligence behind it. Upon spirit all the various scientific ribs hang beautifully and make coordinated sense; without spirit we have fragmented nonsense.

Perhaps the scope of this work sounds a bit broad for a single volume, and I can hear complaints (similar to those made of my less ambitious *Magical Child)* that this book attempts too much. But I argue that all too often we attempt too little. Better an impossible task of splendid proportion than a sure but piddling one of no consequence. We learn from failures as well as successes.

Another problem is that words are not always the best tools for presenting these ideas. I continually search for metaphors, models, examples, and analogies that might help readers grasp rather intangible functions, and I have devised a number of sketches to display these models visually. Even though models and sketches always betray the functions they represent, they do give us visual footholds in otherwise slippery terrain.

Here, for instance, is a sketch of our triune brain system.

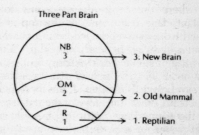

Three Part Brain

NB
3   → 3. New Brain

OM
2   → 2. Old Mammal

R
1   → 1. Reptilian

Can you think of anything more ridiculous than representing the most complex structure known in the universe through such a model? Yet we cannot grasp the meaningful functions of the brain if we are mired down in that incredible complexity. And here is a sketch of our first fifteen years of development, those critical biological years which give the foundation on which the post-biological rests.

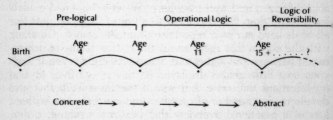

Pre-logical   Operational Logic   Logic of Reversibility

Birth   Age 4   Age 7   Age 11   Age 15 + ... ?

Concrete → → → → → Abstract

• = brain growth spurt

Can this skinny little diagram in any way represent the richness of our experience as children and adolescents? Yet these are valid and valuable aids, signs by which we can thread our way through a maze of otherwise abstract descriptions.

Sketches and models can trip us. I recall a workshop in Sydney, Australia, the audience for which included a psychologist who began to fidget from the moment I introduced MacLean's triune brain as my basic model of child development. Finally, the good man could contain himself no longer and blurted out: "But what about the fontanels?" Ah, the fontanels. Our psychologist had had a course in anatomy once and remembered the fontanels. (Fontanels are those points of the skull where the bones do not come together in the uterine infant. One major one, at the top of the head, remains after birth, the well-known soft spot where the blood can be seen pulsing beneath the skin. Thus the term fontanel—little fountain. Not actually a brain part, just a temporary condition; the lack of relevance to development made the psychologist's distress all the more ludicrous.) I was going full steam down the developmental track, riding this engine of the triune brain, with its physical, emotional, and intellectual passenger cars, but where were those fontanels? Our good man missed the train, wasted his ticket, and floundered around back at the station, trapped in the baggage of his own information.

I am aware that my models betray the functions represented, that I don't address the fontanels. But my models do help indicate those developmental functions in a concrete, tangible way that makes them available to our observation. So, arbitrary as they are, follow along with my oversimplifications; withhold those obvious qualifications that cry out to be acknowledged until you see where my over-simplified models lead. Time then for fontanels and all our qualifying pets (for all of us have our own repertoire of qualifications). Go along with the notion that age seven is the statistical line of demarcation between pre-logical and operational child, even though your own little genius displayed all this at age five. Myriad qualifications will arise, but within the framework that also develops, any number of qualifications can be made without loss of a functional overview that bestows meaning, order, and purpose.

Readers of *Magical Child* and my earlier *Crack in the*

Cosmic Egg will find few research references or names in the text of this book. I draw on a wide spectrum of current research, and numerous footnotes refer the reader to my sources. But a constant academic name-dropping, which our consensus security seems to demand, clutters the reading and obscures the line of thought. So, again, I urge you to follow the string all the way through the maze here before you plunge off into the myriad byways. Remember that once we have awakened from a dream we are not required to go back into that dream to straighten out its mess. Once awakened within us, post-biological development invites us, in turn, to wake up. My bibliography and footnotes—in fact, all words entirely—may eventually pale to insignifice and become superfluous, once we glimpse, even briefly, the state beyond our current dream.

1

Agenda
for Action

Nature has built into us an agenda for an intelligent unfolding of our biological and post-biological lives. Her agenda takes place through a simple, unvarying formula: the agenda within must be given a corresponding model from without to bring about our individual structure. Her inner agenda holds all possibilities for our experience of a self, world, and reality, but the particular experience we will have depends on the models we are given. Everything and every event in our external world are specific examples, or models, of some general possibility within us. Every person we meet is a model of our own possibilities. From birth on, our inner blueprint prompts us to search the world outside for appropriate models and interact with them. Our interaction with that world is the bridge that arcs the gap between our inner field of general possibility and the specific realization of that possibility we are given through our models.

We are overwhelmed with biological models—good, bad, and indifferent. My own post-adolescent blues, however, resulted from a failure to find any post-biological models at all. I found nothing that matched the great longing of the heart, or that met the needs of the grape bursting in my throat. I projected this great expectancy on various targets only to be disappointed anew each time. If no model is given us at the stage-specific time of need, that aspect of our blueprint atrophies, sinks back down into its dormant state.

Nature's agenda within us is like an architect's blueprint for a house. We cannot live in those lines drawn on paper, but if we follow the blueprint's agenda and fill in the blueprint with proper content, a house will be realized. In the same way, we actualize our house of intelligence by filling in nature's blueprint with content, which we do by responding to our models. The quality of our structure, and the kind of experience we have living in it, is determined by the quality of the content with which we build; that is, by the quality of the models we follow and by the nature of our interaction with those models.

Nature's blueprint within us offers unlimited possibility. She does not specify the particular materials we should use to fill in our individual realization of her plan. (For her purposes she doesn't want any two realized structures of ego to be alike.) She does ask, though, that the materials we *do* use be appropriate to the section of her blueprint we are filling in. Glass makes fine windows, for instance, but not much of a foundation. And she does ask that we follow her general order of construction, which is but common sense. That is, we should put in the foundation before we try to hang a roof or put in walls.

At age seven, for instance, my sense of betrayal on being forced to sit at a desk all year was because the blueprint within me set up a tremendous expectation for something different. Schooling could elicit no response from my blueprint because there was no match between model and agenda. A mismatch of stimulus and response brings on a sense of outrage, a violation of self, for the growth of self is thereby truncated or retarded. All that my early schooling did was to teach me to hate schooling, for we hate anything that thwarts our development, which is the basis for our survival. This learning to hate school, which is practically universal among children, is doubly tragic since we equate school with learning and the brain is constructed to do one thing—learn. So a double-bind sense of despair is the only result. If the model for learning matches the needs of the learning period, then learning is spontaneous, natural, and impeccably thorough.

Speech, for instance, is considered the greatest human achievement, but none of us *learned* language, in the sense of school learning. All of us imprinted language automatically, beneath the level of direct awareness, and we did so according to the models for language given us. Speech is my favorite example of the model-blueprint formula, that stimulus-response by which all intelligence unfolds, since speech generally takes place before this natural function has been interfered with by adult intellect. From sometime around the seventh month in the womb the human infant responds with physical movement to his mother's speech.[1] Every phoneme—those basic sound-parts out of which language is constructed—elicits from the infant a precise muscular response. By birth, the infant has a complete repertoire of muscular movements made to every phoneme out of which language forms.[2] The sound *ma*, for instance, might elicit a movement of the left toe, the right arm, or what have you, and exactly the same movement will be made in synchrony with that part of speech every time the mother speaks.

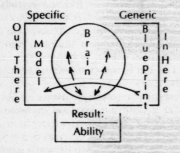

We call this phenomenon sensory-motor learning. The mother's speech-sound comes in through the infant's sensory system and the infant makes an automatic motor response to that stimulus. The combination of the two effects, stimulus and response, is etched into the neural circuitry of his brain as a repeatable pattern. (Muscular movement proves a key to all infant-child learning.) This sensory-motor pattern gives the concrete foundation on which language is built. Only phonemes will elicit this response; arbitrary sound fragments will not. The sound coming in must match the general field of language-possibility to act as content for this particular blueprint.

This underlying foundation of speech is universal, and unfolds in a fairly standard pattern.[3] Yet no two infants develop the same repertoire of muscular responses, even when the same language is used by the mothers involved. Just as no two snowflakes are ever the same yet are all similar, the blueprint function never repeats itself in its realizations, yet uses the same formulae.

If we take our infant from, say, a German mother and place him with a French mother, his outer model for language development will be French. His resulting structure of language will then be French, which is fine with nature. All she asks is that language be given to the infant-child at the appropriate time. All language is arbitrary; any language will do; but *some* language *must* be given from the outer world if the child's inner response is to take place. Development of that child's language will follow the same logical unfolding all language must: Foundation will be followed by walls, roof, and finally the niceties of logical-semantic trim-out, the furnishings and decorations, whether they be French, German, or Swahili.

This same pattern holds for all our development and experience. Between our inner blueprint and outer realization there is a two-way flow, a dynamic of sowing, reaping, and sowing. We follow the models, mirror their essential nature in our own unique variation, and become the model in turn. Each stage of our blueprint opens us to a qualitatively and quantitatively different kind of experience. And each stage requires its own kind of model to act as stimulus for that type of potential. The models we need for our foundation period of infancy are different from the models we need later. Since the models we are given determine the character and quality of our reality, everything in our lives, without exception, hinges on those teachers and guides who furnish the content for our blueprint.

Nature cannot program for failure, such as our failure to find a suitable model at the appropriate time. Her stages unfold on her own schedule; for optimal development we need appropriate stimuli at the appropriate time. You can compensate later but it is a lot harder to shape cold iron than white-hot; you have to beat that object half silly to make any impression. On the other hand, when we force our children to try to put a roof on their house of intelligence when there is not yet even a foundation, we again violate nature's agenda. (And, as before, nature cannot provide for our failure to respect her agenda.)

By mid-adolescence our house of intelligence is supposed to be ready for full-scale occupancy and employment;

at this point we are supposed to enter into a full-scale agenda shift. A dramatically different form of intelligence, and a dramatically different set of possibilities for our development open once the initial building stage is over.

As the newborn infant is the product of the inner realm of the mother, who can produce child after child, our outer world is a product of an inner realm that can also produce state after state. As we are born from our mothers to grow, mature, and become the parent in turn, so biological maturation leads us to enter the post-biological stage's realm of possibility and become the one who creates. Once identified with the creation, we should move on to identify with the creator. Nature's agenda shifts us automatically toward both forms of maturity in their respective turn and in regular stages. Consider, for instance, that well-planned physical sequence: baby teeth, six-year molars, twelve-year molars, and wisdom teeth around age eighteen. All we need to do is give the proper nurturing from without and nature's plan from within takes care of the rest. Intelligence during both our biological and post-biological periods is designed to unfold in the same logical way, provided we are given the proper nurturing, which means the proper models and guidance. In this way we are integrated in regular stages to our final identity with the creative source of life from which we came.

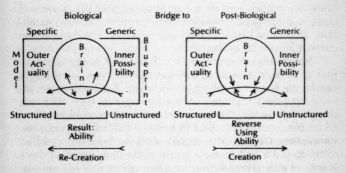

Nature's formula for this mature second stage remains the same as that for the biological period: As usual, the inner plan must be given its outer model. Such a requirement

seems contradictory; we would think an inner model necessary for an inner journey but all learning is from the concrete,
or sensory-motor, to the abstract, or purely mental. The
model required by nature for inner development is someone
among us who has already accomplished it. For this second
stage, the outer model must be much more precise, since
only a fully matured person can guide us to our own full
maturity. Post-biological development leads to a quantum
leap of logic and a major shift of orientation. So nature gets a
bit more particular in her model requirements.

To grasp the nature of the post-biological plan we must
clearly understand the earlier biological one. Biological development moves from inner possibility to outer actuality.
Once this plan is complete, we use it to move from our outer
actuality *back into* the inner fields of possibility. When we
complete re-creation we move on toward creation.

Play is re-creation, but actual creation is also play. The
child plays with the given materials of his world while our
post-biological stage moves our consciousness into realms
beyond all given materials. Nature's second agenda develops
in us the ability to play in the generic interior realm from
which the outer world springs, and this is creation itself, the
goal of our lives.

We have built-in blueprints and we generally find many
models—good, bad, and indifferent—around us. Ability, however, cannot be built in; we must develop ability, and we do
this by interacting between inner blueprint and outer model,
the stipulation holding for all development. We must use our
biological system as the bridge by which we can pass beyond
all biological systems. Point for point, each ability gained in
early life becomes the means through which we develop the
ability to move beyond all physical life. Each ability we gain
by responding to a model of our blueprint gives us the means
to move back into that aspect of nature's open blueprint.

We develop our sense of being individuals by interacting
with our world and with specific models of individual people.
We build our conceptual structures of self and world from an
inner sea of potential that contains all possibilities of such
constructions. Our concepts of self and world are like little
islands from which, in post-biological development, we reverse the earlier process and launch out into that inner sea of
possibility itself. Once we have completed our structures of

reality, we move back into an unstructured possibility for reality, and to enter that realm of possibility is to create our experience within it. Lucid dreaming is a good analogy of a primitive form of this reversal. At first our dreams simply happen to us (and our very earliest dreams may be in only one sense mode at a time, with full sensory dreaming not appearing until as late as the third year of life). With attention, training, and guidance, we can develop the ability to retain our conscious ego awareness in dreaming and enter into our dreams as an active participant, and control them to some extent. The imagery is still given us, however, and only in a final maturity do we become the imagery-making faculty itself, both producer and receiver. In the same way, we create our experience of the unstructured states according to the nature of our conscious entrance into such experience. All perception is a creative act and we find in the inner realm only that which we are capable of finding. We see according to our ability to see; such perceptual ability must be developed, and it is developed according to the nature of our models for such development.

At birth our egos are, in effect, an unformed possibility within that unstructured state out of which we must establish our existence. The word *existence* is from the Latin: *ex-sistere*, to set apart. Our structure of existence is ego. Once our ego structure is firmly established, firmly set apart as an integral, autonomous self, we can move into that unstructured possibility from which we came and give it structure by our conscious movement. Such a movement requires integrity of ego, and integrity is more than a politician's catchword. Integrity of ego means structural unity of ego. Autistic and schizophrenic children have fragmented or split egos, and many adults have multiple personalities that struggle for dominance.[4]

Once we can maintain the integrity of our awareness and move into these inner fields of open potential, we can enter into the final section of nature's agenda: development of autonomous awareness. Autonomy means self-sufficiency. Only when we are no longer dependent on our bodies and the outer world for sustenance are we truly autonomous. Such an autonomy sounds impossible because our biological concepts are all that most of us have and because they can relate us only to biological processes. So the job of post-biological development is to build in us a conceptual system for grasping and realizing this possibility of autonomy. From the beginning our biological development must set us apart from the inner realm of possibility to create our outer world of tangible experience. Then our development must separate our awareness from our identification with the world we make in childhood. By the time we reach adolescence, our identities are separated not only from our world construction, but from our own bodies, which we then look on as our possessions. We then stand ready to identify with the inner world of creation through our post-biological development. At this point our ego awareness is integrated into that realm from which we were originally set apart at birth, but we are integrated as a fully developed, autonomous self-system. Then we can hold our matured egos intact and move into the outer or inner world; we can leave existence (our world set-apart) for a realm of being not set-apart, a realm of possible existence. This is the truly autonomous ego, which, when the time comes, can leave body and world behind.

In order to understand being whole and sufficient to one's self, one must grasp the meaning of post-biological development, for only that stage leads to maturity. Since post-biological development is based squarely on our initial biological growth, I will need to sketch out how our early development should unfold (recognizing that it doesn't always unfold as it should) to show the kind of base our later development must have, at least for optimal development on schedule.[5]

We have been violating nature's agenda at an accelerated rate in recent centuries and particularly since World War II. As a technological culture we have lost all trace of a post-biological development and have no machinery of mind to grasp such a notion, nor words to refer to it. Further, our biological development has been seriously disrupted through our ignorance of any goal or direction for such development. We have created an all-pervasive cultural dysfunction. Worse, we have become resigned to our dysfunctional state; we have accepted dysfunction as our natural condition. We have no notion of a fully functional state because our concepts of world and self have been shaped according to dysfunctional models. Having no concepts of normal functioning, we propose as a model for our children our own dysfunctional state;

thus dysfunction is mirrored back from every direction. Taking our abnormality as our norm, we look on human life as a sequence of mounting crises, disasters, and problems. For instance, we face the bizarre sequence of an outbreak of premature menarche (the beginnings of menstruation) in early childhood; a current epidemic increase of pregnancies in nine-year-old children; an outbreak of violent sexual aggression by males under ten years of age. This has been brought about at least partly by chemical interference with our natural body chemistry, through the synthetic growth hormones by which we speed up growth of our chickens, cows, pigs, and other food animals; but instead of acknowledging the serious breakdown in genetic unfolding our interferences have wrought, our scientists search for yet another chemical to stop menstruation in children.[6]

To try to make feasible the awesome dimensions of our inner blueprint for post-biological development I need to outline nature's biological plan. In making this sketch I will cover some of the ground covered in my earlier book *Magical Child*. Anyone familiar with that work will find the present one somewhat different in presentation, content, and certainly intent, for in writing *Magical Child* I was unaware of a post-biological stage, and as a result, I misinterpreted some data. Consider how an archeologist might someday stumble on a well-preserved spark plug, somehow left over from our gasoline-alley age. He and his colleagues might debate for years the implications of the strange object. (They would, perhaps, conclude that it was a religious fetish of some sort, involved in primitive magical thinking.) Should they discover a functional gasoline engine somewhere, whose workings were found to depend entirely on that little plug, their notions of that plug would change. Context of a part is a major consideration in understanding function. In the same way, there were parts of child development that I overemphasized and misinterpreted in *Magical Child*, which I now see in a different light as a result of my own experience in post-biological development. Items I overlooked or dismissed as insignificant now seem important. Current research into the brain and mind multiplies year by year, and with a knowledge of the post-biological stage added to the data of child development now available, the pattern originally sensed in *Magical Child* isn't so much completed, as though we were just fitting in some missing pieces, as it is markedly changed.

Both sections of nature's blueprint—the biological and the post-biological—are built in, designed to unfold on schedule and move our awareness forward into ever greater realms of possibility and power, regardless of our potential skill in utilizing them. None of us had to pass an entrance exam to be born into this world, nor do we have to do so to enter our second stage of growth. Further, once we do move into post-biological development, under the guidance of the model/teacher, nature patches us up as needed for further growth. This repair work takes place as we move forward in the new development. For instance, our intuitive stage, unfolding between ages four and seven, may have been sadly neglected and largely undeveloped because it lacked models and guidance. But some intuition always develops and whatever scant threads were established provide the needed bridge on which post-biological development will quietly expand beneath our awareness. Little by little we will manifest a mature intuitive capacity far beyond the limited form intended for children. Or our childhood bonding with parent and family may have been deficient, leaving us alienated and unable to relate to others; but in post-biological development a far greater bonding unfolds, embracing an infinitely wider realm and making the old deficiencies of no consequence. All that is required is that we put our shoulders to the plow of the post-biological stage and not look back. No matter how crippled our earlier development may have been, no matter how severe the ensuing nightmare might be for us now, there are no criteria for responding to nature's post-biological plan other than our willingness to respond. No therapy on our part is required, and no turning back to try and patch ourselves up will do any good.

If our years up to now have bred for us a bad dream, all we are asked to do is leave that dream behind. The post-biological path to maturation is a process of waking up. In no way are we required to go back into that dream and straighten out its mess. Once we make the shift to the new agenda, we can walk away from that dream with impunity.

2

Threefold System

Our development unfolds for us in the same way that life unfolded from its beginnings on this earth. A mind-numbing aphorism—ontogeny recapitulates phylogeny—tells us that everything that has come before is repeated by us as we develop.[1] We begin as single cells in the womb and move up through all the forms of various species: At one point we display gills, at another a vestigial tail, and so on. We recapitulate life's whole show and then we go beyond it.

To start at the beginning of this brief evolutionary overview: Buried deep in our brains we have a tiny complex of cells involved in the perception of light. This ancient prototype of brain is called the *pineal* gland. A major function of this gland, found even in the most primitive creatures, is its production of *melanin*, a key molecule that, among many things, may be the link between mind and matter, the medium between brain and mind, thought and reality, and so on.[2] Melanin can do extraordinary things: translate sound waves into light waves and vice versa; translate electrical energy into either sound or light waves; and possibly relate and intermix all our sensory signals, to mention only a few of the capacities of this tiny molecule. Melanin is found in all life forms, is distributed throughout our body and brains, but is found in particularly heavy concentrations at key points in the human body. Chief of these are three gateways in the brain through which information is processed. There is a heavy concentration of melanin in our hearts, and another in our genitalia. These concentration points for this key molecule are keys to our overall development.

Research into how sight works reveals that when we open our eyes and see the outside world, the light that makes up the imagery of this seeing does not come *from* out there.[3] The light we see as "out there" is an inner response to what we can only assume has to be an outer stimulus. But the images seen as outside are put together somewhere inside, translated by the brain, with all its melanin molecules, and projected on that screen of mind we call our perceptual awareness.

All this activity creates the effect of an outside source of light, and to that kind of source we respond. Consider, however, those colorful images we see in our dreams at night. Consider as well the more brilliant images of hypnagogic and meditative experiences, three-dimensional and breathtakingly real; or the chaotic flashing lights and images reported from psychedelic research.

From where does the light come in this kind of imagery? To say it is only illusory is to beg the issue. The fact is that the production of inner and outer imagery is identical in all cases. The source of that imagery is sensed as different according to the placement assigned it by our brain, but in fact is the same. We place it in "outside" and "inner" categories according to the nature of the imagery, the brain organ involved in translating that imagery, and the resulting nature of our state of awareness while we are receiving and responding to such imagery.

Our lives are based on three types of imagery: physical imagery relating to a physical world; imaginative and dream imagery relating to an inner world; and a pure abstract imagery related to thinking and creativity. And we have, within our skulls, brains to handle, or translate, each of these types of imagery. What we think of as the single brain in our heads is actually made of three completely different brains, the three major brain types developed in evolutionary history.[4] The oldest of these, and the foundation of our brain system, is the *reptilian brain*, which ruled for hundreds of millions of years. Superimposed on this is the *old mammalian brain*, which took over with a quantum leap of new possibilities; and, finally, a *neo-mammalian brain* bringing about the discontinuous leap to dolphins, whales, and humans. The reptilian brain is overlaid by the old mammalian brain and is utilized by the newer system for new possibilities and power. In turn, our new human brain is built around the old mammalian and so utilizes both older brains in yet another leap of possibility and power.

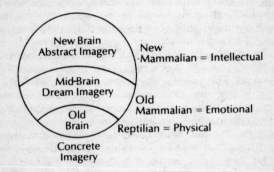

Briefly, we can characterize our three-fold system this way: The reptilian brain handles physical imagery and is the brain through which we sense our physical world and respond to it. The old mammalian brain handles internal images and all emotions; and the neo-mammalian (neocortex) is our intellectual brain, which handles imagery so abstract we cannot place it as quite interior or exterior.

The foundation of our house of intelligence is the reptilian, or old, brain. All our senses, except that of smell, take place through its gateways. Much of the work of our automatic pilot—those things we learn so well we can do them without thinking about it—takes place here.

The old mammalian, or, for simplicity, the mid-brain, evaluates quality, esthetics, or feeling tone.[5] Feeling can be concrete and objective, as touching with the fingers, or emotionally abstract and subjective, as in having our feelings hurt. By feeling tone I mean a third state, a relational quality, character, or condition existing between subject and object, as the relation between things or events, or between ourselves and our experience. All relationship is of an emotional nature and emotion exists only through relationship.

Our mid-brain handles our loves, hates, fears, attractions, and aversions. It handles all our bonding (an important subject that must have its own chapter): bonding of parent and child, male and female, person and society, and so on. The mid-brain is the cohesive brain, the one that ties things together. The sensory information coming in through our old brains is given its meaningful shape through the emotional energy of this mid-brain. In turn, the abstract imagery of the new brain is given its initial concretization or actualization through our mid-brain. The mid-brain ties together the physical and thinking brains.

Our mid-brain is the "heart" of our brain system and, interestingly enough, has direct nerve connections with our actual heart. This physical connection proves a vital key in the function of bonding. Tradition has always connected emotion with the heart, and recently we found that the mid-brain actually does take directives, moment by moment, from our hearts.[6] Conversely, the mid-brain is constantly sending information to the heart. The two form the center of our life system.

Our new brain is the instrument through which we compute, play, analyze, dissect, make syntheses, create, and, in general, think about the materials furnished by the two animal brains. Far more important, our new brain plays a vital role in post-biological development. And, as we shall see, when research finds the new brain grossly underused and almost expendable (we once thought it the whole show), we find the reason for this in the neglect and failure of our post-biological development.

The new brain is divided into right and left hemispheres that seem to have different specialties.

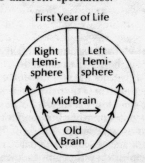

First Year of Life

Right Hemi-sphere | Left Hemi-sphere

Mid-Brain ←→

Old Brain

Less attention has been paid to the fact that at birth these hemispheres are separated from each other, share only their common connections with the mid-brain, and undergo some early parallel development. After about the first year of life, however, a bridge of connecting nerves, called the *corpus callosum*, begins to grow between these two hemispheres. This bridge is very slow in its formation, though, and not until the fourth year of life is the corpus callosum completed. The late appearance and slow growth of this organ are of major significance. Once this growth is completed, the right and left hemispheres can fully relate, communicate, or compute their activities directly back and forth without reference to the two primary brains they encompass. This independence of the two hemispheres will eventually lead to a pure intellect, our ability to think without reference to the activities of either of the two animal brains. Eventually we achieve the ability to translate nonsensory information beyond all biological process.

After 1st Year

Corpus Callosum
Begins

The timing of this corpus callosum's appearance and growth gives us a major clue to child development. For now, bear in mind that this organ does not even appear for growth until toward the end of the first year of life, and is not completed until the fourth year.[7] The significance of this timing and slow unfolding of so important a brain part will become apparent as we continue.

The old brain and the mid-brain are richly connected by communication links; they function in a neat synchrony. Between the mid-brain and the new brain, however, the connecting links are far more sparse. The left hemisphere of the new brain seems only casually connected with the mid-brain, while the right hemisphere has, by comparison, a much richer neural connection with that mid-brain (though far less than the mid-brain has with the old brain). This, too proves a valuable clue to our development, and indicates the meticulous planning that nature has invested in the timed unfolding of our blueprint.

Since the mid-brain responds to the activities and/or the needs of the physical brain, on the one hand, and the intellectual brain, on the other, we can refer to it as the supportive brain. It is the critical link, the median, the ambassador and translator between the sharply different languages and images of the old and new brains. When we open our eyes and see the images of a physical world, we engage in an old brain activity. When we close our eyes and produce images of things not present out there, this is *imagination*. (The dictionary defines imagination as "creating images not present to the senses.") We recognize the importance of translating images of the outside world, but translating internal imagery is equally important. Creativity, logic, intellect, and our post-biological, or spiritual, development and survival depend on this generally misunderstood function.

The imagery of thought and the imagery of a world are qualitatively different and they require mediation; one must be translated into the other. The marks on paper "c-a-t" are instantly translated as cat, which, in turn, opens up a wide variety of semantic possibilities. But the marks in themselves have no meaning. Meaning must be added to them. The old brain brings the plain marks in; the mid-brain and new brain give them meaning.

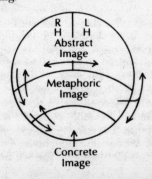

But, for the new brain to add its part, the mid-brain must translate those concrete marks brought in by the old brain into the abstract images of the new brain, or into an imagery available to that new brain's abstract imagery. In the same way, the mid-brain translates the abstract images of the new brain into the sensory motor responses of the old brain, as we put *our* marks on paper, for instance. The mid-brain functions in this two-way fashion through a metaphoric type of imagery-language—which is of such importance it will have its own chapter later.

Our three-part system is designed to operate as an integral unit according to need. Activity in one brain brings the necessary support from the rest. Consider a gas-filled light bulb that has a central filament activating the gas. When the filament lights up, all the gas fluoresces, amplifies the light of the filament, and gives an overall light brighter than would the burning filament alone. The human brain system is like that light bulb in that the diverse parts of our brains are activated as needed to support any other part. But in our light bulb brains we have, so to speak, three filaments. Energize the old brain filament and all three areas respond as designed, with their respective supportive glow. The same holds for any other combination.

The wattage of each brain changes as we move up the evolutionary scale. The old brain is the most stable, but also the weakest. The mid-brain is less stable but more powerful. The new brain is the least stable and most powerful of all. The old brain is not only amplified far beyond its original reptilian design by this integrated circuitry; it can be modified or distorted by its more sophisticated neighbors. And, logically, the actions of any of the three can be modified or distorted, as well as amplified and/or clarified, by the others.

Sleep-dream research indicates that those filaments can light up one at a time sequentially, or all together, or in various combinations. Our energy of attention and the locus of our ego-awareness shift back and forth between those brains. When we go to sleep, we withdraw the bulk of our attention from our old brain. This shuts out the world and many body signals. Our locus of awareness shifts into the mid- and new brains. We may lie there at night thinking over events of the day for a time, ruminating on vain concerns and imaginings. Our supportive mid-brains, having no sensory

information to respond to, react to these mental wanderings
with corresponding emotional images;

we thus lose our thought to this emotional show and dreaming begins. Our eyes move about, following this ongoing
imagery of dreaming, in a process called REM (for rapid-eye-
movement) sleep. Our breathing may speed up and muscles
twitch as mother-in-law chases us with a hatchet. The old
brain makes whatever peripheral supportive action is needed
by its neighbor's carrying on, while dutifully keeping the
world out. (If that old brain's shadowy response gets too
dramatic we may sleep-walk.)

Next, the energy of attention seems to withdraw from
the mid-brain entirely, and the locus of our ego-awareness
resides only in the new brain. Muscles collapse and the body
slows to its lowest ebb. We used to refer to this as *deep sleep*
and thought the state free of dreaming. Recently we have
found something the ancient Eastern yogis knew quite well:
Dreaming goes on during this stage of consciousness as well.[8]
The dreams translated into our awareness during this stage of
deep sleep are essentially geometric in nature, and are abstract in design. They are usually three-dimensional and change
continually within their single frame, require no eye movement to follow, and thus they are harder to detect (research
people can easily spot the eye movements of emotional dreaming). These geometric-type dreams have no emotional character (unlike mid-brain imagery), no relation to our ordinary
world at all, and are numinous. That is, they have an awesome, mystical quality. A fourth state has been implied in
some early research, a period following or even a part of this
deep sleep period. This fourth state has not fit any category

available and has not been further researched, since nothing tangible could be found.[9]

Following a period of deep sleep and its possibly elusive fourth state, our energy of attention swings back into REM sleep and emotional dreaming. The old brain makes its supportive twitches as called for, until we awaken briefly, enough to roll over, and perhaps glance at the clock. Then we repeat the entire cycle. This sleep-wake cycle takes about ninety minutes to run its full course, forty-five minutes up and another forty-five down. Further, we continue this cycle twenty-four hours a day. Fortunately, during our waking hours we go through only partial or mini sleeps and dreams without a full shift of locus away from our attention to the outside world.

Note that the locus of our awareness is not static in our brains. Nor is our awareness and attention energy evenly distributed. In addition to this sleep-wake cycle, a slight shift in weight of attention between right and left hemispheric dominance takes place on another cycle, independently of the forty-five—ninety-minute cycle.[10] In this way nature arranges a regulated balance between all her various organs of consciousness and their specialties.

Now this shifting capacity of our energy of attention and locus of ego holds great significance for the story of development. For nature's blueprint is organized around our three brains and their interlocking actions. The point here is that the development of intelligence follows the same logical, sequential unfolding we find in the evolution of the planet. Each stage of child development is a time for concentration on, for the development and perfecting of each of these brains, and in their logical, evolutionary order of appearance.

First, we must develop the capacity to bring in raw information, which is an old brain job. Second, we must learn to organize that raw information into meaningful categories, which is a mid-brain task. Third, we must learn to play with the structures built up through the other two systems—a new rain job. This three-part task takes an average of fifteen years to complete, and sets the stage for the post-biological system to take over.

Of course, all of the brain is involved from the very beginning of brain life, which is around the fifth month *in utero*. The brain always operates as an integrated unit. But integration in this sense does not mean homogeneity or equal distribution of attention and energy. And in our initial development nature concentrates on one major area at a time as necessity dictates. For each brain must be exercised, employed, developed, until the automatic pilot can take over in each case and free our awareness to concentrate on the next stage. So the locus of our egos, the kinds of tasks we are involved in, and the models we look for as guides, all shift accordingly.

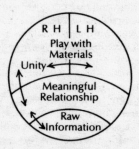

All stages of development, then, are periods of concentration on particular brains, brain parts, or interactions between them. Our blueprint prepares for the next stage of its unfolding, even as we are engrossed in the present one. At the same time the character and needs of coming stages sharply influence the earlier ones. Thus, because of my new brain the reptilian brain in my skull has a dramatically different history of development than it has in a dog, which lacks so huge a new brain, and is vastly different from that in the black snake in my backyard, which lacks even the mammalian addition.

The first year of human life clearly is devoted to the physical-sensory system related to the old brain. A complete synchrony with the mid-brain is certainly needed at the same time, but the locus of infant awareness is solidly sensory-motor, or reptilian. Once this sensory-motor brain is established and operative, the locus of awareness shifts an equal weight of attention to the mid-brain. Now two entrainments, or organizations, take place at the same time; one physical-sensory, the other emotional. The child is then aware of being both a sensing body and an esthetic center.

Next enters *will*, an emotional drive, the instinctual force to overcome obstacles to development. Like and dislike, esthetic qualities overlaid as a judgment on experience, begin at the same time. This esthetic polarization puts the information sensed through the old brain into meaningful relationships, and out of this a sense of ego, as distinct from the physical-sensory world of the reptilian brain, begins to take shape. Once this shift of locus to the mid-brain takes place, the corpus callosum, that great bridge of connecting nerves between the two hemispheres of the new brain, begins its first, tentative growth. Now we have two separate processes taking place, self as emotion and self as physical body, and these two function require some specialization of hemispheres, though the intricacies of this specialization have not yet been firmly established.[11]

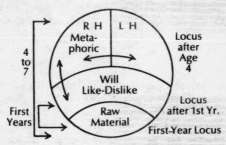

By around age four, eighty percent of the child's structure of knowledge of the physical world, language, and ego-awareness distinguishable from the world is complete. There is then a further shift of the locus of awareness into the new brain for the development of intellect as an independent possibility. During this period the corpus callosum is completed as a structure and from about four to seven the child's ego is evenly distributed among the three brains. His locus of awareness is that of self as body, emotional center, and an intuitive thinking center. The major task of development is to bring this four-year-old's three-tiered system into a perfect synchrony. This involves development of intuition, which opens the child to levels of awareness and information not available through that reptilian brain's outer orientation. At the same time the child develops an analogical language system, a metaphoric-symbolic system of imagery transference center-ing in the mid-brain and right hemisphere. The grandest part of childhood is this period from four to seven, when a perfect balance is achieved between body, mind, and feelings. This is the Garden of Eden state, from which the child is by necessity expelled, at about age seven. For around age seven the locus of ego-awareness shifts out of our primary brains.

From about age seven on, our blueprint moves toward *mind* as a point of objectivity, a state of awareness where ego can act as though it were separate from the brain. Mind as the receptor of all perceptual activity is initially identified with the action of the brain that gives it its perceptions. Development can be seen as the formation of ego-mind re-lated to each brain in succession, followed by a series of dis-identifications of ego-mind from these related brain parts. Finally, ego-mind will stand within its own identification, outside the brain, in effect, in a position of objectivity.

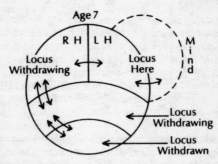

We can think of our ego-minds as being born in the old brain, in effect, the weakest system, and indeed we are then at our most helpless. Even when the child can get about a bit, to crawl around on the floor, getting his snake's-eye view of the world, he is restricted and weak. But when he is moved into an equal energy of attention in his mid-brain, and that new power manifests, he gets up on his hind legs; becomes emo-tional, self-assertive, and willful; and begins talking.

Once his emotional center is well established and his rela-tions with his world are worked out, he is moved into the new brain. With the power of the new brain we bring all three systems into synchrony, through storytelling, fantasy,

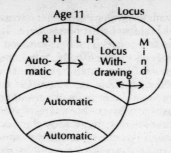

imaginative play, and mirroring our parent and sibling models through imitative play. Our adult behavioral engineers complain that we resist their behavior modifications: "All they want to do is *play!*" they fume, and right they are; children are driven by millions of years of genetic encoding to follow intuitively their only road to survival and intelligence—which is play.

By about age seven, synchrony among the three different imagery systems has been established and our identities withdrawn from direct association with those primary brains. The erratic behavior and non-logical willfulness of early childhood fade; a new logical behavior unfolds. (The capacity for measurement of the world, and the concepts of time and space, unfolded automatically.) In our pre-logical years *quality* was the criterion of experience, our esthetic response the standard of our relations. Now, at seven, *quantity* enters as the main focus, making possible a form of concrete logic, a way to grasp the nature of the physical relationships taking place. Between seven and eleven, nature withdraws our locus of awareness from the right hemisphere and concentrates development on our more isolated left hemisphere. Mind, as a point of objectivity beyond brain function, begins to manifest. Our right hemisphere is left on automatic pilot somewhere around eleven and we move into creative thought, abstract logic, and semantic language—the world of the mind. Our identification with the brain has been withdrawn by around fifteen and we are left only with our objective point of view; our minds have, in effect, no particular locus other than vaguely in our head. Our brains are, then, the physical aspect of our experience and mind the subtle counterpart, at which point we are ready for post-biological development.

Post-biological development opens us to creative power, a power of consciousness related to possibility rather than to what has already been created. As we shift our orientation away from the fixed physical world to the fluid mental world, the more power we have at our disposal. Through the subtle power of the post-biological development, our identity as an entity distinct from brain or body manifests and becomes stable, just as ego was gradually articulated and separated from its earlier identifications with the sensory-motor and emotional systems. Whatever we call this post-biological identification of ego—the psyche, the soul, or the spirit—it is a matter of semantic choice; the function is the same. I will use the term *Spirit* because I like it; but I refer not to some vapid, vague, insubstantial ethereal body emanating in a seance, but to the exuberant, explosive creative power bubbling up from our hearts in adolescence, when we manifest the first inkling of our identities with the creative power bringing our universe into being. This identity is also present from the beginning of our lives, of course, but in latent form, awaiting, like all aspects of our blueprint, its stage-specific turn for concentrated attention and development. We finally shift into development of Spirit once all its necessary support systems are functional.

Post-biological development is based, point for point, on the biological foundation then established. The weaker physical system is the basis for the more powerful spiritual being. Through a process I will call reversibility we will shift our identity and awareness from the particular experience we have gained to the generic field from which the particular arose. We will move from the specific to the general, from the concrete actuality to the abstract possibility, from the physical to the subtle.

No development of any kind can take place without a physical model out there with which we can interact enough to make our own approximate construction of what that model represents. The reason for our complete dependence on models is the nature of our generic blueprint. Our blueprint encompasses any and all possibilities, which is too broad to be the basis on which to build a structure. We can build a structure only of some particular, selected possibility. Just as total wealth is a kind of total poverty, so existence is a setting apart of something specific. Were you to describe to a child the same event under a different name with each encounter, language confusion would result. Any name for an event works, but one name for the event must predominate for imprinting to take place. In the same way, we select from possibility by discovering through our senses a tangible, specific example of that possibility. We cannot comprehend "all possibility" until we can fully comprehend many different forms of a limited but realized possibility. Throughout our lives we then select our continually expanding reality according to the nature of the model originally followed.

Throughout both biological and spiritual development, the formula follows this pattern: the blueprint within, plus the model from without, equals a structure of knowledge. Our structures will be in keeping with the models we find or are provided, and will always only suggest the openness of the potential field of our blueprint. We always leave an infinite number of possibilities unrealized as we carve out of this potential a tangible worldview.

Post-biological development gives us the ability to conceptualize directly out of the infinitely open blueprint realm. Conceptualization then becomes the criterion for reality. In addition to our tangible outer reality, we open to an interior reality in continual creation. To build this capacity, our awareness must continue its series of dis-identifications. We must shift our identities from the structures of knowledge we made in the biological period if we are to identify with the blueprint realm itself. But dis-identification does not mean eradication or annihilation of the self so identified; it means a shift of criterion or reference point. As the child shifts criterion and reference point from family to society and peers, we can grasp inner vision only by giving up our established reliance on outer vision as the only source of seeing. Of course we must still use our outer senses as needed, but we learn to keep our systems distinct. Creative insight, for instance, is literally a "seeing-within." The interior visual world is the creative possibility of vision itself and unfolds for us constantly anew, provided we allow this to become our criterion for development and use our biological orientation as the necessary support system. (Generally we reverse this order, and thus bring about our downfall. That is, we try to adopt inner vision as an adjunct to our outer worldview, or use insight as a support system of ordinary mundane seeing.) We must dis-identify with our fretful, fearful, and limited ego-self, in order to identify with the Creative Self underlying all process. Then, and only then, will our ego stop its fretting.

We can do this only by standing on the concrete structures of knowledge gained in biological development. All growth is from the concrete to the abstract. Imitation precedes originality. Re-creation precedes creation; child play must precede divine play.

To enter the spiritual stage we must give up our specific achievements on behalf of the non-specified. We must give up our early physical life for a greater spiritual life. We must give up our childhood emotions of like and dislike for that emotion of love, the bond of power in the heart. We must give up our isolated intellect for the intelligence of the whole system. Integration of our ego-mind with ever higher structures can take place only as we leave that which we know for that which we do not know. Just as the child is weaned from the breast to discover the wider gastronomic world, so we surrender our conceptual bank account in exchange for the treasury itself.

This natural movement, carefully worked out by nature, is inborn, waiting its own turn to unfold sequentially. As with all other developmental sequences, however, this spiritual state remains *in potentia* until the usual two requirements are met: one, for the proper sequential time to unfold; and two, for the appropriate outer model around which to build a coherent, specific experience.

3

Bonding
and Attachment

In my book *Magical Child*, I described an American mother,
Jean McKellar, who observed newborn Ugandan babies being
carried in a sling next to the mother's breast. No diapers
were used and, since the infants were always clean, Jean
asked the mothers how they managed bowel and bladder
movements. "We just go to the bushes," answered the mothers. But how, Jean asked, do you know when a tiny infant
needs to go to the bushes? The astonished mothers replied:
"But how do you know when you have to go to the bushes?"[1]
In Guatemala, mothers also carry their new infants in that
manner, and if a newborn should still soil a mother after two
or three days, the woman is considered stupid and a poor
mother.[2] Colin Turnbull, in his book *The Forest People*, tells
how the mother anticipates the infant's needs and responds
before the infant gives any detectable signs of being in need.[3]
And in that statement lies the heart of the issue of bonding.

These mothers have bonded with their infants. Delivery
practices vary widely among cultures and it is hard to find a
standard we can call natural, other than a minimum of interference. A natural birth, though, is one that allows bonding
to take place. Bonding is an instinctual function directed from
or through our mid-brain, following essentially the same form
in all societies, and, like breathing, will manifest if allowed to
do so.

Bonding gives an intuitive, extrasensory kind of relationship between mother and child. Bonding is a felt process,
not available to discursive thought, language, or intellect. It

is a communion that bypasses our ordinary reasoning mind.
The mother senses the infant's need to evacuate the same
way she recognizes her own bodily needs, but the communion of bonding goes beyond just physical processes.

Bonding, however, is biological. It involves a direct,
physical connection we have between our mid-brains and our
thumping hearts.[4] Bonded persons connect on intuitive levels
that operate below the level of ordinary awareness; the awareness resulting from the bonded state is qualitatively different
from the awareness of attachment behavior. The bonded person's center of operations is in the heart, the mid-brain

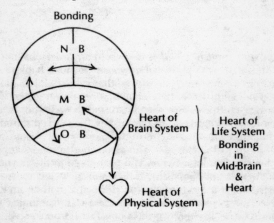

emotional center. In terms of physics, we can say the bonded
person's awareness is rooted in a wave-form energy that
underlies and gives rise to physical states. From such a
precursive and intuitive position, the bonded person responds
to physical stimuli in a qualitatively different way than does
the attached person.

Attachment occurs when bonding fails to take place at
birth. It can also occur at any point where there is a breakdown in the ongoing sequence of bondings that make up our
development. Attachment arises from processes in the old
brain and the lowest levels of the mid-brain, and thus the
attached person can only relate through specific, overt physical signals.

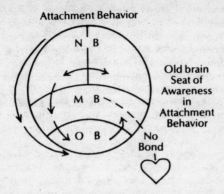

He cannot perceive subtle or intuitive signals that are the precursors of physical experience and is always aware only after the fact. He is, you might say, locked into hindsight. He reacts to stimuli, since by the time he has registered and processed an event, the time for response to that moment is gone. He compensates by trying to anticipate, predict, and control events in the outer world.

The physical energies of the old brain are weaker than the powers of the emotional mid-brain with its heart connections. This means that the attached person is left unaware of an inner power, has no trust that his needs will be met, and so moves aggressively to seize and possess. Vulnerable to an unpredictable physical world, the attached person attempts to incorporate into his ego defense the events, persons, and objects of his outer world. He treats the other person as an object for domination or as a device in his protective strategems. The attached person lives like an armed crustacean eternally on the alert.

Learning is a process of movement from that which is known into that which is unknown. The bonded person can make such a movement because his orientation is based on the non-physical realm of relationship that underlies and comes before all physical events. So any event fits the bonded state and can call forth a response, as opposed to a reaction. Bonding provides a capacity to flow with events on a precursive level. The attached person attempts to analyze the upcoming event ahead of time, predict the probable outcome, and try to enter into the flow to alter it on behalf of a supposedly preferable outcome. Since attachment behavior is always aware after the fact, this intellectual meddling is disruptive, always too late to alter what has taken place, and gets in the way of what should take place *next*. The attached person attempts to incorporate the unknown back into the known, to squeeze experience back into a tight frame of stable reference, which is always sensory-motor and tangible to the senses. The underlying, inherent essence or pattern of events is relational; it is, so to speak, wave-form rather than particle-form, abstract rather than concrete. The attached person fails to develop the ability to integrate the relational patterns into his interpretation of his world, and learning is difficult.

The bonded person can allow integration into wider circles of possibility for he has an intuitive sense of the underlying, inherent possibilities within situations. The bonded mother is in touch with the precursive, intuitive state and meets needs ahead of time. The bonded person assumes the unfolding moment will meet all needs and is thus open and receptive. This bonding function is the creative principle that holds a diverse creation together. Bonding is displayed from the appearance of the first unit of matter, the smallest sub-atomic particle, on up through galaxies and universes and our own brain/minds.

Bonding begins between mother and infant in utero. By birth, these bonds are well established, but they must then be confirmed and re-established after delivery, to integrate the new psyche into its new surroundings—which is the function of the bond. All bonding must be established before it is needed and confirmed at the time of need. Consider bonding to be a bridge between the known and the unknown. The bridge must be thoroughly anchored within the known ahead of time. And, before it can bear traffic, the bridge must be anchored on the other side as well. Then integration from the old into the new can take place. If this confirmation of the bond at the point of need, in the new terrain, does not take place, the new psyche will have no choice but to try to incorporate the new experience back into that which it knows. In the case of an infant's birth, this means relating all new experience back to the uterine experience rather than bringing that experience forward into the light of day. This regression leads to attachment behavior. For instance, the attached infant's fists will remain clenched—a delivery behavior—for many weeks after delivery. In the same way, the attached child will later cling physically to the parent, in fear of loss of contact, and will not freely explore the world. The bonded child's relations are on the deep intuitive level not subject to time and space, and he will range far afield.

Shortly before delivery from the womb, the infant's body releases a pituitary hormone called ACTH. When ACTH hits the infant's brain, millions of new connecting links between the major neurons form, preparing the brain for rapid change and learning.[5] ACTH also triggers a burst of adrenal hormones associated with stress or excitement.[6] These hormones bring about a series of responses. They signal that departure from the womb is under way, and so the baby's body goes into a high alert: The back arches, feet and toes point back, and fists clench to get digits out of the way. The hormone signal is carried back through the umbilical cord to the mother's body, signaling it, too, for strong, swift muscular responses to help expel the infant. (The distance to travel is about four inches.) The right amount of adrenal hormones produces the necessary alertness and energy for a successful birth. Too much hormone for too long a time will bring on shock, as when someone faints from prolonged crisis. Minor shock retards learning and adaptation as long as the shock continues. Sustained major shock can kill.

This burst of hormones prepares the infant for delivery; a secondary burst begins at issuance into the world. The hormone production then continues until birth is completed. The fulfillment of five simple needs will complete birth after delivery: a thorough stimulation and activation of each of the five senses. These five sensory needs are automatically met through the one, universal, and spontaneous response—placing the newborn in the nursing position. From that position, nature will receive her five signals that birth is taking place, a new life is beginning.[7] Until nature's signals that birth is taking place *are* met, adrenal production will continue at its initial rate, awaiting those signals to shut down this output. Nature cannot program for failure, as we have seen, and unless the birth needs are met, adrenal production will continue until a critical mass builds up which sends the infant into some form of shock, which can range from minimal to severe. Statistically, if the birth needs are not met within about forty-five minutes after delivery, this critical mass level is reached,[8] the infant's sensory-motor system largely shuts down, there is a retreat to a uterine state of consciousness, and adaptation and response to the world largely cease.

The umbilical cord is some eighteen to twenty inches in length, just the right distance to permit the infant to suckle and still leave the cord intact—an important and obvious bridge between old and new. This keeps the infant's supply of blood and oxygen linked with the mother's, as it has been for nine months, and gives him ample time to allow the mucus in his mouth, nose, and tubes to drain, clearing them for the new task of breathing. Then, from that universal nursing position the infant's five signals that birth is taking place will automatically be met. The inner blueprints of sight, sound, touch, taste, and smell will all be given their necessary stimulus, their model-content, from the physical world, anchoring the bonding bridge in the new domain. The necessary functional structures of brain/mind and body will rapidly unfold, and birth will be complete.

We have, in our old brains, two major neural gateways called the *reticular formation*.[9] Four of our five bodily senses are channelled through these pathways, as are our motor

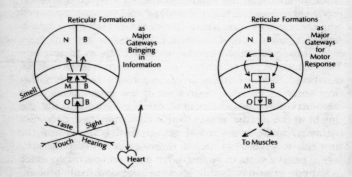

responses to such information. Our sensory-motor systems are, in fact, extensions of these reticular formations. These are key neural areas where sensory information is brought together, coordinated, and the coordinates sent on to other brain areas for further processing. The information coming into the old brain from its various sensors is a kind of rough accumulation of raw materials, giving only the most primitive and crude information in itself. So the old brain sends this conglomerate straight to a reticular formation in the mid-brain, which is the major gateway, probably the central nexus of all brain function.[10] In the mid-brain's gateway, the formative actions of emotion, intuition, smell, and other forces are added, all of which sort the raw material from the old brain into meaningful categories of relationship. This rich synthesis of primary action is then distributed to all parts of the brain for any further refinements and responses.

The job at birthing is to activate this sensory system in its entirety and get the processing of information functional in the shortest possible time. This means having the reticular formations of both old brain and mid-brain operative. The sensory system cannot be activated and completed in utero, for that is a dark, insulated, rather quiet water world. Our skin, with its millions of nerve endings, is coated with a fatty substance that protects us against the constant water immersion. Hearing, movement, and a response to movement develop quite well in utero. The mother's heartbeat, its force and sound, is the major stimulus, and her visceral activity, body movements, breathing, and voice all provide a constant stimulus and a major anchor for bonding. The other senses, however, must await delivery to be activated.

The infant cannot provide himself with any of this sensory activation after delivery. All of it must be done for the newborn, and his system is designed with the expectation that this will *be* done. Activation of the senses takes place automatically and spontaneously simply by introducing the infant to the mother in skin-to-skin contact immediately after delivery. Millions of years of biological encoding ensure the instinctive response of each to the other from that point on.

The five parts of birth can be listed in any order, since activation of one is usually accompanied by activation of all, but I will take them in arbitrary order. First, vision. Our blueprint for vision is open-ended but is prestructured to recognize a human face. Among all possible patterns of visual experience, a face is intended to be immediately cognized by the infant.[11] At delivery the infant can recognize a face, will spend eighty percent of his visual time looking at a face, and, if given a face within a distance of six to twelve inches during the first forty-five minutes after delivery, his entire visual system will be fully functional by the end of that time. The parallax of the eyes (the muscular coordination to focus and follow movement) and long- and short-range vision will fully function. This infant will then smile every time a face is presented, and this smiling, begun usually within that first forty-five minutes, continues. Nature has had one of her signals met.

The second phase of birth, hearing, has been established in utero by the infant's imprinting to the mother's voice and heartbeat. Positioning the infant at that ideal distance of six to twelve inches from the mother's face—stimulating vision—re-establishes and confirms these uterine bonds in the new surroundings. Most mothers put their newborn infants to the left breast, and the majority of infant holding takes place there. Excursions to the right breast are just that—excursions. Home base seems to be on the left side, where the heart is. Re-connecting with this well-known stimulus, and the mother's voice (for mothers immediately begin a high-pitched kind of universal baby talk at this point), help anchor the bond, and nature checks off need number two.

The universal nursing position, which is the place where all five needs are met, triggers the third phase, nursing. The first milk (colostrum) transfers to the infant the mother's immunities gained over her lifetime.[12] This first milk may contain a hormone that counteracts any excess adrenals to bring the infant's system back into hormonal balance, and further, nursing activates the mandibular joint (of the jaw), which is connected with the vestibular rotation factor of the inner ear, which, in turn, is vital to body balance and to orientation of sounds in space.

Human infant digestion is designed to handle only the lightest of nourishment, and human milk is the thinnest of all mammals'. That is because the human infant is designed to nurse between forty-five to sixty times a day.[13] Nature could easily have designed things otherwise. Baby rabbits nurse only about once a day, for instance, and their milk is so condensed it is barely fluid. This is because mama rabbit must forage for food most of the time and may get to the nest only occasionally. Mama human is expected (in nature's agenda) to tote her baby about, carry it along with her, and give a steady supply of that very thin milk. The reason for this weak milk, and need of a steady supply of it, is simple. The human infant must receive a constant activation of his entire sensory system to nurture his brain/mind and ensure the development of intelligence.[14] Frequent nursing automatically ensures a major sensory stimulus on all levels: a constant renewal of the face at a distance of six to twelve inches; a renewal of the heartbeat connection; the familiar voice; and stimulus of the sensory endings of the skin by the continual movement of the mother in her daily routines.

We turn now to the fourth phase, touch. Cross-culturally, on skin-to-skin contact with her newborn, mothers begin an automatic, gentle palming of the infant's body. All mammals stimulate the skin area of their newborns, mostly by constant licking. Prevent this activity and an animal infant will not survive.[15] The nerve endings of our skin cannot be developed in utero, covered with that fatty coating (vernix caseus) as we are in our water world. Our mother's gentle massaging, and the ongoing stimulus of body contact with her, bring these sensory endings to life. Then, with a majority of its sensory system activated, the reticular formation in the old brain goes into full operation. Sensory information from the outside world is channelled properly and sent on to the mid-brain for processing. And, not to be discounted, all this sensory information is benign, beneficial, and exactly what was expected, what has worked for millions of years.

The sense of smell, the last signal, is a mid-brain action. The newborn can immediately pick out his mother's smell from among that of many other mothers and will respond to it. This plays only a part in nature's final birth need, though, for the key to the mid-brain's activation lies, again, in that universal nursing position. The mid-brain's reticular formation, wherein all information is synthesized and given its complete organization, is the real key to bonding, and the bonding function enters directly into the quality of the mid-brain's future work. Bonding is also necessary to complete the midbrain's reticular formation just as it is for the old brain. The mid-brain's reticular formation must have information from the old brain as the stimulus to complete this mid-brain area. And for the rest of our lives all our information from the world outside will be given its qualitative, relational pattern through this mid-brain action. This relational action is the essence of bonding itself, since bonding is that which ties things together. The mid-brain's subtle energy is more powerful than the old brain's material sensing, and the powerful energy modulates, shapes, and gives relational meaning to sensory information.[16] Otherwise the old brain's raw information is largely without meaning and has no coordinating pattern adaptable to the rest of the brain.

The child cannot furnish his old brain with material for its completion at birth; this must be provided by the mother. For the first seven to twelve months of the infant's life the locus of awareness is in the old brain.[17] Once the sensory-motor system is stabilized to some extent, through the mother's nurturing, the infant can initiate his own search for sensory stimulus, and begins within weeks an aggressive exploration of his sensory world. The mid-brain, though intimately involved in sensory processing, is not the locus of infant awareness during this early, essentially reptilian stage. And so emotional-relational stimuli for that mid-brain must be provided and reinforced continually by the mother, until the early sensory-motor period is complete. When nature shifts the infant's awareness into that mid-brain as a locus, along with the locus awareness in the old brain,[18] the mid-brain as a relational function can develop its autonomy as did the old brain—a process which takes two to three years. But during the first year of life the mid-brain—the "heart" of our system—must be furnished its stimulus just as the body must receive its nourishment.

A direct set of nerves connects the heart of the brain system with the heart of physical life, pumping away in our chest. The mid-brain both sends signals to that great organ and receives signals from it in an as yet unknown synchrony, but one which is the obvious core of all bonding. (See illustration on page 29.) Both organs, brain and heart, are places of high concentration of the melanin molecule, the probable interface between consciousness and matter.[19] Affairs of the heart are matters of subtle, intuitive energy, matters of relationship, and melanin is almost certainly involved. Take two live heart cells, place them well separated on a microscopic slide, and you will note that they pulsate, as good heart cells should. But they pulse at random, different rates. Bring the two cells closer together, however, and at a certain critical distance, before they touch, they begin to pulsate in synchrony, functioning as a miniature heart should. They have arced the gap of separation; they are bonded.

The newborn's consciousness is brought about through sensory stimuli that he cannot furnish for himself. Emotional stimuli, which the newborn also cannot furnish, are equally important. The emotional stimuli activate the mid-brain areas as an emotional function, that is, as the organ of relationship. As noted earlier, the mid-brain reticular formation could not be completed in utero since there was insufficient stimulus. But a major bonding stimulus *did* take place in utero: the heartbeat to which the infant imprints. Reinforcement of this sound after delivery is a principal bonding clue. Medical researchers found not long ago that piping a recorded heartbeat into hospital nurseries markedly reduced crying in the newborns.[20] The isolated little systems were simply fooled into thinking that their principal needs were being met. (Similarly, sugar water will reduce hunger crying, but does little for nutrition.)

Consider now those two heart cells on that microscopic slide, and how they arc the gap of separation and communicate. Each is a concentration of the melanin molecule, interface between consciousness and physical process. Our hearts contain billions of those cells with their massive accumulations of melanin. If two single cells arc the gap of distance and communicate, how much more the arc between two actual hearts, if brought into proximity. So consider again that universal left-breast position of the newborn, which gives an ongoing physical proximity of the infant's and the mother's hearts. Through the physical proximity of the two hearts, emotional imprinting of the mid-brain and its major reticular formation does take place in utero, just as do hearing and intuitive sensing. The bond, however, must be re-established after delivery. Hearing is part of this, but the emotional imprinting through the actual *proximity* of physical heart systems must also be reaffirmed. Having had a literal heart-to-heart chat for many months in utero, that conversation must be resumed in the new domain to cement the bond.[21]

If the heart of the bonding process is established, the infant's mid-brain receives its input both from the old brain's reticular formation, which sends the physical-sensory information (largely provided by the mother), and from emotional-intuitive inputs from the mother's own emotional-intuitive outputs. Furnished with both emotional and physical stimuli to activate both reticular formations and complete the birth process, the infant is now equipped to adapt to his new environment. He must, however, *continue* to receive these inputs until autonomy of both primary brains is well under way.

Now we can see why mothers instinctively place infants at the left breast for the majority of the time. All birthing signals are met here, and within a short time the production of adrenal hormones stops. Birth is completed; millions of years of programming have succeeded. The infant is now highly alert (though he sleeps at will), his instinctual responses are in a relaxed learning posture, his eyes are focused and taking in everything. His hands are open, exploring all within reach, and he smiles and smiles at every face in this new, rewarding environment. He has given up a limited life for a greater life, relinquished a safe warm haven for a far more exciting and nurturing place. Learning has begun on a brilliant note.

Learning, as we have seen, is movement, and if this first great movement is successful, the pattern of movement from known to unknown is well established and will be carried through in all the many subsequent shifts of knowing that must be made. Each stage of development is an extension of this birth procedure, and if the bonds with each subsequent stage are established ahead of time and re-established after each shift, that shift will be made in its entirety. There will be no splitting of ego between opposing factions: When nature moves the ego on to be integrated into a higher function, the ego has the capacity to shift. If the bond is not established, there is no bridge to the mid-brain as the intuitive center underlying both known and unknown. That ego will, of necessity, hold to its identity with the sensory-motor system even when nature, unable to program for failure, goes ahead and tries to shift that ego into its next higher stage. Ego will fragment between its old brain identity and the new and more powerful pull of the mid-brain locus. The ego will stay in the sensory-motor mode, so to speak, and try to incorporate into that mode the new possibilities.

Bonding occurs when the infant is met on both physical and subtle levels by his caretaker. Anchored in the power of the subtle heart system, the infant is always anchored in the core of his life. He is rooted within the great subtle intuitive energies that power physical life, no matter how his physical situation shifts and changes. Through nursing, his continual heart connection with the mother signals well-being, the heart-to-heart relations secured, and the infant's heart continually sends these signals of well-being on to the mid-brain, which acts in that emotional grouping of sensory information that gives him his stable world.

A state of euphoric, excited, interested, and enthusiastic well-being results. Anchored in the powerful subtle energies at the core of his life, he can change his physical moorings and relations with ease and skill, encompassing ever larger horizons of experience. He will arrive at the first great shift of blueprint, the division of his conscious awareness between old and mid-brains, at an average of ten to fourteen months ahead of the unbonded child. If his future shifts of blueprint prove to be as successfully bonded, his superior intelligence, social compatibility, nurturing of his or her own offspring, and so on, are assured.

The breast-fed child is always more intelligent than the bottle-fed child, and the longer he is breast-fed, the more intelligent he is.[22] The reason is the continual sensory stimulus and bonding automatically provided. The bonded mother will always (unless some major disaster intervenes) breast-feed her child and for periods up to three years. She will breast-feed against all odds and opposition. The unbonded mother, on the other hand, is virtually incapable of breast-feeding except for, perhaps, two to three weeks at best. Always some perfectly logical reason for not breast-feeding comes up. There are no moral-ethical issues involved here; these are simple biological responses. And failure to breast-feed automatically means that none of the above named processes can take place. The opposite occurs just as automatically—and that is attachment behavior.[23]

Since I covered what happens in the majority of technological births in *Magical Child*, I will give only a brief summary here. My reason for doing so is to point up the nature of attachment behavior, since only through a contrast of bonding and attachment can I clarify the issues of development. Over ninety percent of American deliveries are in hospitals. (Only thirty-four percent were before World War II.)[24] The majority of these deliveries are chemically induced and take place between nine in the morning and three in the afternoon— convenience hours of obstetricians and staff. The drugs used for inducement, and the drugs used for anesthetizing the mother, transfer to the infant in utero in an average of forty-five seconds and scramble the ordinary delivery birth signals.[25]

Most women deliver in brilliantly lit operating amphitheatres, often strapped down to the operating table, knees in stirrups. Almost universally, delivery is attempted with the woman on her back—a most difficult position. Masked medical people use scalpels, forceps, and various machinery in the extraction of the infant. The umbilical cord is immediately cut in the majority of deliveries, creating oxygen deprivation in the newborn. Oxygen deprivation is a major mammalian fear. The infant instinctively gasps for air, prematurely. He may inhale the mucus still in his tubes and gag; suction devices are then employed to meet the emergency. In most cases he is held by the heels and given resounding swats on his backside to stop his gagging and/or to initiate those first breaths. An autopsy of silent crib-death victims showed that eighty percent had died from internal bleeding in the upper spinal column.[26] The result of this type of delivery-induced damage is undetectable by an ordinary autopsy. The slow clotting that results takes some four to six weeks to build up around the major nerve plexes leading from the spinal column to the heart and lungs, at which point the infant quietly stops breathing, there in his isolated crib.

(A majority of the silent crib-death victims in the United States are black infants. A majority of the charity cases in our hospitals are blacks or other ghetto peoples, and a 1976 survey showed that these cases receive minimal care. Since charity cases are often paid for by the state, at a fraction of the ordinary fees charged, many hospitals set a limit on the delivery room and doctor's time allotted to any patient; speed and efficiency become the rule.[27] A young doctor reported to me that he had interned in a major eastern hospital where a large percentage of the ghetto population was delivered. He had been required to deliver some dozen of these charity case women. In each case, he said, the woman was drugged on entry, strapped down, the baby extricated, the umbilical cord cut, the baby spanked for air, handed to the nurse for processing, and, under the direct instructions of his supervisor, he had in every case seized the umbilical cord and jerked the placenta loose, to clear the room for the next patient. Only later did he find that many of the women hemorrhaged as a result.)

Even during more normal delivery in hospitals, the new-born's eyes, unused to any light, open to the brilliance of the operating room. Genetically geared to search for a human face, the infant finds only masked figures. He closes his eyes against the sensory overload; his eyelids are peeled back by the medical men and a harsh chemical is dropped into them. (Seeing, and its related smiling at faces, do not develop in these infants for an average of ten to twelve weeks.) The infant is then washed, weighed, wrapped, and dispatched to the nursery. Here he undergoes two states totally unknown in nature, and for which nature has no passible machinery for compensation: silence and stillness. The infant experiences sensory deprivation, the complete and total opposite of what millennia of genetic encoding have called for.

The trauma, physical insult, and pain send the infant's output of adrenal hormones into a life-preserving burst. Within an average of forty-five minutes, the continued outpouring of adrenaline hits a critical mass in the bloodstream and brain of the infant and the infant goes into shock, a loss of consciousness. He then exhibits two well-known states: massive crying when aroused, and a heavy torpor-like sleep which is not the ordinary rhythmic sleep-dream-wake cycle established in utero, but minimal to severe shock.[28]

I am leaving out here another major cause of damage in male infants, automatic circumcision, an issue covered with remarkable thoroughness in recent studies.[29] Suffice it for now to say that the production of adrenal hormones continues unabated as the infant's system awaits the needed stimuli to complete the birth process, and undergoes continual re-stimulation through trauma. This over-production of adrenal hormones remains at a critical level for an average of ten to twelve weeks—whereas in a natural delivery and birth a majority of the adrenal hormones will be gone within a maximum of twenty-four hours.[30] There is no smiling in these infants for an average of ten to twelve weeks. People in infant research refer to the "smiling syndrome" which then appears, which they think indicates the first signs of consciousness. It takes that long for the sporadic physical stimuli given the infant, isolated and wrapped in blankets, fed from a bottle, and so on, finally to activate the reticular formations and achieve some compensation of the damage done.

Brain damage from oxygen deprivation will have been done in anywhere from twenty to forty percent of deliveries, with the higher percentages among ghetto children.[31] Far more damaging than the obvious physical damage, however, is the absence of bonding between infant and mother. Instead of bonding, the infant will physically imprint to whatever concrete stimuli he is afforded, generally the baby blanket. The infant undergoes deprivation of the emotional-intuitive functions of the mid-brain's reticular formation. Without the emotional-intuitive inputs from the mother, without the constant sensory stimuli and renewal of bonding functions, the basic coordinating and organizing force of the mid-brain on the old brain sensory information is lacking. Whatever sensory intake occurs in those first weeks is chaotic, without organization, and disruptive. Meaning and emotional relationship are the issues at stake.

The shift of ego-identity from the old to the mid-brain will be ten to fourteen months later in the unbonded, isolated child than in the bonded one. All future capacity to learn, to move from context to context, will be impaired. For the pattern of response to stimuli will itself remain locked into sensory-motor reactions at their most primitive level. The child will not be anchored in the deep core of the subtle processes of the mid-brain and heart, from which base all capacity to change, or to learn, is manifested.

From every point the target of damage lies in the mid-brain's reticular formation, the heart of bonding between mother and child, child and world, child and society, eventually male and female, and so on. The result of attachment is the compulsive survival reaction to try to possess physically all phenomena occurring to or around one, to cling to phenomena as the only means of self-identity, since no other form of relationship is biologically available. Bonding uses attachment behavior (all children grasp and cling to their things at times), just as intelligence can use intellect. Attachment and possession are functional when encompassed within bonding's powerful moorings in the emotional center—and deadly when operating only from the reptilian center. Attachment behavior cannot encompass bonding (nor substitute for it) or lead to bonding. The weaker physical energy cannot encompass the more powerful subtle one. The child locked into attachment behavior is limited to the weak physical-sensory system, with an impaired emotional system to relate and balance even physical phenomena.

The unbonded child has no choice but to try to possess his experience, as he grasps that baby blanket, his only stable source of stimuli. But human awareness can exist only through relationship. If denied the relationship given through the mid-brain and heart connection, the infant has no choice but to establish what relations he can on the shallow sensory levels afforded him. He will then treat all encounters as objects of possession, and later, of domination, since emotional bonding, the common unity of experience on the subtle levels, will not be within his capacity. Again, moral-ethical failure is not in the picture at all. We are speaking of biological functions. This inability to relate on emotional levels is widespread. The unbonded male treats the female as an object of gratification, a physical possession to be dominated. And we are now all too familiar with the battered-wife syndrome.

Now, if the ego's first and only stable identity is sensory-motor, then at each shift of ego-awareness into a higher brain function the attached ego automatically tries, as an act of self-preservation, to *incorporate* the new state of consciousness back into its sensory-motor identity.

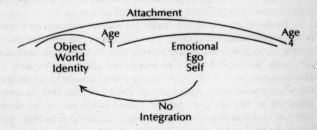

At each shift of the system a quantum-leap of possibilities and powers unfolds. Compulsively trying to incorporate the higher energy structure into the lower is impossible; biologcally, it just cannot be done. At each shift we must relinquish our attachments to our earlier identity and *be* integrated into the higher integral structure. Nature provides for this integration automatically, beneath the level of our awareness, if we are bonded. Our egos are carried along from state to state; we have nothing to do with the process.

Attempting to incorporate the new capacities offered at each stage of development back into the sensory-motor identity splits the ego between the two states while identity remains locked in the more primitive form. We end in an internal struggle between competing systems: an old brain *id* at war with a mid-brain *ego* at war with a new brain *superego* and so on. More insidious is our touch-hungry system, sensorily deprived, locked into sensory-saturation which tries to ease an inner hunger that is never articulated. The compulsive consumer devours the earth, crying "More! More!" yet is never satisfied.

The result of attachment behavior is not simply emotional retardation and anxiety, but rage, the anger of impotency. Identified only with the weakest of our systems, the sensory-motor, we have no way to deal with the vast subtle forces of our lives, and thus feel victimized by the outer world. Rage is expressed in the current epidemic outbreak of battered children. In 1983 there were over a million cases of brutally beaten children, five thousand outright murders known—the average age of the victims between two weeks and two years. By 1980, sixty to seventy percent of all American children under the age of four were in day-care centers for periods up to twelve hours a day, seven days a week. A study showed the adrenal steroid levels of a majority of these children to be at near shock level, the shock coming not from the day-care situation, but from separation anxiety, the psychological abandonment suffered by the children on separation from parents.[32] For the infant or child must have a continual renewal of his basic orientation, his touchstone for reality and his model: the parent. True, were it not for the buffer effect of day-care, which stands between parent and child for the major portion of the day, abuse and murder of infants would be far greater than it is. Even so, day-care as a solution breeds a far more difficult problem for the next generation: Studies show that many day-care children express marked hostility, aggression, and violence toward caretakers and peers.[33]

Meanwhile, parenting has become a major national issue. Institutions, foundations, forums, workshops, college courses, and a staggering output of how-to-parent books flood the market. But attempts along this line are all intellectual, and no amount of intellectual training or effort can replace the automatic bonds of the subtle system on which our surface life is based. The bonding function of the mid-brain and heart is simply not an intellectual process. In 1982, 87,000 cases of violent attacks against teachers by students were reported in American schools, while many school administrations, shielding the public against the deplorable situation, report only the most extreme cases. Fifty percent of all American marriages are now ending in divorce, including remarriages. And thirty-eight percent of all American children are in homes with only one original parent. This list could go on into volumes. I have touched only the tip of an iceberg here, simply to point out that all these effects, now breaking up technological society, are directly related to the mid-brain and its function, and that the breakdown is generated at birth.

In 1979, the state of California, facing an annual budget of four billion dollars for crime and violence (the figures have since nearly doubled), appropriated $750,000 for the first scientific study ever made of the root causes of crime and violence.[34] Two years later a first paper was issued, listing the ten principal causes of crime and violence in our nation. At the top of the list was the violent way we bring our children into the world. The next five causes prove to be the direct result of the big "number one."

A culture can destroy itself through some insignificant, thoughtless little practice. Medical childbirth in the United States is not insignificant, but almost a fifty-billion-dollar-a-year industry. I have touched on this unhappy business not with any intention of bringing the system down, or even changing it, which I doubt can be done. I want instead to contrast bonding with attachment in the hopes of making more credible some of the seemingly incredible material that follows.

The issue is that post-biological development rests on the biological. If our biological development is so damaged that a normal functioning is largely unknown, how much more difficult it will be to grasp the issues of post-biological development. The good news, however, is that post-biological development is based on an energy, a function, a power, which can heal, mend, patch up virtually any damage done in our earlier years. Nature is not easily outdone. Since this healing takes place only through integrating lower structures into higher ones, the answer for us lies not in more and more social therapy and bootstrap operations of an intellectual nature, but in the developmental plan built into our system. So, with only an occasional glance at our mounting disasters, we will move right on into development, where the action is.

4

Snake's-Eye
View

Recently a twenty-two-year-old female was found in a California attic. Normal and bright as an infant, she had been tied to
a potty seat in that attic from about her sixth month of life,
from which time she had had no human contact. A daily pan
of food and water was provided and the potty emptied occasionally. Incredibly, she survived—more or less. When found,
twenty-two years later, she was dwarfed and virtually mindless.[1]
Without models from the world around her to act as stimuli
to her inner blueprint, her consciousness receded back into
that continuum from which it came. Attempts to teach or
train her have not been successful, since the stage-specific
periods for learning had all been missed.

Our awareness at birth can be thought of as the electricity resulting from an electric generator. Coils of copper
wire revolve within a surrounding magnet. Moving the coils
within the surrounding magnetic field creates a kind of stimulus-
friction between that field and the one created by the moving
coils. Stop the movement and the electricity ceases. In the
same way, the stimulus of the sensory system by outside
objects can be said to generate infant consciousness. Remove
the stimuli and awareness recedes. Perhaps the electricity is
not created by the magnetos, armature, brushes, wires, and
all within that generator, but movement of that gadgetry sets
up the conditions by which electricity is conducted. Our
nurturing of the infant or child does not create awareness in
our child, but it sets up the conditions for awareness to
manifest itself.

For general consciousness to become specific awareness, the consciousness must relate to something already available. Infant consciousness must be given models of manifest consciousness, which in turn elicit consciousness into awareness. Since there is no awareness without stimulus, infant awareness and the outer stimuli that elicit that awareness are a single entrainment in the brain. By entrainment I mean an interlocked sequence of responses organized around a specific activity, such as our shift of balance in going up a step. Put the entrainment into motion and its lock-step character must play itself out in its entirety, as a unit. Thus the infant's awareness of self and awareness of the object which elicits that awareness are a single unit; the infant's identity and the object's identity are the same in the infant's experience. This is concrete consciousness, our earliest and most physical form of awareness. Ego identifies first with the objects and events that stimulate and maintain the awareness of self. This is the period of egocentricity: The child is the center of a world that radiates out from him.

People who study child development have wondered why the human infant is helpless for so much longer than other mammals. The reason is the kind of foundation the human must establish. A frog's brain, for instance, registers movement in specific objects that match his food-blueprint, and the frog responds accordingly. Movement not fitting this food category is registered as suspect and the frog takes protective action. As we move up the level of brain evolution, the level of complexity and extension of possibility increase. *Our* frog brain must register movement and size also, but of an infinitely wider level of complexity and possibility.

I drop a spool of thread on the floor. The frog would make a quick leap for safety. Our infant spots the spool with her long-range sense of vision and is impelled to interact with that object with her other senses. She is driven to build up a full sensory knowledge of that spool. She crawls over to grasp it, tastes it, smells it, touches and feels it in every way, intently looks at it close up, and listens to see if it has anything to say. If allowed this compulsive interaction, she will end with a full sensory structure of knowledge of that spool. Through her interaction a pattern of this object is etched into her neural circuitry, ready for re-employment. Her next encounter with a similar object will require less energy of attention. She will have a pattern for assimilating that kind of information. She will have a concept.

I take that spool away from our crawler and she immediately scans for another object of appropriate size, moves to interact with it, and builds her full sensory structure of knowledge about it. The blueprint is generic; its content makes it specific. Nature is not specific about the actual content so long as it fits the general criteria the blueprint encompasses. The world is the human child's oyster, whereas the early chick just out of the shell will peck at any appropriately sized object that resembles a seed or tiny insect. Everything the child experiences teaches her something; the world teaches the child about the world. Any object will do for our crawler and she will relinquish one object for another willingly. "Out of sight means out of mind," since any object fills her entire perceptual field. That single object requires all the energy of her conscious attention. Single entrainment is the rule of the reptilian brain, so if the object is removed attention simply shifts to another.

At some point, statistically around the end of the first year, our infant accumulates a critical mass of such constructions. All at once, out of sight is *not* out of mind. *Object-constancy* takes place.[2] The object of interaction, heretofore casually expendable, becomes a permanent part of awareness. Our child will search for a removed object or will protest its removal. No longer does a single object fill her perceptual field. The object is now only one part of a larger perceptual field in which objects become permanent fixtures. The infant can now conceive of something that exists even though it is not concretely evident.

Object-constancy takes place in a single shift and brings in an entire chain of different behaviors. The infant's locus of awareness, the center of conscious attention, shifts from its single entrainment in the reptilian brain into a parallel, equally conscious involvement in the affairs of the mid-brain. Now, self as perceiver sits in the mid-brain and self as world-perceived sits in the old brain. A first separation of consciousness has taken place and a full development of the emotional mid-brain begins. Self as perceiver translates through the mid-brain and makes an emotional overlay on the experiences registered by the old brain. Mid-brain's emotional power has always organized old brain's raw materials, but now that

organization becomes self-conscious and will include the esthetic response, including likes and dislikes, which have been
made possible by the relation between the two functions of
self. Through this division of labor between old and mid-
brains, the child can perceive any number of objects simultaneously and make a qualitative evaluation of that experience.
An esthetic overlay on her world appears; she experiences
reality.

The stimuli needed to bring about object-constancy can
be quite different in different cultural settings—a New York
City apartment in winter, or an African bush world. But
when it forms, the universal perceptual field of a world will
be essentially the same for children in all cultures. We all
play our games on the same given stage. We view the same
world, but in different ways. Our worldview is an overlay that
begins when we shift our locus of awareness into the mid-
brain esthetic center. We participate in creating our own
reality, but not the world.

After object-constancy, the child still interacts with objects through all five senses in order to build a full-sensory
knowledge of the world. But now these interactions will be
made from a new evaluative impetus. The child is aware as a
self interacting with the object, rather than totally identified
with the object of interaction. As the object becomes constant, so does individual awareness. Ego arrives.

At this point the corpus callosum makes its initial appearance. Until this time both hemispheres of our new brains
have imprinted the same information given by the old brain
and mid-brain. After object-constancy, two different types of
conscious activity are taking place—object encounter and emotional response to that encounter. A distinction between object and self begins to formulate, and the hemispheres of the
new brain begin to translate this differentiation.

That a completely new set of abilities unfolds at object-
constancy is easily explained by the different natures of the
two primary brains. Logic, for instance, is based on relating
things or events and requires some form of separation. Our
most elementary logic of relationship begins in this first division of our awareness between self as sensory world and self
as esthetic response to that world. Through this logic we will
organize our world into meaningful patterns, patterns of emotional relationship based on likes and dislikes. And, almost

incidentally, our ego will be articulated through this esthetic judgment, defined as an integral structure separate from the world.

From the time of object-constancy the model that draws out the ego structure determines the nature of that ego. The world teaches the child about the world, and the world-field appears automatically as a shared, common backdrop or universal playground. This is not the case for all future structures of knowledge. All future growth of intelligence will be determined by the esthetic models by which the child's own esthetic sense is developed. She will relate to her world according to the models she has for such relationship—and on such relations she will build her structure of reality, her emotional, intellectual overlay on her world structure. From object-constancy on we become what we behold emotionally—our parents and society.

At the time of object-constancy the child begins to walk, emotional language is completed, and word language begins. (The sequences vary.) Above all, our child is driven to make a non-stop exploration of the world around her as *will* enters the picture. Will is the grosser or more physical form of emotion; in the early child it is the instinctual drive to overcome obstacles to development. Development can only take place as the child constructs a knowledge of her physical world by interacting with it, then acts on that knowledge esthetically, and builds a knowledge of self-awareness as distinct from the objects of awareness. An ego structure, a sense of self-awareness, must be built up. Ego is achieved through the relationships established between self and world. So a knowledge of the outside world is the only way by which a knowledge of an inner self can form. Survival of self is at stake.

Our child brooks no interference, then, in her insatiable drive to interact with her world. Her irrepressible will has no logic to it at all. She is in no way separate from her will, nor is her will amenable to adult logic. This willfulness of the early child is grossly misunderstood. Parents interpret the drive as willful disobedience. Many a battered, even murdered child results. But the child has no choice in the matter. Her willfulness is non-volitional and drives her as we are driven to move our hand from a hot stove.

Parent says, "Don't touch, dear," and this negative initiates a powerful drive to overcome the obstacle to her exploration of her world. Little dear must explore in spite of these warnings, and *does* touch. In our high-tech age "Keep Out of Reach of Children" is our most common sign, and the child is likely burned, electrocuted, mangled, or, at best, beaten for disobedience.

A contradiction takes place between two powerful drives. On the one hand, children are driven to construct their knowledge according to parental guidance and modeling. The parent is a touchstone for reality, a cornerstone of the house of intelligence. The child is driven to follow and maintain the bond with this model. Without modeling the ego fragments in confusion. On the other hand, the will drives to overcome obstacles to development. The child cannot resolve the issue: Body seems moved in spite of self, while such a move threatens the bond. So the parent must resolve this issue for the child. For instance, if real danger is involved, physical removal and involvement in another exploration are a common-sense course. The discriminating parent will guard against creating double binds, and will be less concerned with teaching the child obedience and more in developing the child's curiosity and intelligence. Millions of years of survival-encoding work for the benefit of the parent, for the child is designed to learn and learns by following his models. His will to follow the model is the same will that drives him to explore the world. He is, we might say, genetically disciplined. Just as the word "discipline" comes from the word "disciple," so the disciple or student follows the teacher when real learning takes place. Will is the child's mental muscularity, his power for following, which must be nurtured as any other capacity.

When the student does not follow, there is no discipline, and learning breaks down. Discipline has become a mania in our day since learning has faltered. But if models do not match the needs of the student, or if the model leads into a no-win double bind that negates any response, then how can there be following or discipline? When we say we must then discipline the child we mean, in effect, force her to follow or break her will. And a broken will is a broken mental muscularity for learning, a lost capacity for adaptation, socialization, and creativity.

5

Concrete Language

Our language blueprint unfolds as all intelligence does, from the concrete to the abstract. The word grows from a sensory-motor reflex begun in utero, using the old brain, to an emotional overlay made by the mid-brain, on to a full-fledged word structure, related to the new brain. Words are sound and sound affects our physical system in many ways. Through the melanin molecule, for instance, sound can be converted into light, spatial qualities, and other sensory phenomena. The unique sounds we call phonemes, out of which language is made and to which we are genetically geared, participate in a wide spectrum of the creation of the child's world.

As we have seen, phonemes initiate muscular response in the infant, and the muscular movement imprints on the brain the content associated with the movement. In this way the name for a thing and the thing so named form as a single pattern in the brain/mind and we call this singleness *concrete language*. Langer and Cassirer once proposed that language arose from emotional outbursts, as in singing.[1] Insofar as the way language forms in us, this is the second stage, the mid-brain's role in the game. Listen to the *lalling* of the early infant, those random sounds produced from birth on. Even here emotional tone soon enters and lalling will begin to cover a wide range of expressiveness. Sound as expression precedes language as words, just as language as muscular movement precedes expression.

Long before words appear, we hear squeals of delight, rage, or pleasure. The first speech is emotional exuberance, or, occasionally, complaint. Our toddler continually talks as she plays about the house. Seldom does a recognizable word occur, but words are not necessary. A wide range of inflections, pitches, emphases, scoldings, purrings, frownings, and excitements pour out. Intricate statements are made in declarative or dramatic style, questions are asked in plaintive tones, comments are thrown about, but few if any articulate words result.

An early aspect of language learning is pointing. The earliest pointing is generic, an automatic gesture that is nonvolitional. The child's arm just flings out in some direction, index finger extended. After object-constancy, pointing becomes more specific and volitional. She begins to point toward things and finally begins that incessant "What's that, Mama?"—asking for a name for the thing toward which she points.

Matching word with object is the third stage of language construction. The name the adult gives to the child in response enters as an integral part of her construction of knowledge of that object. The name serves on many levels: the name's sounding, the actual wave-effect of the word's sound, acts on the sensory-motor system (we saw its beginnings in utero) to coordinate the myriad bits of sensory information coming in from those various sensory sources concerning that event named. The sound waves seem to weld together the sensory bits from smell, taste, sight, and so on into a meaningful and repeatable unit.[2]

As a result, in concrete language if you "punch the button in the brain" for the event, you get its name; conversely, punch the button for name, you get some approximation of its event. A single entrainment holds between name and thing. Ask our two-year-old to say the word *hand* and she will move her hand as she says the word. This unity of word and thing holds throughout the pre-logical years. Ask six-year-old Fred whether he could have been named Jim, and he will be both offended and emphatic in denial. He is Fred! How could he be Jim? Nor can you, by any logic, convince pre-logical Fred that his name is arbitrary. (He might agree with you outwardly, but inwardly he will know you are silly.) Name and identity as Fred have grown as a single structure of knowledge.

The name label that coordinates those senses into a unit

of meaning will be used to coordinate that structure with larger groupings of named structures. Names form structures among themselves and establish relationships. All cats attract our toddler's attention and *kitty* names them all. But the neighbor cat who comes to visit is specific and is both kitty and Flo-Bo. Names identify phenomena out of context and give the child a way to refer back and reflect on. As Vygotsky says, for the early child, to think is to remember. For the later child, to remember is to think. Name and memory fuse.[3]

Every bit as important is the fact that when the parents name a phenomenon, they establish that event as part of their own worldview. The parent is the child's model and the child is driven to construct his world, self, and language systems according to the model the parents give. Naming a phenomenon for the child establishes that the phenomenon is shared by the parent's frame of reference. This grants parental sanction to that phenomenon. Sanction gives weight, importance, and significance to the pattern taking shape: The word-name shows that the event is an acceptable part of the parent's worldview and therefore a shared event. This disposes the child's sensory system to cue in on the outside world for repetitions of such sharing. Each use of the shared name elicits parental response and reinforces the mutually held phenomenon. Our toddler quickly picks up on the name we have given the new stuffed animal. "Pooh-Bear," she says over and over, checking out our response to establish the mutual link.

Sanction is an emotional overlay on the concrete thingness of an event. Sanction makes one event stand out above others. We carry the power of the parents into the event sanctioned by them through naming, and this sanction strengthens our bond with the parents and gives *their* power to our structure of that named event. This selective power of sanction helps give our open possibility for experience its finite shape of actual but limited experience. William James suggested that our awareness is selected from a wide range of possibility. But only as specifics within that openness are selected out for stable construction can a world structure be built. The content of our worldview is bought at the price of all that continuum left out, but to make a specific possibility actual requires this kind of decision. Decision comes from the

Latin *de-cidere*, to cut off from. To decide is to cut off alternatives.

Researchers refer to the "quasi-hallucinatory fantasies" of the early, pointing child.[4] Our child points toward something and insists on a name. We look to respond but nothing is there. That is, nothing available to our conceptual system is there, so we cannot respond with the desired name, sanction, sharing, and so forth. Our child's construction of that event will then lack its sanction by her models. In the ongoing rush of interactions with an infinitely open possibility for phenomena, her sensory system will tend to cut off such a phenomenon in favor of full-sensory, named, sanctioned experience. Nature has no priorities; one phenomenon is as good as the next. The universal field that opens at object-constancy is simply a backdrop for an ongoing filling of that scene with specific, named events subject to the model given.

Language construction follows a cycle of competence found in all development. This cycle unfolds in three stages.

Cycle of Competence

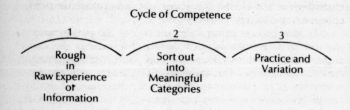

1	2	3
Rough in Raw Experience or Information	Sort out into Meaningful Categories	Practice and Variation

First, there is a *roughing in* of a mass of raw sensory data, information-experience. Second, there is a *sorting out* of this rough mass into meaningful categories of relationship. This stage may require some filling in of gaps with additional raw information that is related. The third stage is a time of *practice and variation* of that which was learned in the first two stages. This cycle can be found in all learning, whether of a one-minute duration or a large cyclic learning lasting for years.

My favorite example is a short-term learning of a nonlanguage sort. Our child toddles over to the kitchen cabinets at floor level. The doors are held by magnetic catches. She has seen her mother open these and she moves to emulate her model. She grasps the handle, tugs, the door opens, and

down she plops on the floor. Up she goes, pushes the door
shut, tugs again, opens. She pushes it shut, opens—pause;
wheels turn, lights dawn. She has roughed in her raw information, then sorted it out into a category of meaning. Now
what does she do? She practices: She stands there and pounds
that door back and forth until Mama's patience grows thin.

Observe the next step, for on it hinges development.
She leaves the door of her triumph and moves over to the
next door to see if she can work it in the same way. Pound,
pound! Then the next. She has practiced the new behavior
until her automatic pilot can take over (all the millions of
neural connections now thoroughly entrained). Conscious attention is now freed from the single entrainment that a new
skill demands. She can now "stand back" from her own
learning and extract from her new behavior the essence, the
idea, behind that behavior. (Remember learning to drive a
car? Particularly a stick-shift? All those movements to coordinate required a single-minded attention that left nothing over
for polite conversation. Once all the movements were synchronized and could be taken over by the automatic pilot,
conversation could be added.)

To move to the other door and repeat the performance,
she first had to make a logical abstraction, though of a concrete, sensory-motor sort, out of her own motor learning.
And she then correlated her abstracted pattern with another
context involving a similar setup. She extracted a blueprint
out of her concrete context and filled the blueprint in with
other content. She moves from door to door, and then on to
other types of doors; on to hinged objects of all sorts—potty
seat (no stuffed animal is safe now!), box tops, covers of
things.

This is the uniquely human *variation stage*, when she
moves beyond her animal brains entirely. She separates her
experience from her learning of it; that is, she exercises logic.
She employs genuine thinking, however rudimentary it may
be.

Language construction follows this same cycle: The
roughing-in period begins in utero when gross muscular movements respond to mother's spoken word. The long experiment with lalling matches sounds, rhythms, inflections; the
emotional period roughs in the esthetics of feeling-tone on
this sensory field. Then the formation of word appears and

the rush to name-label everything: "Whazzat, Mama?" The second phase, sorting out into meaningful categories, opens around age three. By now the acquisition of name-label becomes automatic in the same way that world construction became automatic at object-constancy. Now that incessant "What's that?" query gives way to "Why?" The question "Why?" demands a highly particular category of answer. The nature of the answer we should give hinges on the nature of the logic operant at this age, and how the child's practice and variation period must be nurtured.

Why? asks for meaning, purpose, design, pattern, reason. *Why?* puts the event named into a larger frame of reference. The nature of the question is shaped by the developmental period of the three- and four-year-old, which, in turn, determines the nature of the answer we should give. *Why?* is intricately connected with the third stage of the cycle of competence, with which that question overlaps.

The third stage, the period of practice and variation, opens at about age four and runs until about age seven. (These ages are, of course, statistical only.) Some eighty percent of the language structure is completed by age four, and the child must now practice and vary those great constructions made to this point. The nature of this practice-and-variation period of language structure can be grasped only by realizing that what I have called the structures of self, world, and language are totally intertwined; it is a single structure of knowledge, the active intelligence of that child.

I have left hanging here an important thread to the tapestry, and must pick it up before moving on. At object-constancy, *will* arose as the drive to overcome obstacles to development. The emotional twin of will is esthetics, our toddler's response of like and dislike so readily displayed. Once the dual entrainments of self as emotional center and self as body-world center begin, our child begins to employ arbitrary likes and dislikes regarding all her experience. Her mid-brain seat of awareness begins to sit in judgment on her old brain sensory reports. Qualitative evaluation becomes more and more pronounced as she grows older, more arbitrary and willful. For through this she helps organize her major constructions of knowledge, world, self, and their interrelation into meaningful categories.

Increasingly she will announce, often without apparent

logic, "I like this. I don't like that." Though arbitrary, she exercises esthetic discrimination and self-determination. Also, she begins to gather around and support her ego with those likes and push away and not identify with those dislikes. In this way her sense of separateness, or independence of ego, is shaped.

At about age four, our child's ego awareness shifts its locus into the new brain as well as in the two primary brains. Ego is now identified with all three brains. She is now aware as a body, a soul (or feeling center), and a mind. That is, she is equally an acting, feeling, and thinking center. The imagery of that new brain, which now comes into its own for a concentrated development, is completely different from the imagery handled by the old brain.

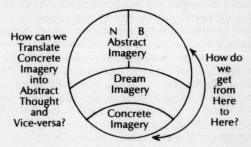

How can we Translate Concrete Imagery into Abstract Thought and Vice-versa?

N B Abstract Imagery

Dream Imagery

Concrete Imagery

How do we get from Here to Here?

(Recall from Chapter 2 the concrete imagery of the old brain and the pure, abstract and geometrically based imagery of the new.) The issue between age four and seven is: How can the concrete information, or images, of the old brain be translated into the abstract images of thought in the new brain? And, how can three so distinctly different systems be brought into synchrony?

The period of practice and variation—third of the large cycle of competence occupying the first seven years—must accomplish both this harmony and this transference of imagery, if further growth of intelligence is to take place. As we shall see, nature accomplishes each of these tasks through the other, in her usual economy. The success of this third stage, practice and variation, is based largely on the nature of the sorting-out stage which precedes and must support it. The question "Why?" is the key to sorting out, and the nature of our response to that question must be determined by the needs of the stage for which this prepares. The period from four to seven is the age of metaphor and symbol, the language of analogy, the language of the dream. And our answers to the *Why?* question must be symbolic, metaphoric, or analogical.

"Where does the sun go in the evening?" our child asks, and we must answer her analogically. We must not roll out a model of the solar system and launch into Newton's Laws of Planetary Motion. "Old jolly red Mr. Sun is tired from his hard day's work warming all of us, and nestled down in his bed over there in the west." This puts the child's world into meaningful relationship on the qualitative, esthetic scale of values by which she lives. Measurement, time, and motion belong to the period after age seven, and nature's timetable should be honored. Analogy is the language of the dreaming child, the language of the heart; it is the center that holds all things together.

6

Analogical Language

Miguel Serrano, the Chilean writer, reports that when he was about five years old he had a nightmare in which words were surrounding, smothering, and cutting him off from his life.[1] I had a similar dream when I was five, and it recurred intermittently until I was eleven. Mine was a night-terror that would continue even when I was apparently awakened. It ran its course like a pre-set film, beginning with a rhythmic thumping which I later discovered was my own heartbeat. Then a huge red mass appeared that was everything that had ever been or would be. I was being cut off from this totality of things by billions of simultaneously sounding words. Over-riding this chaos of sound was a powerful voice, demanding of me, "What is it? What is it?" over and over, in synchrony with the pulsation underlying the whole scene. On being separated from that totality I was both isolated in nothing-ness, and, more terrifying, forced to turn and contemplate that grim immensity and somehow answer to what it *was*. I was eleven years old before I could remember the dream afterward, for its terror created a kind of amnesia in me and I would be forgetful and vacant for days following.

Across several cultures, four- and five-year-old children have been found to have dreams of separation, which range from dreams of falling off the earth into empty space to becoming separated from the mother.[2] Around this age the locus of our identity shifts into the new brain, while we maintain our locus in the two animal brains as well. Our awareness will now identify with the new brain's capacity for

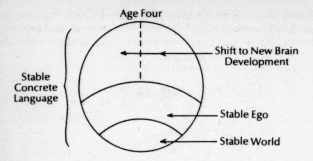

objective thought. This thought, however, will relate exclusively to the two primary brains for some time to come, as several major developments must unfold. First, by the time

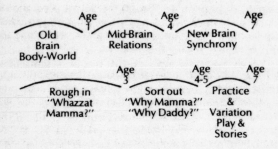

**CYCLE OF COMPETENCE AND
SHIFTS OF LOCUS**

the child is about age four, his structures of knowledge of the world, his self, and language have been roughed in and sorted out. Practice and variation of these structures will occupy nature until about age seven. Second, a way must be created to relate the abstract images of the new brain to the concrete images of the old brain—because, third, the locus of the child's awareness is going to shift away from the primary brain around age seven. His sense of self is going to be separated from his sense of the world outside himself. The child's bonds with that world structure in the old brain must be thoroughly established for the shift to be successful.

Fourth, the shift of ego at age seven will be away from parent and family as chief models, to society in general, and preparations must be made for this model shift ahead of time. As

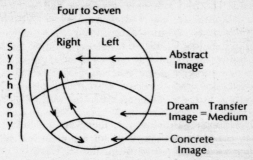

usual, in nature's economy, all these disparate needs will be met by the simplest procedure.

At about age four or five some children seem to sense intuitively that this separation from their first matrix, mother and earth, is beginning. Though the actual separation does not take place until about age seven, intent precedes the ability, and the child senses this new intent with some uneasiness; hence his dreams of separation.

The child's world and his self are in fact at a perfect balance at age four; there exists here a symbiotic subject-object relationship like that of the mother and the late uterine infant shortly before birth. The child is in a world that is both "other" to him and yet also an aspect of his own consciousness, a work of his own construction. Around age seven this happy synchrony ends as the social ego appears. The locus of ego is withdrawn from the old brain, leaving that brain on "automatic pilot," and the child will sense that he is different from—and separated from—his world.

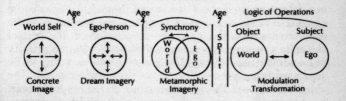

Once separated from his structures of knowledge of a physical world, that world becomes an object of his new, separated self. This new subject-object relationship ushers in concrete logic, and the child will have no choice but eventually to contemplate his outer world as something other than his own being. On many levels he will be driven to ask, "What is it?"

How, then, does nature manage the multiple tasks in the period from ages four to seven: to bring about a sufficient practice and variation of the structures of knowledge gained in the first four years; to learn to transfer concrete imagery into abstract imagery; to bond with the world structure in preparation for a separation from it; to bond with the coming society in preparation for a union with it; and to develop a synchrony of all three brains in preparation for the unfolding of operational logic at age seven?

Around the last part of the third or early in the fourth year, some ninety-seven percent of the characters in children's dreams are animals. Even parents, surprisingly, seldom enter the dreams of this period, until, at about age seven, animal dominance gives way to human figures. The animals of these dreams are generally personifications: They represent human persons, including, occasionally, parents. Through these animal figures the child's psyche may resolve problems of relationship with his all-too-human daily situations. The dream characters work out the functional relations between the outside world, his emotional center, and the new brain with its capacity for objective and abstract thought. He does this through an animal imagery that can function *analogically*.

Logic is a form of reasoning. Through logic we can infer that things that are alike in some ways can be alike in other ways. *Analogy* asserts some partial agreement or resemblance between things that are different. To say that "food is to the body as fuel is to an engine" is to draw an analogy. The word *metaphor* comes from a Greek word meaning to transfer. A metaphor is a figure of speech in which a name or characteristic of one object is applied to, or transferred to, another object to suggest a likeness between them. The animals in the intuitive period's dream are metaphoric in that they act as if they were human.

Logic can unfold only when there is separation between a subject and an object. The pre-logical child has no clear sense of a difference between self and world, but at age seven a separation between self as subject and the world as object takes place, making logic possible. A striking difference exists, however, between the concrete images of the old brain and the abstract patterns of the new brain, the two poles of experience that are involved in this split. And the basis of the new logical thought is an intermediary analogical thought, a system of metaphor and symbol that can transfer concrete imagery into abstract imagery, and vice versa.

From about two years of age on, our child begins an incessant plea (once she has had a sample): "Tell me a story, Mama; tell me a story, Daddy." By age three this plea becomes a compulsion I doubt many parents have met adequately. Storytelling is probably as old as our species. The story has the power to create an internal world into which we, as listeners (and the teller as well), can enter; an inner space travel into adventure. The child's desire and demand for this adventure are compelling, and the need for parental response cannot be over-emphasized.

Examine the nature of the stories handed down for centuries, or the nature of successful children's books. Beginning with that earliest *Three Bears*, a great percentage of the characters of children's tales are animals. And the animals are all anthropomorphic. They display human characters in animal shapes. Furthermore, everything in the story is animated. The word animation means filled with life. The sun is Jolly Old Red Mr. Sun; it is Old Mother West Wind that blows; Babbling Brook laughs and reports the latest woodland gossip; the trees are austere personalities, while rocks have faces and are silent witness to events.[3] The action may weave around Peter Rabbit and his sister Molly Cottontail; or Sammy Squirrel, Freddy Fox, Woody Woodchuck and his Aunt Polly. Each animal has his or her all-too-human foible, idiosyncrasy, failing; the impetuous foolishness of Tigger; self-pitying Eeyore; the fumbling indulgences of lovable Pooh-Bear.[4] All are embroiled in intrigue, crises, adventure; problems of relationship with self, others, the outside world.

There is a striking relationship between animals and the child in his intuitive period. I am sure stuffed animals are treasured by both boys and girls as much as dolls. From the earliest age animals fascinate children. Watch a five-year-old and his dog and you can begin to detect an almost disturbing affinity, as though they are on the same wave length in some way lost to us adults. The animals in the dreams of the intuitive period and in the stories told to children serve to work out the children's relations with world, parents, peers, siblings and so on. This is to say, these images are the tools the three brains use to relate to one another. Jungian psychologist Frances Wickes found that many later childhood dysfunctions resulted from a lack of storytelling, fantasy play, and imaginative ventures in the pre-logical years.[5]

In the beginning of life, language helps give shape to our sensory world. When we tell a child a story, language plays the same role, but now it gives shape to an *internal* sensory world. Just as the word helped shape outer experience, in storytelling the word creates inner experience. The little girl who said she liked radio better than television because the pictures were so much more beautiful gives us many clues. Speak the Word, and the inner reality forms. The little girl does not, of course, consciously fabricate an internal imagery to match the words. The creative process within her, the blueprint, is ready for activation by the appropriate models at that time. Her blueprint responds to the word and she is the delighted witness to the play.

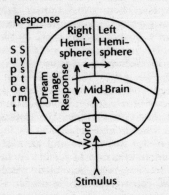

This inner appearance is creation itself, freely given. To translate this creative gift is a skill, however, and must be developed as must any other capacity to receive creation. We adults take the image of our outer world for granted, forgetting that we had to build up and practice our world structures. We forget that if a person born blind is later given sight through an operation, that person must learn to see, in a long and often difficult experience.

Just as external imagery could develop only if given the proper stimulus, so the blueprint formula holds for internal imagery. If no stimuli are given, no imaginative structure will form; that child will have no imagination. Without the capacity for internal imagery, and so *transferring* imagery, that child will remain locked into sensory-motor modes and identification by simple default. Intelligence will develop no further.

When we tell a bedtime story to the child, the child internalizes the action of the story through spontaneous image-making. The bedtime story, told when the lights are low, has tremendous power. I told my youngest daughter (of my first family) bedtime stories every night for years. We had a "tune in tomorrow night" series that involved the same characters who went through many adventures. The more I got into this storytelling, which was difficult at first, the more vivid my own inner impressions of the action became. For years afterward I would have memory flashbacks of these scenes and confuse them with actual memories. The incidents would appear in my dreams as well, for I had unwittingly incorporated them as parts of my own experience (as indeed they were). This daughter (now grown) and I recently discussed the striking clarity of the images evoked by those stories. We were struck by the suspicion that we may well have shared the same internal imagery during those tales, a sharing that had given them their power. (Sharing internal imagery is one of the subjects of Chapter 9.) The mid-brain and right hemisphere of the new brain seem involved in this activity; these are the primary organs of bonding. Storytelling almost surely strengthens the parent-child bond.[6]

The word of the story acts as a blueprint that draws on the inner materials available to fill in the needed content. The similarity between the action taking place in storytelling and our original construction of knowledge is obvious. The external word evokes from the internal structures according to the nature of the word stimulus. Whether our imagery process is called on to create images of a world out there or a world in here is arbitrary; the function is the same.

An ability to make internal images and the ability to

transfer meaning through these images are the functions of storytelling. This is the basis of abstract thinking, the sign of a mature intellect. Information, social mores, conventions, morals, ethics, and such are *not* parts of nature's agenda in these late pre-logical years. The ability to abstract and create is nature's goal. The content used to bring about such an ability is relevant only insofar as the content matches the general blueprint of the period.

Animal-human interactions dominate myths and folklore. We draw on a deep, archetypal consciousness that lies beneath the threshold of our ego-awareness. Animal imagery is the key to this stage of bonding with the earth and to the development of intuition, since our animal brains must be brought into alignment and harmony with our unfolding new, or human, brain. Through practice and variation the child must connect the different neural patterns of the three brains until the connections become autonomic. When the automatic pilot can take over the synchrony of the system, the child's awareness is free to move on into higher forms of operation.

The mid-brain and right hemisphere will be the main support system for this movement, and will hereafter be the heart of our operations. This supportive brain will organize and transfer the physical images from the old brain and the abstract images of the new brain. The supportive system will do this through its analogical language—imagery that can transfer back and forth the meanings of concrete to abstract imagery. When the new brain's abstract images must be communicated to the world, the supportive brain must translate those abstractions into a concrete form available to the old brain, and to the old brains of others in the world outside.

So the animal imagery of both dreams and stories serves metaphorically. The animals stand for higher life processes. *Father Bear wears a suit and carries a cane!* The images can stand for both our animal natures and our human natures. They can stand for complex intellectual, social, and psychological relations through their capacity for transferring imagery. The imaginative activity of storytelling (and play, to which we will turn next) builds a metaphoric and symbolic language system through which concrete images can be used in the service of abstract images and vice versa. This analogical language structure is, in turn, the means by which the three disparate brains are brought into that perfect relationship of the pre-logical years. This intuitive communion gives us a paradisaical state of unity, the integration of body, soul, and mind.

Equal to storytelling and fantasizing, and directly involved in analogical language, is *play*. Play calls into being the field of imagery transfer; the child begins to see one thing in another. How children long for constant fantasy plays of "Let's pretend," particularly with parents. At breakfast we reenact with our two-year-old the Three Bears: "Oh! That porridge is too hot!" Every mundane item is turned into a reflection of an animal story or is a trigger for a spontaneous one. The Big Bad Wolf dominates the scene for months, linked into every daily event. Clouds become dragons, animals, figures, castles; tigers lurk behind every bush; everything is significant, animated, filled with life.

The child needs mediated experience to establish this play world, and the parent is that mediator. The parent is the unchanging rock of reality, the one who makes the excursions into the dream world meaningful, safe, and shared. Our neighbor, three-year-old Patrick, plunges into the pile of leaves, emerges with them stuck all over, and, delighted, sways around, arms outstretched, shouting, "Look, Daddy, I'm a tree." The child posits fantasy play against the stable parent. "Look, Mama" not only shares the creative venture but touches base with the common domain Mama represents.

The period from ages four to seven prepares the child for the shift into the social world. A major part of childhood play is to pretend to be an adult. Much of our adult world is unavailable to the child, so he creates a representation of our world that *is* available, a world in which he can practice being an adult safely—a world where errors are of no consequence. His play is metaphoric.

How impressive road-rollers are to a five-year-old! (They used to be "steamrollers.") How we longed for that great day when we would be grown and could drive such an impressive machine and build roads for cars! Road-rollers were unavailable—until . . . here is an empty thread spool from the sewing chest! Immediately the spool represents the road-roller with its huge cylinder on the front that mashes everything flat. The spool furnishes the roller part, and imagination—the capacity to create images not present to the senses—fills in the missing parts and we lose ourselves to our transformed object. The child enters into his play world over which he has dominion, and builds roads happily by the hour.

This is not abstract thinking, but symbolic, metaphoric thinking. Metaphor and symbol are the cornerstones on which true abstraction and creative thought will later rest. Spool stands for road-roller; the child acts as if one is the other. The image, essence, or idea of road-roller is extracted out of that lumbering, unavailable giant, and these essential features are projected onto some available item which shares enough of a similarity on which to hang the transference. In play the child overlays an external object with an internal object and plays in the modulation so created. This is a form of "creating reality." The child creates play reality, his modulated version of the creation given him.

He is, or course, perfectly aware that a spool is a spool. There is no failure of mind here, but rather the joy of creative modulation, overlaying one process with another. The activity is perfect for the child because this is the way creative ability is developed. The ability must be developed, practiced, perfected according to his stage of development, to lay the ground for future stages. From age seven on, *all* development is creative, and unless creativity can take place, development cannot.

Just as Michelangelo was said to see the statue in the stone before he began his work, so the child sees the road-roller in the spool. Transference of imagery precedes our ability to create our own image to transfer. Learning to extract images out of actual concrete events prepares the child for extracting images out of the very capacity for imaging. All learning is from the concrete to the abstract, from the physical to the mental.[7]

Imitation precedes originality. In every facet of life we imitate our models until that time when our ability can stand alone. The capacity to see one object in another object, though the two may have only the faintest similarities (or none at all),[8] calls on that capacity we observed as *variation* in the cycle of competence. Every object the child comes across can serve in the great game of image transference and play, and this capacity operates even more fully in the years from seven to eleven. A porch swing was an obvious airplane, and Jim and I, age nine, would swing wildly for hours, flying into the clouds in adventure after adventure. Our hero-models were the barnstorming pilots of the old World War I derelict planes that landed in the ball park back in the 1930s, or the ace heroes of the Saturday afternoon movie. (We do well to temper the use of manufactured toys with the child, as a result of this need. The manufactured toy generally represents that future world in a perfect miniature. Michelangelo would not have been able to see the statue in the stone, were the stone already a statue.) "All they want to do is play," the behavior-modifying educational engineers lament, as they devise an endless stream of motivational devices to try to trick the child's system into making pre-adolescent responses of brain/mind during this period of intuition and dream. "How can we make them abandon their fantasies and magical thinking," the modifiers ask, "make them attend to the real, brass-tacks, no-nonsense world?"

Nature's agenda for the years from four to seven is to practice the structures of knowledge already achieved, and to vary them by arbitrarily overlaying the inner dream image on the external structure. At the same time, this establishes the bonds between world structure and ego structure, and prepares for those social adaptations destined for age seven. Nature accomplishes this complex job by a means as simple as play. The imagery capable of transferring thought and shaping reality resides within that dream mode of the midbrain and right hemisphere where Father Bear wears a suit and carries a cane. Abstract imagery is not present to the senses; it must be created from within. We must then process that imagery, transfer it into images available *to* the senses out there. If we cannot, we have no imagination, and if we have no imagination we are automatically grounded in sensory-motor imagery. No matter that we might develop sophisticated ways to manipulate the material stuff available to such primitive imagery, we will still be grounded in a sensory-motor frame of reference. No merging of animal into human will then take place. Instead, we will incorporate *aspects* of our human potential, piecemeal, into those lower animal-brain operations, in service of that sensory-motor identity, and serious trouble results. (A case in point is the fact that an estimated 500,000 scientists are involved in weapon production on our planet. The highest products of our system are therefore involved in the apparent destruction of all our systems.)

I mentioned that too many manufactured toys tend to bypass development of the child's metaphoric-symbolic play, but a far more serious block to this development has arisen. I will close with a cursory glance at this, the most destructive of all processes outside hospital-technological childbirth.

Note how in all pre-logical play the child talks out his play world. He or she maintains a constant, unbroken chatter concerning his moment-by-moment play world. He is, in effect, continually furnishing himself with the outer stimulus word through which his entire metaphoric process takes place. Every aspect of the child's life revolves around this stimulus-response play of language. The Word is the creative key.

Consider then, that instead of feeding that magical stimulus of Word into the child's old brain, bringing about the vast responses of creative imagery, giving that vast interior world of space-journey the child longs for, building up the whole structural capacity of metaphoric imagery by which and through which the mid-brain can do its great supportive work later on—suppose instead that we furnish the child with *both* word and its corresponding imagery complete and intact as a single sensory unit. That is, suppose we feed into the child's old brain both sensory actions, the stimulus *and* a response—a response he then need not make. Suppose we give him simultaneously the magic Word *and* all the associate imagery?

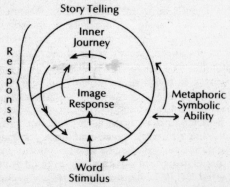

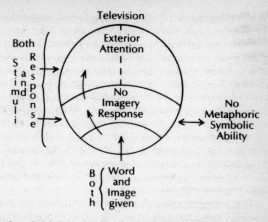

Put the child down in front of a television set, the great American baby-sitter, and forget about him, as so many of us do. You can also forget about development. Programming on television has nothing to do with the issue at stake here. The imagery is what does the damage, since you flood the system with that which it is supposed to accomplish itself.[9] Nor is it just that TV builds a shallow-dimensioned worldview based on only the two long-range senses of sight and sound. (The toddler, exposed to television, tries to get at the phenomena to taste, smell, and touch in order to make a full sensory structure of knowledge.) Functional, intelligent abstract thought and logic can only be built on a full-dimensioned, five-sensory world structure. All thought is imagery. Even the blind think in images. All reality structure is imagery. Reality is imagery. The world is imagery.

The mechanism of TV itself, as an imagery counterfeit, is what kills intelligence and grounds a populace in sensory-motor modes of thought. (*Intellect* can still develop, but this will be an intellect devoid of intelligence. Again, our enormously sophisticated super-weaponry of global destruction is the product of a high intellect—but one devoid of intelligence, since intelligence will not operate against the well-being of its species.)

Radio proved an enormous boon to creative imagination. The little girl likes the images on radio so much better than TV because her creative power is being exercised as designed. Back in the 1930s our Saturday afternoon movies were a great boon to creative imagination. The high point of our week, we sat for three hours engulfed in a momentous event, a venture into fantasy, an excursion into a different world, an abrupt and complete shift of orientation, a purposeful journey into play. (We always went in groups.) We then brought back into our whole week's play and imagination the rich stimulus those movies provided. Had we had them reflecting on the walls of our homes constantly, though, like parts of the furniture, not only furnishing our fantasy needs but reporting to us what we were led to believe were the real facts about the real world—the accepted criteria and model— then the damage of movies would have been that of TV today.

The average American child sees six thousand hours of TV before going to kindergarten at age five. And he maintains close to that average thereafter. The child imprints to a box while in a totally passive stage. The imagery/sound comes in as a single, condensed, one-way impression with no possibility for interaction. His mid-brain function of creative response to stimuli is bypassed and doesn't develop. Stripped of his capacity to create internal imagery, vital to survival itself, he becomes compulsively *attached* to TV, since TV is the only source of imagery then available, and we cannot stand only bare, concrete material reality. Television is naturally addictive—not on a psychological basis but on a biological one.

Then comes the video game: The young person can grab those two levers and—for the first time in his imprinted existence—turn the tables, establish at least some simulation of interaction with that to which he has imprinted. He can do partially that which he was supposed to learn to do in childhood—assume dominion over his world. Note that most video games center on some act of violence or destruction. If you manipulate the levers with skill, you can wipe out, destroy, annihilate, and dominate. The pent-up rage factor is loosed in the strangest compulsion yet to sweep our sensorymotor, compulsive culture.

When no internal imagery ability develops, and when we deny the child his long period of dreamlike "messing around" that childhood must provide, no merging of the animal and human brains will take place. And the necessary merging of animal with human is only the first step in the far greater integration of human with divine—that realm of consciousness that needs no object.

7

Intuition

When my first son was five years old, I was deep in the midst
of an intellectual-spiritual search, reading such works as theologian Paul Tillich's monumental *Systematics*, devouring Søren
Kierkegaard, Dietrich Bonhoeffer, Alfred North Whitehead,
Carl Jung, poet William Blake, and so on. The problem of the
relation of God and man had seized me completely. My
dreams and inner experiences reflected this absorption and I
had been in a pitch of intellectual excitement and spiritual
bewilderment for several years. I had an exceptional rapport
with my son and, as I was dressing for my class one morning,
he came in with a detached look on his face.

"You know, Joe," he said, sitting down on the edge of
the bed, at which point he launched into some twenty minutes of unbroken, publishable speech; structured sentences of
perfection followed without pause, without groping or emotional coloring. He delivered to me the most perfect articula-
tion of the relation of God and man I had ever heard or
hoped to hear. He used long, involved theological terms, and
the overall pattern that emerged staggered me. Immense,
vastly beyond my dilettante dabbles, he was telling me everything there was to know.

As I listened, and began to grasp the impossibility of
what I was hearing, the hair rose on the back of my head,
ripples of goose bumps spread over me, and tears began to
fill my eyes. I was in the presence of the uncanny; something
numinous and unaccountable was taking place.

He finished, his car pool honked outside to take him to

kindergarten, and he left. I remained there for some time, confused and stunned. I tried to recapitulate what he had told me, but it was too enormous; his account exceeded my grasp of mind. I could only stand there and feel that revelation washing away from me, back into whatever state from which it had arisen. I was late to my class that morning, came home early, and paced about waiting for my son to come home at noon. When he rushed in, in his usual exuberance to hop on the piano stool for a romp with Bartok and Bach (which always preceded lunch), I interrupted him and tentatively approached the subject of his morning talk with me. He had no idea what I was talking about, nor did he ever recall the experience. All I had as verification of the event was his mother's observation that he had talked with me at length that morning.

The child psychiatrist Gerald Jampolsky related how four- and five-year-old children were brought to him by disturbed parents because the children reported experiences we would call extrasensory. Eloise Shields reports that many children show telepathic and clairvoyant capacities at age four but that such potential usually disappears around age seven. Similarly, a colleague of mine did her doctorate in musicology and found that virtually all normally hearing four-year-old children had perfect pitch, but almost all lost it at around age seven. The reason for the loss seems to be lack of development and stabilization of such intuitive ability during its specific time for development. If no model is given to stimulate and stabilize the capacity, it atrophies. The loss seems to occur at age seven as the child's locus of awareness shifts away from the primary brain system in order to develop the new brain and mind. If intuition has not been developed by then, through proper modeling and guidance, the possibility for such action generally atrophies, as the weight of attention shifts to the new blueprint.

In his book *Never Cry Wolf*,[1] biologist Farley Mowatt described how an Eskimo "minor shaman" placed his five-year-old son with a family of wolves for twenty-four hours. When he returned, the child was playing happily with the wolf cubs, the adult wolves casually watching the antics of the children. Later, it was this son who could interpret the calls wolves use to signal from pack to pack over long distances, informing each other of the whereabouts and movements of the herds of caribou. This was vital information to the Eskimo, too, and was available through the boy, who had in some way been plugged into the wolf communication network at the appropriate time.

This is a cultural phenomenon unique to the Eskimo, of course. The father knew precisely what the maneuver was for and how to go about it. That was part of his calling as a shaman, his legacy and heritage. He did not prime the child with a set of expectancies, prerequisites, or instructions. He simply placed the child with the wolves, and the child spontaneously played with the cubs. The issue was not a matter of intellect but an affair of the heart—the heart of the life system that moves for the well-being of all. Of course, at five years of age, human and animal have much in common.

My five-year-old son provided for me an archetypal link which was equally a cultural phenomenon. He gave the particular delivery he did because of the particular passion that had moved me for so long. He was in the middle of his intuitive period, and I was his primary background and criterion. (I must make clear that my son's mother did not share my spiritual enthusiasms and I never mentioned my pursuits around my family, for this offended her. So my son was not echoing oft-heard sentiments on my part, or giving me a glorified synthesis feedback of my own rhetoric. Not until after the death of his mother, when I was left as the sole parent of our rather large brood, did I begin to talk with them of my interests.)

For upward of thirty to forty thousand years, Australian aborigines operated out of a mind-set they called Dream Time. By shifting back and forth from the present moment into Dream Time, the aborgine had at his disposal information "closed to our senses five," as William Blake would say. This capacity was a development of that very intuition that opens around age four and disappears for most of us at about age seven through lack of such cosmologies as Dream Time and aborigine models. By means of Dream Time, the aborigine knew the location and direction of travel of those animals he was allowed to kill in his particular clan, though those animals might be miles away. He knew the closest and most economical point of interception to take his quota of the proper food, and while cutting across the desert sand he knew the location of water, not by some acute ground reading of exterior cues alone, but by shifting into Dream Time, an eminently practical function.

My favorite story of the aborigine is of an English research group investigating the aboriginal ability to track and ground read.[2] The aborigine, like the American Indian, considers the earth sacred and so fosters its ecology. He leaves little trace of his movements because he believes the earth was laid down in Dream Time and one must honor the precepts of Dream Time. Being a hunter-gatherer, he is always on the move: Wherever he is, is home; and he does not foul his nest. Yet, going across a wilderness area, a tracker would point to an area and remark that his kinsmen, the so-and-so group, were there so many days ago; so many were in the group, they did such and such, and went off in such a direction. The research party could detect nothing at all, and were impressed at this ability to detect such subtle signs and read so much from them.

As an experiment, the English had one member of their group walk a pre-selected, one-hundred-mile course, carefully mapped out, that would encompass every type of terrain: desert, rocky areas, swamp, ocean beach, and so on. Care was taken to leave no more visible sign than possible. One year later, when all signs of this walk would almost surely have been obliterated, they asked a famous tracker if he would undertake to follow such a trail if they took him to the beginning of it. He agreed only if they would give him an article of clothing worn by the man who left the trail. Holding the article of clothing, the tracker went into Dream Time. Then, in his economical fashion, he ran, following the trail unerringly. Never could the research people detect him stopping to search for a sign.

The researchers came up with their theories and then the aborigine gave his own explanation: "Holding the article belonging to the man, I go into Dream Time where that man leaving the trail is a permanent event. I simply translate that aspect of Dream Time into now. But I am not following a trail. The man and I are leaving that trail together." In our logical split, we demand either-or; we can't tolerate the paradox the aborigine presents. Paradox, I have been taught, is the threshold to truth, the breakpoint between logical sets. At paradox we must shift logic. The person who tries to carry one logic into the set of another logic loses the best of both worlds.

The aborigine was bonded with the earth. He maintained a state of unity between earth and self, or unity between his three brain systems. He provided his children with models that stimulated and nurtured this intuitive function at the appropriate time. The aborigine believed that every man, woman, animal, blade of grass, water hole, or tree had a counterpart, a subtle or *dream* image. The plan of the world is laid out in this dream form and enacted now, in the physical world. A perfect coordination and cooperation with Dream Time assures man a perfect relation with the form which shapes our world, with creation itself.

Dream Time refers to the general blueprint out of which life springs. Intuition is our innate capacity for becoming aware of this subtle energy as needed for our biological well-being. The optimum period for the development of this possibility is from age four to seven, and every facet of aboriginal life acts as the model, guide, and ongoing stimulus for the function to develop in the child. Yet the aborigine does not introduce the concept of Dream Time, with its elaborate rules and regulations, until a rite of passage at puberty. On the other hand, Dream Time is not developed at puberty; the capacity itself has been developed in the pre-logical years. The rite of passage that introduces the young person to the concepts of Dream Time takes place at the unfolding of the intellectual process around puberty. The rites encode the earlier development into a systematized, formalized, intellectual (and arbitrary) cosmology unique and perhaps indigenous to the aborigine. The function forming naturally within the child is made conscious as an intellectual structure at puberty, when abstract, intellectual capacity naturally unfolds. Through the rites, the natural, largely unconscious development taking place in the pre-logical years is incorporated into an abstract system of meaning, purpose, and design totally beyond the grasp of a five-year-old. The five-year-old's job is to lay the functional groundwork on which the later abstract principles can be built. By fully living the stage of Dream Time as itself, the state is made available to a fully conscious analysis later.

Rites of passage, observed in many different ways in different cultures, serve a double purpose. The natural developments taking place around age seven and again around age eleven separate the ego from its state of pre-logical unity. The child's awareness must be split off from his world structure in order to develop the kind of intellect that can create and grasp cosmologies of an abstract sort—the very cosmologies through which the ego is reintegrated. So rites of passage are movements forward into maturity; they reunite processes previously separated by integrating them into a higher structure.

The grounds for this reintegration are laid from age four to seven, before the periods of separation begin. This takes place through the development of intuition, which is again a way of relating the energy of the three brains. As the old brain is a physical energy system, the mid-brain is a subtle energy system.[3] It would be analogous to say that the mid-brain is a wave-form energy where the old brain is a particle-form system. In physics, wave forms are less restricted and more powerful than particle forms, and thus from the beginning, we find the fluid images of the mid-brain acting on and shaping the more restricted images of the old brain. Now at age four the new brain enters the scene as a third and equal center of child awareness and the focus of new development. The imagery of the new brain is abstract and far more fluid and powerful than that of either of the animal brains. From this new position of power, intelligence can use the support-

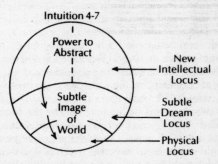

Intuition 4-7

Power to Abstract

New Intellectual Locus

Subtle Image of World

Subtle Dream Locus

Physical Locus

ive mid-brain to give information concerning the physical world which is not available through that old brain's physical sensory system. This subtle sensing of physical relations is called intuition. All the higher animals develop some aspect of this mode of sensing, though they have only a minimal amount of that gray matter we call the new brain. With this huge new brain, and an elaborate extension of the animal brains, we have available a wide range of subtle capacities, though they must, as usual, be developed, and can be developed only through models of such capacity given at the appropriate stage.

The careful organization of nature's plan can be seen in the late appearance and the long, slow growth of the corpus callosum. From the beginning of life, both hemispheres register and imprint the input from the two primary brains, but the left hemisphere, with its sparse connections, has a reduced role in these interactions. Once the corpus callosum begins its growth, the left hemisphere imprints from the mid-brain as usual but increasingly through its connections with the right hemisphere. So the left hemisphere has an ongoing and increasing access to the unified interactions of all three brains taking place in that unifying right hemisphere. With its weaker imprinting and reduced interplay with the primary brains, the left hemisphere is less committed, so to speak, less involved in that concrete construction of the early years, except as that action is translated through the unifying and supportive right hemisphere.

The right hemisphere maintains intact, throughout our life, all those imprints and interactions with the primary brains we made from our beginning. It maintains the perfect unity and functional rapport all three brains achieved in the first seven years. The right hemisphere preserves, unchanged, its earliest imprintings of that concrete language of body movements begun in utero; the emotional language of the late infant; the named-thing language; the analogical language of imagery transference; and the function of intuition developed during that same period from four to seven. This single, synchronous intelligence maintains the unity and well-being of the play of consciousness unfolding in the child. And all of this unifying action should be available to the left hemisphere as needed, after the shift of ego's locus at age seven. Then the blueprint of the left hemisphere and mind can unfold for the development of operational logic—the logic of separation—and all previous systems will act as support for this next, higher integration.

Any left hemisphere specialty, such as abstract language,

requires a continual feedback and cross-indexing with the right hemisphere, and the right hemisphere requires feedback and cross-indexing with the rest of the brain. The abstract language of the late child, unfolding fully at about age eleven, is one set apart from this unified system. Without the left hemisphere and mind separations, the materials of that holistic right hemisphere would become circular and repetitive; while without those materials to draw on selectively, the operational possibilities of the mind would have nothing to work with, nothing from which to build an abstract language or logic.

So we do well to reconsider our talk about a failure to develop right-hemisphere thinking in our schools; the development of the right hemisphere may not be an academic proposition. Its classroom is the living earth, its teaching material matter itself and models of intuition. The curriculum for this development is built within us, and has an explosive, universal longing for expression. And its expression is through play, storytelling, and "Let's pretend"; its "prime time" is the first seven years, with a secondary time from age seven to eleven. Our problem is not that we have over-emphasized the left hemisphere and starved the right, it is that we have hardly touched on the capacities of the new brain. Things will not change until we allow each modality to develop as designed in those pre-logical years, and we rediscover the post-biological blueprint and its development, wherein, alone, the new brain is fully utilized.

At each shift of blueprint the brain apparently undergoes a "growth spurt" that prepares the brain for new learning (as we found happening right before birth).[4] The capacity for new learning parallels the growth spurt and is followed by a plateau period in which new learning is not only inappropriate, but difficult, since the previous learning must now be practiced and varied to be completed. The brain/mind cannot undertake new learning in the practice and variation period, since the entrainment of brains is tied up in the incomplete structures of knowledge awaiting their completion by repetition and variation.

There is a brain growth spurt around three or four and another around age seven. The learning appropriate to the four-year-old is connected with bringing the new locus of

awareness in the new brain into synchrony with the rest of
the system. This is the practice-and-variation stage discussed
above.

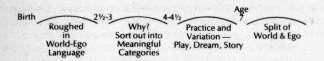

Birth   2½-3   Why?   4-4½   Age 7   Split of

Roughed in World-Ego Language   Sort out into Meaningful Categories   Practice and Variation — Play, Dream, Story   World & Ego

During this time, particularly during the fifth and sixth years,
new learning, other than practice and variation, is highly
inappropriate and difficult. From all standpoints we find that
this period, from ages four to seven, is designed for that one
purpose to which the child is compulsively driven—play.[5]

Over the past forty years, however, this is the age at
which we have insisted on putting the child into a school
desk, restricting his movement (and we know learning takes
place only through movement at this age), and forcing that
dreamer into abstract pursuits suitable to pre-adolescence at
best. Combined with the effects of hospital delivery, day-
care, television, the collapse of family, and so on, the collapse
of childhood itself has been accelerating. Since in each case
the general area of damage has been the mid-brain where all
bonding, including social bonding, takes place, the collapse of
society is a logical counterpart of this pattern of damage.

We must face the fact that damage to mid-brain development is damage to species survival and personal survival.
When the mid-brain breaks down in its bonding, the right
hemisphere breaks down in its unifying job and cannot support the left hemisphere's movement into logical abstraction.
The left hemisphere leads to independence of mind, and
mind alone leads to Self. And Self, the goal of all development, is the only possible realm of integration, the final
maturation of ego. So we must rediscover the truth that the
teacher of the child is the earth and nature, whose language
is first concrete, then emotional, then analogic and intuitive,
long before word is split from its thingness to give a semantic
language. And we must learn again that nature's didactic
method is play, the re-creative play of childhood that alone
leads to the divine creative play of maturity.

We will discover this not by turning backward intellectually and trying to patch up our adult system with that same fractured intellect. We will discover the road to the divine play of maturity only through those teachers, those models, who have gone that road themselves. Only through contact with such models will our blueprint for that divine play leap up to us for its unfolding.

8

Concrete
Operations

One evening in the fall of 1982, I was invited by my neighbor Robert Monroe to meet with some twenty-five other neighbors and three military men, two majors and a colonel. The officers were from Delta Company, a small department of the army set up to investigate new theories about consciousness. The three had undergone some shifts of consciousness themselves. The colonel in charge, who holds a doctor of philosophy degree and is soft-spoken and gently persuasive, stood in the center of the circle where we sat and created for us a receptive atmosphere for an experiment in non-ordinary phenomena. Each of us had brought a piece of stainless-steel cutlery, and within about twenty minutes, simply by stroking them, twenty-three of us present had bent those pieces of tableware into every conceivable shape.

The first to succeed was an eight-year-old girl who neatly creased the bowl of her spoon across its middle and folded the end portion of the bowl back over the shank portion, giving a double-thick, truncated bowl. We then watched her younger brother corkscrew the handle of his fork from top to bottom, and the effect spread around the room, generally from the youngest to the oldest. People bent knives into knots, interwove the tines of forks, rolled the handles of spoons tightly into the bowls, and generally messed up twenty-three pieces of flatware.[1]

It came as a surprise to me when my own spoon bent, though I was familiar with the extensive literature on the subject. The sensation of steel getting warm and malleable was strange. Many of the shapes cannot be duplicated with instruments, for the metal bends erratically and often snaps prematurely from metal fatigue when forced. Metallurgical analysis of the steel bent in this non-ordinary way shows, in fact, a different type of molecular surface than steel mechanically bent.

Robert Jahn, Dean of the School of Engineering at Princeton University, has recently published the results of research into paranormal phenomena taking place in his laboratories.[2] Under controlled conditions, people change the readings of magnetometers, instruments that register the magnetic fields of the area, simply by looking at the dials and willing them to shift. Apparently the magnetic lines or fields around the device shift accordingly, which makes little sense. A Fabry-Perot Interferometer projects circular images on a screen. Individuals look at the images and change their shapes without physical contact with the electronic gadgetry projecting those images.

Jean Piaget[3] used the term "Concrete Operational Thinking" for a capacity that opens for development in the seven-year-old. This is the ability to operate on concrete information and change that information through use of an abstract idea. That is, through an internal image we can change an external image. Piaget's classic example of this operation is mundane and well-known but I will repeat it here. Present the pre-logical child (statistically before age seven, but don't count on it) with the following experiment: Take a tall, thin flask that holds a pint of liquid and a short, fat flask that holds the same amount. Fill the tall one with water, then pour that water into the short, fat pint flask. Ask our pre-logical child to observe that the two flasks hold the same amount. "Oh no," he explains, "the tall one holds the most." He views the world qualitatively, and big tall things are the most and little short ones are least. So you pour the liquid from the short flask into the tall one and ask him to observe that nothing is left in the short one and that the tall one is exactly filled. Therefore, they must hold the same. "No," he insists, "the big one holds most." But, you point out, how could that be when none is left over from the tall one? "Some just disappears," he patiently explains.

Our pre-logical child's situation is roughly analogous to the late uterine infant. The infant is largely functional, yet still symbiotically tied to the mother. The child at five or six years of age is still symbiotically connected with his world construction, since his locus of awareness and identity is evenly distributed among all three brains. At about age seven, with the analogical and intuitive connections established, separation of this symbiotic unity takes place. Identity shifts into the left hemisphere, leaving the rest of the system on automatic support. Since the left hemisphere's connections with the mid-brain are sparse, consciousness can shift its energy of attention from mid-brain inputs, and so can operate independently of all physical process. No trace of egocentricity now remains; world structure and self structure are two processes. Separate from the old brain, ego can now treat that world construction as an object, and the logic of separation unfolds.

In the pre-logical child, the relationships between objects and between self and objects were qualitative, centering on esthetic response. At age seven, due to the separateness ego can employ, quantity enters the picture; quality is now less an issue. A summer's day could last nearly forever for the pre-logical child, but after age seven, time becomes an issue. A concept of space enters too, as the distance between objects or events can now be considered objectively, rather than through the older esthetic, subjectively.

The shift of locus to this new point of objectivity is equally the first shift toward *mind* as a state separate from the brain. The seven-year-old can begin to grasp abstract patterns, provided that those patterns are given through concrete, tangible models and applied to concrete objects. Then the child can operate on incoming information from his world and change that information according to the abstract ideas for change given by his model. The formula still holds: Blueprint plus model equals structure.

The current interest in metal-bending arose some fifteen years ago when an Israeli, Uri Geller, performed widely on television, bending spoons and keys. He may or may not have been genuine but the effect he had on many hundreds of children was genuine enough. Since TV is the principal source of information, criteria, and social modeling for most children of technological societies, when they saw Geller bend metal on the screen they emulated his example spontaneously. The effect has been reproduced in laboratories for some dozen years now, though the spontaneous effects in groups of around twenty-five persons are more spectacular.

The seven-year-old cannot yet create his own abstract ideas for concrete operations. Nor can he operate on his world information simply by being presented with an abstract idea for doing so. You must demonstrate the operation physically, or the operation must be a part of natural process available to his five senses, as in the case of the law of conservation—that those two pint flasks hold the same amount of liquid, for instance. Once the shift to concrete operations takes place, we can present this example to the child and immediately he knows that the amount of liquid is the same. The law of conservation is simply a capacity of the logic inherent within the blueprint of this period. You do not teach such laws, or any aspect of concrete operations; as with the response to a face in the newborn, you present the child with tangible examples. (The two children who first bent their spoons at Robert Monroe's were the children of one of those army officers, and had seen spoon-bending before.)

Piaget also referred to concrete operations as a capacity for measurement. The seven-year-old can grasp the spatial relationships between objects and can take the measure of things. The child in utero has a rich relationship with his mother but it is a limited relation. He could not, for instance, stand back from her and take her physical measurement. Once he is born, however, he could, in theory, pull out a tape measure and do so. Through separation he achieves a point of objectivity to her, and can treat her as an object of his subject self. In the same way, so long as the child's ego structure and world structure are a single unit, as found in the pre-logical child, he cannot measure his world any more than the uterine infant could measure his mother. At seven, the child is borne out of that unified relationship by the shift of locus away from his primary brains into that left hemisphere/mind viewpoint. World and ego are now separate entities, and the child views his world structure as an object of his self.

All logic depends on separation, and the higher integrations of intellect are gained through logical processes. To develop a higher intelligence the child must be thrown out of his paradisaical state and enter into the experience of separation. This process gives him objectivity.

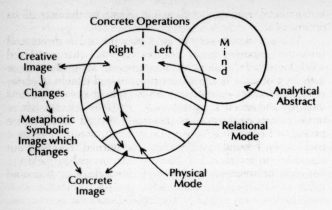

Young Mathew Manning bent metal without touching it and on occasion moved metal from one room to the next without contact. He did this time and again while wired up to an electroencephalograph (EEG) brain-wave recorder, both in an English laboratory and at a Canadian university.[4] When Manning moved or changed physical objects, the EEG registered large bursts of activity from his old brain and cerebellum, which is as it should be: The cerebellum (among many things) seems connected with movement, the old brain with physical matter.

My favorite example of concrete operations is one followed by the Nestikare dancers of Bulgaria (a tradition handed down from mother to daughter for millennia); by peoples in ceremonials throughout Africa, South America, Indonesia; by Polynesians, people of India and Sri Lanka; and lately by a neurolinguistic programmer in weekend workshops, beginning in California (where else?) and now nationwide. I refer to people walking across beds of white-hot coals without injury or pain. My critics speak scornfully of my continual pulling out of this old chestnut. "Everyone knows," wrote one sage, "that fire walking is just autosuggestion." (So what is autosuggestion?) I like to talk about fire walking because it is probably one of the most widespread and oldest nonordinary practices on earth. Many thousands of people walk fire each year. Movies, photographs, video clips, scientific instrumental readings, and so on, attest to the fact of its occurrence.

When I was twenty-three I experienced a direct and prolonged exposure of my flesh to live coals that registered 1380 degrees Fahrenheit. The setting was simple, a college gathering of some dozen of us sitting around a table. A series of non-ordinary events had occurred to me within a few months, and when I again found myself in a world where ordinary processes could be reversed, I used up an entire package of cigarettes (they were, I recall, about 17 cents a pack) when I found that I couldn't be burned. I ground out cigarettes on my cheeks, on my eyelids, my palms, held the hot ends between my fingers, and, for a finale, got several going at once, puffed them to white-hot pitch, put the glowing ends between my lips, and blew showers of sparks over my companions. It was an exalting experience where, rather than an anesthetizing of my senses, they were heightened enormously, an intense sensation with no pain. And, of course, no damage afterward. (It has been years since I smoked and even longer since I experienced that reckless "high brass wire world" that spontaneously mixed inner and outer processes.)

I like to refer to the ceremonies in the central temple of the god Kataragama on the island of Sri Lanka, where from eighty to one hundred people spend some three weeks in preparation for the event, then walk out onto a bed of coals twenty feet in length, six feet wide, recessed into the ground.[5] (The fire will melt aluminum on contact.) Some walkers dig their feet in deep; others dance across quickly. Some hang out there for a while; some scoop handfuls of hot coals and pour them over face and body. Neither hair nor the light cotton clothes they wear burn or singe. Failures do occur. An average of three percent of the walkers "lose their faith" out on that bed; most of those are killed by the heat. I refer to those as the control group, as the psychologist would say. The *National Geographic* ran a photographic essay on fire walking and other non-ordinary ceremonials in Sri Lanka.[6] No one suffered from the lesser event photographed by the *Geographic* (it was held in a private courtyard), but optical pyrometers registered 2400 degrees Fahrenheit internal and 1380 degrees external temperatures.

When Brian Josephson, 1973 Nobel laureate in physics, observed Mathew Manning moving or changing objects without touching them, he called for a rewriting of the laws of physics.[7] Princeton's Robert Jahn recently made the same comment concerning the paranormal events mentioned earlier. In June 1982, the University of California Education Department at Berkeley gave a closed (invitation only) conference on education, to discuss latent potentials in children. (The Institute of Noetic Sciences, and Willis Harman, were co-sponsors.) Following a presentation by Jahn, I gave a brief outline of my developmental theory, relating brain/mind, physics, development, and so on. My claim was that the laws of physics are adequate to operations of physical stuff. The materials of our world and the interactions between them fit physical laws well enough, but when we add *operational thinking*, even as it unfolds haphazardly at age seven, we must refer to *modulations* of physical process.

Modulation of physical law may follow laws of its own. I don't know. I do know that people are trying to explore this phenomenon, since an awesome unknown energy is involved. Soviet Russia has long been pursuing these phenomena, and they are, ironically, free of the ideological restrictions that our scientific-academic community is subject to. Some eight weeks after that Berkeley conference, and long before the proceedings were published, I received a request from a biologist at the University of Leningrad for any and all information I might be willing to share concerning my proposals made at that conference.

When one performs any of these non-ordinary operations (and I have mentioned only a few), a new brain process acts on an old brain function. The action itself is a transfer of imagery. We have an image of people walking fire, and extract from this the essence behind it, the blueprint of that action. We then fill in this blueprint with the content of our own action. The function is essentially the same as that of overlaying the image of the road-roller on the spool except that now instead of image overlay there is transference of image as movement. Instead of an overlay of imagery there is an operation *on* imagery which changes the image. The changed image changes reality.

In frequency modulation we take one radio wave and modulate its frequency with another. In concrete operations we can modulate physical process through mental process. We can change the interactions between self and world, as in fire walking, or change aspects of the world itself, as in metal-bending. We can change our notions of physical laws over and over and never arrive at the modulation of physical process brought about through this non-physical process.

The Sanskrit word for measurement, *Maya*, means to unfold our experience out from us in measurable units. Maya splits us off from our actual unity, but the split is illusory. The word Maya has come down to us through its Latin equivalent: *illusion*. Illusion comes from the words *in ludere*, meaning *inner play*. The ancient sages understood that what was taking place was an inner play of the brain/mind, between self as thinking brain and self as physical brain. Thinking brain can play with physical brain through its supportive brain, once our locus of identity has shifted from that physical brain itself—once, that is, Maya has fallen.

The outside world reflects this inner play since that world is translated for us through our old brains. Arguments about the primacy of the "real" world out there and our "internal imaginations" drop away as insubstantial.[8] The same relation exists between inner and outer that exists between blueprint and content or between nature and nurture. Dualisms break down, as reality is perceived to be a dynamic between possibility and realization.

The law of conservation is but one expression of the limitless possibilities for measuring our world. And this particular expression is not dependent on showing flasks of liquid to the child. Children of non-technological countries develop the same capacity with regard to the kinds of proportions used in their society. Fire walking, metal-bending, and paranormal phenomena are in general simply inherent within the natural structures of our brain/mind. You cannot have a structure such as ours without including this possibility. This does not mean, however, that such a particular expression is necessary or at all even preferable. Any language fills the language blueprint. Development of a functional concrete operational thought is not contingent on these sensational events just mentioned, nor is any part of overall development necessarily enhanced by them. I used to think such paranormal operations were important and vital, and that we were cheating ourselves for not making a full-fledged development of them.[9] I now believe that I was wrong.

Earlier in this book I discussed the open-ended nature of

our blueprint for language, and how any specific language as a model would bring our blueprint into play. In the same way, whether the child's concept of concrete operations is built up by modeling clay, glass flasks and liquids, Erector sets and cooking classes, fire walking and metal-bending, or what have you, is not the issue. I have concentrated on these non-ordinary aspects because such phenomena give the lie to the mechanistic, behavioristic nonsense that pervades most thinking today. Such events demonstrate that an awesome capacity *is* built within us; the whole show is tucked away in our own consciousness.

Fire walking is the most stable non-ordinary event, yet few adepts can walk fire with impunity at will, and failure at any time is always a possibility. Neither adults nor children have been able to stabilize, predict, or control these odd phenomena. There is a strong element of poltergeist, random foolishness here, and a stable, predictable development of such may not even be intended by nature at all. The great teachers and saints of history seem to have possessed paranormal capacities yet seldom used them. One and all they cautioned against dabbling in such matters.

The unity of the creative process within us is demonstrated at every fire walking, though, so we would do well to consider what the larger signs for us are. For, as we have seen, while each stage of our development is complete to itself, each also takes on its full significance and power only as it is integrated into the next higher structure, and supports further development. The meaning and use behind these prankish outbreaks probably lie in the higher integral structures of knowledge built into nature's agenda. The entire developmental period through adolescence is but the grounds for a later integration of breathtaking dimensions. At that stage, and only then, these peripheral magical tricks take on their true depth and significance.

9

Formal Operations

In Chapter 6 I mentioned a childhood night terror from which I had difficulty awaking and which I could not remember afterward. Since the dream was seriously disturbing, I felt, as I grew older, that I must somehow come to terms with it, so I determined to hold on to my senses, follow the sequence, and remember it, rather than letting it take me over as it had. I began to keep paper and pencil by my bed, determined to remember the dream the next time it occurred, and to write it down. After some time, my project worked. During my dream I held to my awareness, witnessed the event, and immediately wrote out an account of it. The dream faded from my life at that point. In later years I would have rumblings of its overture, but nothing more.

At age eleven the locus of our ego-awareness shifts into that objective point of view called mind. From this position we can, in effect, stand outside of and operate on our own brain functions. I was eleven when the notion struck me that I could gain control over that night terror, stand outside it and witness it as an event separate from me. Piaget called this ability to operate on the functions of the brain itself "Formal Operational Thinking." My ability to stand outside my own dream state was a characteristic of this capacity to manipulate the very machinery for thinking. Such notions require maturation and separation of ego from brain mechanisms. By age eleven, body and brains become supportive instruments of this higher integration from which we view everything, even our own thinking, as "other" to us. Ego is now identified with mind, which is a mirror of the brain in the same way that a television screen mirrors the translations from the set. Now ego-mind must move on toward freedom even from that screen itself, to a point where ego can punch the buttons of its brain components and switch stations in a fundamentally new way. Ego, born out of the brain as a child is born out of the womb, can now move to an objective point beyond the bias of the brain systems, and come into resonance with the very waves of consciousness being translated by the brain. This is the next logical step in the growth from concreteness to abstraction, but, just as the television screen is a useless blank without the input from the component parts, ego-mind at adolescence is still dependent on its brain for its source of awareness. The new freedom of consciousness is an ability that must be developed.

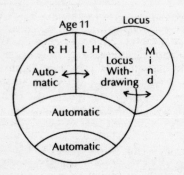

Between ages seven and eleven, nature constructs a language of abstract meanings and connotations we refer to as semantic. Such notions as morality, ethics, quality, meaning, virtue, transcendent, and so on are semantic. They have no referent other than states, conditions, or attitudes of mind. They are rather a mature form of the early esthetic ("like and dislike") polarizations of the two-year-old. At age eleven this semantic system arrives full-blown on the scene. Word is born out of its physical matrix and can now act in a formal way, that is, as a way by which we can operate on the very functions of our brain. This gives rise to intellect, a way of thinking outside emotion, free of the need to relate qualitatively, and beyond the limits of physical referents. Thinking can range freely, and the young person can think about thinking by examining his own mental machinery. The child has used many variants of this earlier, but the process now moves into universal implications and broad causal fields. Intellect can now use thought independently of all previous systems, balances, and checks. It can draw on its support systems without having to answer back to them, in effect. As a result, unless intellect is integrated into the next structure, as designed, it will operate without regard to consequence, or balance, and can easily become demonic.[1]

Since all learning is from the concrete to the abstract, our first formal operations are essentialiy concrete. Intellect refers to our previous structures of knowledge. From that point, intellect can become increasingly creative and move on into ever more abstract realms. This should prepare for the integration of intellect into intelligence.

We can categorize formal operations as science, art, and philosophy and religion, the three broad subjects that constitute a culture or society's body of knowledge. We open to a full conceptual grasp of these areas of thought around age eleven, with the separation of word from its physical origins; we are geared, by our blueprint, to turn to our society's body of knowledge at this stage in the same way we turned to the parent in infancy and childhood.

We can consider these three categories as mind playing with its three brain instruments: science with the material old brain; art with the emotional, dream-time mid-brain; religion and philosophy with the abstract concepts of the new brain. Since we are all familiar with our culture's body of knowledge (all schooling is based on it in one way or another), I will take it for granted that we can examine less conventional forms of playing with the brain, and so stretch our horizons.

Tim Gallwey, author of *The Inner Game of Tennis*, tells of a fifty-five-year-old woman who had no prowess in sports, had never held a tennis racket in her life, and felt too old to be taught new tricks. Following training (which can be considered a variation of neurolinguistic programming), she picked up a racket for the first time and, with cameras recording, beat everyone around.[2]

Sports psychology is becoming quite a fashionable field. Professional athletic teams are trained through the neurolinguistic approach. ("Neurolinguistic" refers to the effects of language on the nervous system.) Plays are outlined, and each player makes an image of his part of the action over and over in his mind's eye until all movements are seen clearly. Then he moves onto the field to apply his practice directly; he projects his internal world onto his external one with something like a forty-percent increase in efficiency and none of the broken bones of the ordinary forms of practice.

The sports psychology phenomenon is only once removed from the bedtime story. Internal imagery is a form of thinking, and thinking requires muscular movement. These movements, generally microscopic in proportion, are always present. Brain activity elicits body activity in sympathetic response, since body is an extension and instrument of brain.

Of itself, the brain will make the same instinctive muscular-glandular survival reactions to an internally produced image (of, say, a tiger) as to an externally given image. Apparently the mind, or a hidden observer, arbitrates in these matters, and informs the brain that because the internal image is not real, flight is not necessary. (At night, in our dreams, this arbitration largely disappears, but so does a full response from our old brain's motor systems, since they are largely suspended.)

The phonemes of language have brought about muscular-neural responses since our early pre-natal times. The two-year-old moves his hand as he says the word "hand." The play of the brain/mind and body through neurolinguistic programming is an extension of this and of the activity of our five-year-old's bedtime story, where we speak the word and the image appears.

Concrete language is retained in the right hemisphere's synchrony with the primary brains, as well as the analogical language of imagery transference. In his inner practice, the athlete plays out his inner action in perfection that transfers to the old brain's world image and muscular systems. In the same way that the early child projects his inner image of the road-roller on the outer image of spool and plays in his modulation, so the athlete projects his long-rehearsed internal game onto the external game. The micro-movements become macro-movements with ease and precision, for they have been rehearsed without opposition, and in the precursory, subtle dream world that underlies the real one. In the face of opposition, the player's inner imagery, being subtle, is more powerful than the external and modulates that external image to varying degrees.

We read of the Aikido master who "dances through" his attackers in slow motion so that no one can lay hands on him. Mathematician Ralph Strauch, a master in martial arts and the Feldenkreis movements, claims that we must unconsciously accept the idea of attack in order for an attack against us to be carried out.[3] Without this unconscious agreement there is no conscious agreement. So our Aikido master's inner image wins agreement from his attackers in spite of themselves, since he has developed a powerful image of his own actions.

Group imposition of imagery has a more creative application. An English psychologist traveled in India a number of years ago, making movies of fakirs, magicians, and non-ordinary practices.[4] His ambition was to photograph the famous Indian rope trick, but he could never find it being performed. About when he had decided it was only a folk tale, he heard that the trick was to be performed in a nearby village. He rushed there with his big camera on its tripod and worked his way to the scene. The fakir stood in a clearing with the stock tools of his trade: a large basket and a small boy. The crowd grew quiet, suspense grew; finally the fakir moved and the Englishman turned on his camera.

The fakir opened his basket, withdrew a large coil of rope, held one end of the rope in one hand, and, with the other, expertly threw the coil into the air with great force. The coil unrolled as it went up, and the end simply disappeared "up there" somewhere, the rope suspended in mid-air. The little boy then broke his stance and climbed the rope, all eyes following him. And he simply "disappeared up there" somewhere, like the end of that rope. The fakir again reached into the basket, took out a wicked looking, curved short sword, tucked it into his sash, and also climbed the rope, all eyes on him. He, too, simply disappeared.

A long pause, tension reached a breakpoint, all eyes turned up. Suddenly there was a gasp from the audience. Down came a bloody leg, apparently that of the little boy, all eyes following as it crashed to the ground, splattering blood. Then came another leg, then an arm, another arm, then the bloody, dismembered torso, and finally the pitiful little head. The audience moved their heads as one, following this drama.

After a pause, the fakir appeared, climbing down the rope. Casually, he reached in his basket, took out a cloth, wiped the murderous instrument, put it back in the basket, and, with indifferent nonchalance, drew the rope down, carefully coiling it into a neat, tight coil. He placed the rope in the basket and, almost as an afterthought, looked around at the mess of the little boy's parts. With a shrug he gathered these, one at a time, and deposited them, too, in the basket; closed the top and stood, quietly, eyeing the audience impassively. Suddenly the basket top flew open and out sprang the little boy, whole, intact, smilingly alive. The audience burst into a great shout, applause rang out and coins showered in, the little boy scrambling to pick up every one. The crowd then broke, making way, and the actors left the scene.

The Englishman was entranced; too much so—so he questioned a sample of the audience, noting down their observations. All experienced precisely as he had. He hastened back to the city to have his rare film developed, and projected the film on the screen. He saw the fakir move, bend over, come up with the coiled rope, throw it mightily into the air, at which point two things happened: The rope fell smack down on the ground in good Newtonian fashion, and the fakir and his boy stood absolutely stock still, without moving a muscle, from that point on. The film showed the audience, meanwhile, all move their heads up, then down, then up—then the look of horror, then up and down, and so on. Finally the film showed the fakir move, wind up the rope from the ground, applause, coins, and departure.

"Aha!" the materialistic tough-minded brass-tacks, nonsense scientific believer says: "Illusion." Of course it is illusion!—a little play, an inner play taking place entirely within the brain/mind of an entire group. The scene was projected by a master projectionist and received on the screen of mind of all participants. The storyteller uses words and the internal image making is produced accordingly in the listeners. In the rope trick the storyteller uses image only and all share that image.

Our tough-minded behaviorist says this illustrates our problem. People are deluded by such trickery on many levels. They should let this be a lesson that the mind is untrustworthy and cannot give a true, objective picture of the world as it really is. What the mechanist claims, of course, is that the lifeless camera, that poor mechanism, is the proper criterion for what is real! At which point the mechanist allies with—and limits himself to—the least conscious aspect of our living world as the only reality.

The story illustrates the fact that reality is a production of the human brain/mind, a production infinitely rich, which opens to incredible vistas and potential spaces. None of this, alas, is available to that machine, the poverty-stricken camera, which cannot take part in reality. It is limited to some pre-set, inflexible, unchangeable world of matter as itself— whatever illusion that might be. The same goes for any other technological device, including the greatest supercomputer that will ever be achieved. At each shift of brain mode, there is a threshold that is paradox. Nothing on one level can in any way account for the next. And the behaviorists, with all their posturings and bravado, peering through their triple-thick lensed glasses at a world they cannot see—maneuvering money, public image, governments and education; chronically award- ing medals back and forth for their restrictive foolishness— they are locked into a one-way world that leads only to death. In that world available only to and authenticated by that camera, the film must surely run out.

The above progression leads logically to the next step in the possible play of mind. I refer to his experience in every book and workshop, and see it on a continually broader basis. This is an experiment Charles Tart, psychologist at the Uni- versity of California at Davis, ran years ago,[5] which Jean Houston has reported on, and which a group of friends and I duplicated. I will condense Tart's experiments into one typi- cal venture, using an actual episode (from many that took place). The experiment is in mutual hypnosis.

Two graduate students, male and female, were found who could go into deep trance and could also put other people into trance (a rare combination). In preliminary ses- sions, both agreed to keep tuned in to Tart and accept his directions. (This agreement broke down at a certain point, as you will see.) Tart tells the young woman to put the young man into trance. She does. In order to do so, the man must be willing; he must, in effect, surrender his will over to the young woman. And he must surrender his ordinary reality in order to go into a trance state. One of the things that takes place in hypnosis is a reduction of attention paid to the old brain's physical sensory system; that system is drawn on selectively according to suggestions from the hypnotist. The bulk of conscious attention then resides in the mid-brain and the new brain.

Tart then tells the young woman to tell the young man to put her into trance. She, like her partner, then gives her will for what shall be real over to the young man, restricts her level of attention to his suggestions, and Tart's, and goes into that suspended state. Each has then surrendered his will for what shall be real to the other. Each would then go all the way to sleep, having sharply reduced sensory intake. So Tart instructs the woman to put the man into the highest trance she can. "You have a golden rope ladder," she tells her partner, "and you are going up that ladder into higher and higher states of trance." His supportive mid-brain, translator of imagery, translates the word into imagery; he enters into the inner journey and imagines going up the ladder. They have a number system for gauging extents of trance, and he arrives at the top figure, a state of complete surrender to her words.

To stabilize his state, and prevent his going on to sleep, she tells him to imagine that he is on a beautiful beach and should stay there. This occupies his energy of attention and keeps him in his trance. Since each has surrendered his or her will, and thus volition and desire, to the other, nothing more would happen without a coach on the sidelines. This is Tart's role. So Tart tells her to instruct the young man to put her into the same state. The young man goes through the same routine with her: the golden rope ladder, higher and higher, the beautiful beach, the same state.

Then something surprising happened. The couple found themselves together on the same beach. And at that moment, the beach, heretofore just another imaged notion, shaky, shifting, insubstantial as any imaginary scene would be, leaps into full life, fully real, available to all five senses, in three dimensions, and stable, as real as any event of their lives. Except, the beach is psychedelic: The sands are diamonds, the ocean champagne, crystal rocks range the shoreline, heavenly voices sing overhead. All is tangible, available to every sense, indistinguishable from any other reality, but like none they have known. They have created a consensus reality, or rather, they have set up the conditions by which such a creation takes place (an important qualification).

Dreaming seems related to the mid-brain and its right hemisphere interactions. In lucid dreams we manage to achieve some objectivity and, to some extent, can operate on the materials of the dream. The scenes of lucid dreams are experienced in isolation, though, and are transient; they fade quickly. In mutual hypnosis, we have two projection points of mind creating a mutually shared scene. The participants set up a field effect between them. A relationship between the internal imagery of each system is established. For here the mid-brain is involved, and that is the brain that opens to intuition and other shared field effects. This mutuality is what gives the permanence and the full sensory dimensions to what would otherwise be a transient, shallow dimensional image.

Either of the parties involved in mutual hypnosis can go back later, in a self-induced trance state, and find these mutually created states intact, full-dimensional, fully real as they had experienced them together. (Neither permanence nor full-dimensional structures can be achieved in individual, private hypnotic dreams.) Months later, the mutually created states are unchanged and stable, available either singly and self-induced, or together, in mutual, hypnotic states.

During one experiment of Tart's, another young woman graduate student came into the study while a mutual state was taking place, sat down to wait for the conclusion, fell into a trance, and found herself in their private world. The two resented her presence and asked her to leave. Tart lost touch with the two each time at the point of the formation of their mutual dream image. For at that point they no longer used their physical bodies for communication, so they lost touch with Tart. They were then in their so-called dream bodies, or "subtle bodies" (of which more later). In this state, only their heads and hands fully materialized; their bodies remained slightly diaphanous, a bit transparent, less than substantial, in spite of the solid materiality of their dreamlike surroundings. (Their physical bodies, back in the laboratory, were slumped over, apparently sound asleep, on automatic pilot while the owners were away.) Written reports, made separately after the experiments, always tallied point for point.

Two people taking drugs together often enter into the

same non-ordinary reality experience. A third party, not under drugs but physically present with the other two, may fall into the same state and share their experience. In my years of living and traveling with my meditation teacher, Muktananda, I had several strikingly real experiences through which I would be taught—through clear, tangible, sensory-motor imagery—some teaching that I had not been able to grasp from verbal or written description. All learning is from the concrete to the abstract. Sufi and yoga teachers use this practical method to teach students about states, processes, or functions not available through ordinary sensory ways.

In 1983, reports on large-scale group dreaming were published.[6] All members taking part must be adept at lucid dreaming. As many as ten people at a time agree on a "target" meeting place, such as a bus, and a specific time. While meeting in the dream they exchange specific information with each other, the test being to awaken from the dream and write out the information received, as well as an account of the event. One of the persons involved remarked that one might develop the procedure to eavesdrop on other people's dreaming. There may be a sharp shift of modality, however, from the ordinary "psychic flatulence" making up most dreams, and true lucid dreaming.

In all these cases listed here, including the fakir's rope trick maneuver, the experiences are not our creations, not even in the most tightly controlled lucid dream. The experiences are given and we are the recipients; but they are given only when we set up the conditions for that giving and reception. Our ability to then enter into and influence the direction of that creation is significant, for that is a next step. This ability to participate leads to an eventual merger with the creative process, to becoming that force which is the goal of human maturation.

Ability to stand outside and operate on our conceptual-perceptual instruments moves us into an area of creativity that does not require mediation through physical means. Then mind can experience outside its own brain process, the logical next step in the overall progression of separations and entry into ever more subtle, non-structured power. By adolescence, mind is a reflector of the brain; brain is the translator projecting its translations on the screen of mind. Mind now prepares to bypass this mediation and perceive on its own directly out of creative possibility. Mind will develop as a two-way mirror, one toward the world of physical process, the other toward the inner realm of creation; post-biological development will open.

It will sound like the most puerile and fatuous nonsense to say that the fakir and his rope, or Tart's young couple on their beach, or the lucid dreaming shared by a group, or my meditation experiences brought about through my teacher, represent a more advanced evolutionary function than our super-computed rockets to the moon or planets. But no matter how inordinately complex and sophisticated, manipulation of one physical process by modulation with another physical process never moves beyond physical function, the most elementary, primitive mode we have. No matter that technology represents brilliant intellect; that intellect turns us back into our most primitive process and devotes the new brain's power to concrete levels. The child bending the bar of metal opens to a realm of mind vastly beyond chemical explosions of rocketry, and into that inner realm is where we are designed to go. No amount of physical manipulation can take a single human psyche into his next matrix—that non-physical mode in which we must be able to maneuver when our physical apparatus goes down, like a used-up rocket.

10

Power and Possibility

Development for the first fifteen years of life is a series of shifts into greater personal power and possibility. We begin in a sensory-motor mode, crawling about, interacting with one object at a time and identifying with those objects. Once this weak and most restricted mode is stabilized, nature shifts us into our dreaming brain, and new power manifests. We overlay our sensory-motor images with internal ones and play in the modulated imagery that results. Around age four we shift into the new brain as our locus and develop an analogical language of symbols and metaphors that can transfer sensory-motor imagery into abstract imagery, and vice versa. At the same time, we develop intuition, perceptions outside direct sensory-motor stimuli, outside locality in time and space. We bond into a single unit our three different means of perception: concrete image, dream image, and abstract image. The resulting state is more powerful than the preceding ones.

Around age seven, we begin to be able to take an internal image and, rather than simply superimpose the external image for a play reality, we may actually change the concrete object through superimposition. At that point, the source of the sensory-motor image is itself altered, and along with it our sensory-motor reality. To walk fire or bend metal requires access to an energy greater than that through which the chemical-molecular structures of fire and flesh, or bars of steel, are ordinarily maintained. A weaker energy cannot modulate a more powerful one.

By about age eleven we can stand outside all our modes

of perception and play with the modulations possible between these systems. We can then create forms of art, or systems of logic such as mathematics, philosophy, or religion. Our awareness has now extended from our original sensory-motor identity into an abstract mental process that needs no reference outside itself. We can then create internal sensory worlds and enter into them. This is a long way beyond our earliest, crawling state. Our power and possibility have increased at quantum leaps at each stage of development. But where does the power come from?

Consider, first, that the physical world we know is the external form of an inner projection taking place through the primary brains and projected on the screens of our minds. All that we can ever be aware of is that we interact, using our sensory system, with perceptions we know are an internal production, a play between the three brains and mind. We perceive the world, but this is a perception given us, and perception is creation. We cannot claim to create physical reality through our awareness of that reality, nor can we assume that physical events take place outside our awareness of them. The event we know as reality is a dynamic between possibility and realization. The creation cannot be pinned down by intellectual premise nor split into pieces. The dynamic is our reality and our questions should center on the nature and process of this creative dynamic that constitutes our consciousness.

Common sense refers to a shared reaction to sensory stimuli. Common sense demands that we recognize the source of our physical stimuli to be external to us, and it certainly is. But this externalization is also a product of our brain/minds. The brain places stimuli according to logical necessity. Some sensory information is placed as an outside event, some as inner imagination. Under certain circumstances we can mix our mediums and share a common perception that arises from within us. The fakir with his rope trick, groups in mutual dreaming, the teaching experiences given me in meditation— all are cases in point. By and large, though, we share a common physical world, and the history of physical science has revolved around discovering what these commonsense systems are. Even the experiences explored by scientists are expressions of our three-fold brain, however, and the relation between inner and outer image embraces our whole experience.

In our expanding scientific model of the world we can find many parallels between the energy of physics and personal power. Some three centuries ago, Isaac Newton commented, almost marginally, that matter and energy were exchangeable. More recently, Henri Poincaré worked out a mathematical equation for this exchange. Albert Einstein picked up on Poincaré's work, rewrote the equation as $E = MC^2$, and now receives full credit for the idea.[1] Back in 1940 my eighth-grade science teacher wrote ENERGY = MATTER on the blackboard, held up a tiny lump of coal, and announced that according to atomic theory there was enough energy in that tiny lump to run a steam engine such as a freight train for a year. Then he snickered and we snickered since that was the silliest statement we had ever heard.

In 1940 few people understood or believed in the theory of atomic energy. Einstein scoffed at Enrico Fermi's proposal which eventually gave us the bomb. And Fermi's process was not, as commonly believed, based on Einstein's theories. In 1945, we dropped a couple of Fermi's brainchildren, took out a few hundred thousand Japanese in a matter of seconds, and every schoolchild then knew that energy and matter were, indeed, interchangeable.[2]

The atomic proposal that the most energy arises from the smallest bit of substance was a logical offense, but *quantum* physics held even bigger offenses in store. Truly *big* energy, the evidence from quantum mechanics suggested, comes not from matter at all, but from the empty spaces between the particles of matter. Break up an atom, our littlest item, and we get our biggest bang (to date). But within the spaces of an atom, or in spaces without atoms, quantum physicists said, lie far larger fields of energy. The most comes not from the least, but from nothing at all.

Early in our century, physicists had found what they assumed to be the basic particle out of which atoms, molecules, cells, and bodies are built. In a major logical offense they found that this building block would, under one set of laboratory circumstances, act as a particle should; under another, it acted as a wave of energy. Energy functions as either particle or wave according to the experiment we set up, which defies all classical logic.

Today physicists accept that a wave field of energy underlies all particles of energy. A *field* is a continuum of energy that has no localization, no place. To be localized or placed, the energy must manifest as a thing, a specific, singular event. The field embraces the range of possibilities for *thingness* or manifestation which that expression of energy contains within it. In order to manifest as a thing or event, all those variables appropriate to that field are eliminated, and the field is said to "collapse" to the particle event then expressed. The particles present themselves as more restricted than the wave forms, since the open potential has closed to that single configuration.[3]

The fifty or so phonemes that underlie language can be considered a field of appropriate variables. As the child imprints to the given language model, the variables possible within the field close to that specific configuration. Without the model, the field retains its potential but has no existence. Once expressed as a particular language, the field closes, yet is always there in some manner as the substratum from which its expression springs. (Condon and Sanders find our sensory-motor response to phonemes present on a microkinetic level all our life.) In the same way, quantum physicists say the wave collapses into particle form yet the particle also resonates as its own wave form. The particle-wave possibility displays as one or the other according to the display we set up.

The electron, for instance, does not swing around the nucleus of the atom in an orbit like a planet around the sun; it resonates as an orbiting wave field around a nucleus which is also an expression of a wave form at its own level. Under certain circumstances, that orbiting wave field can be observed to be a particle, but we must set up the conditions for that observation to manifest. We can consider a particle a thing set apart from its wave form and so having existence in a measurable time and space. The particle is the localized expression of the non-local wave field. From the wave standpoint, none of our language or logic applies, since our language and logic are the results of our experience with particularized expressions of energy. The wave form is not any thing and does not exist as a measurable time-space phenomenon. Yet the wave form participates in and precedes all things and brings about those particularizations that give time and space.

All phenomena we know are the results of energy interactions of this kind. The first energy interactions available to us on being born into this world are particle in form—that is, sensory-motor. This physical or concrete state is the most restricted, contracted form of energy, and, since our awareness is brought into being through such stimuli, we have no choice but to identify with this contracted state as our first expression of being.

Once this concrete level of experience is stabilized, around the end of our first year of life, our consciousness is free for further development. We then move into that dreaming midbrain, with its capacity to translate highly fluid, flexible images. This opens to us a more fluid, flexible reality. The mid-brain translates subtle energy, wave forms that act to give meaningful shape to the constricted, concrete imagery of the old brain. But this shaping force is not available for measurement by instruments or even our ordinary sensory observation, since our observation is a result of the process we try to view and the instruments we use are physical properties. The flexible imagery of the mid-brain has no localization, no placement, but can be superimposed on those contracted images of the old brain for a flexible reality. The mid-brain opens to the field of variables appropriate to the physical phenomena to be modulated. We begin this superimposition of images by the second year of life; it is a movement beyond the restricted particle expression into a greater realm of possibility, a greater freedom of conscious awareness. Through fantasy, storytelling, and play, the child is driven to develop ever more unrestricted modes of consciousness, learning to handle ever more fluid forms of experience.

We know that our eyes register only a small part of a spectrum of light waves. In the same way, we register only a small part of a possible field of energy through our restricted reptilian-mammalian sensory system. As physicists Kafatos and Nadeau point out, a field (as a continuum of appropriate variables) is logically antithetical to the construct of matter as a discrete, localized entity in space and time. Thus, in physics, " . . . when we seek to understand the field aspect of a phenomenon, nothing can be known about its discreteness (as matter) and vice versa." In the same way, our blueprint for intelligence, as a field of possibility, can only display in discrete, set-apart events, and does so according to the models of discretion given. The blueprint, as an open potential, closes to that model's expression. If we should remain related only to this closed expression, however, we would be restricted to an extremely contracted state of consciousness, which would create despair. The whole point of the development of intelligence is to move beyond this either-or split displayed in physics, even in quantum physics. Consider matter and energy. Each is needed to understand any event, and yet one displaces the other in a given instance. In the quantum domain, as Kafatos and Nadeau point out, the description of a state splits into two mutually exclusive classes which are complementary to one another, since both are needed to describe completely the state of the system. This principle of complementarity applies equally to human development. The inner state of power and possibility is complementary to the outer, realized models of that possible power. Both are needed for development and both are needed to explain who we really are.

From the standpoint of particle reality, the absence of particles means a vacuum state, a state of nothingness. Classical physics assumed, rightly, that no energy existed in a vacuum. The particle is set apart from the wave state as a discrete thing. A vacuum is devoid of particles and so devoid of the energy inherent in things. On the other hand, since nothing is set apart in a vacuum, it has no restriction within its continuum; there is no contraction of its field of potential. Coming into existence sets it apart. To realize an event is to select from, and so close, the continuum of variables. Existence *(ex sistere)* means decision, in effect a cutting off of variables. (Decision is from *decidere*, to cut off.) We restrict the potential to the limited but specific expression of that energy. So any appearance is bought at the price of the open continuum of possible appearances. The field "collapses" to that specific. So, from the standpoint of a quantum *potential* of energy, an absence of matter automatically means a freeing of the potential inherent within the field. The more perfect the vacuum, the greater the potential.

Furthermore, the more compact the wave itself, the

closer together its peaks and troughs, the greater the power inherent within that wave spectrum. Long, slow waves (such as photons) are weaker than fast ones. Max Planck estimated that waves could reduce to a final, irreducible length of 10^{-34} centimeters (which is less than nothing at all). Take the figure one, follow it with thirty-four zeroes *minus* centimeters, and you have the estimated size of the final wave forms before the compaction is complete and no movement manifests. At this point of compaction, called Planck's Constant, a single cubic centimeter of empty space contains an estimated 10^{93} ergs (energy units). Though only potential energy, from a physical standpoint, this is far more energy than computable from all realized matter within the entire conceivable universe, with all its untold billions of galaxies.

Recall my story of my eighth-grade science teacher in 1940, with his talk of running a steam engine for a year on a tiny lump of coal. The quantum-theory statement that a tiny cube of emptiness contains more potential energy than all matter in the universe is simply a logical extension of the earlier atomic notion. As we reduce down to the heart of matter, the energy increases. To get to the source of that energy, though, we must reduce down through and beyond that heart of matter, into emptiness, or no-thingness—at which point energy is infinite and beyond computation. Physicists hasten to explain that this is only potential energy and not available as such. But, as we shall see, the energy is not available only if we adhere to a logic drawn from physical matter. The fields of energy are not just potential; within their own logic they simply *are*, they exist. At a point in our development we are designed to shift from this orientation which considers anything not physical as "only potential." That is, we must shift from the primitive view which can comprehend, or grasp, possibility only when it lends itself to physical application. Our first stage of development places physical realization as the focus of life, and rightly so. Once this physical orientation is stable, however, we are designed to orient to the energy field itself as the focus, and recognize that physical realization is only a temporary platform or training ground from which we can move beyond such restricted forms.

Einstein did not like quantum mechanics and, with two mathematical friends, Rosen and Podolsky, came up with a mathematical disproof of quantum mechanics by showing a basic contradiction, a true paradox, within its terms. In 1964, nearly thirty years later, a mathematician-physicist, John Bell, came up with a theorem showing that Einstein's paradox proved, rather than disproved, the case for quantum mechanics. Eight years later, John Clauser, then at the University of California, using his own variation, gave the first substantial laboratory proof that Bell's theorem was true. Since that time a steady succession of experiments has established the validity of Bell's theorem and quantum mechanics. Many physicists have referred to it as the most significant discovery of Western science.[4]

A stream of paradox pours from Bell's theorem and a logical shift for all of science looms large. For instance: If two particles of energy are brought into proximity with each other, as part of a relating system, and are separated from that physical relationship and sent off in opposite directions, traveling away from each other near the speed of light; and the spin or polarity of one particle is changed by an interference; then the spin, or polarity, of the other particle will simultaneously shift in the same manner.

We assumed that nothing could exceed the speed of light and the particles are moving apart at that speed. Yet when one is changed, the other particle mirrors that change with no time lapse. This indicates some kind of communication outside the restrictions of time and space. Further, mathematical extrapolations of the laboratory events show that even though the particles should move an entire universe apart, they will still mirror each other simultaneously, once they are brought into this proximity as part of a closed system.

Recall that if we put two live heart cells on a microscopic slide, well separated, they pulse randomly. Bring them closer together and at a certain point they arc the gap between, communicate, and pulse in synchrony. They establish a bond that arises as the relation between the two cells, a relation which is initially dependent on proximity (though not actual contact), but which then holds outside all physical restrictions. Bonding is not restricted to time and space, yet it participates in both. In the same way, the particles in Bell's theorem bond by coming into contact on a physical, or localized level, and the bond, once established, holds outside the limits of localization. The bond is established within the wave field from which the particles arise. Time and space of a particle nature do not apply within the wave field. The non-local state is not subject to the restrictions, or laws, of the localized, physical state. But the bond cannot be considered *in* the wave state, since the bonding relates to particle forms. Without the particles, without physical forms that are set apart from each other, bonding is meaningless. Bonding is the dynamic, or participates in the dynamic, between the two states. Bonding is the dynamic of relationship, the force that relates apparent separations to the underlying state of unity. Bonding is the force that encompasses and participates in both particle and wave field and so enters into the material configurations that result.

The general principle of complementarity in physics shows that we have either one state or the other, physical or subtle. Yet we must have both to explain fully any situation. The full explanation, which leaps the logical paradox of either-or, is the principle of bonding. Bonding arcs over and beyond all complementarities. Through the bond our consciousness moves from the restriction of realized forms into the open and fluid potential of the wave field, not as "material" for use in the restricted physical mode but as the grounds for non-restrictive awareness, the freedom *from* physical form. Wave and particle are mutually exclusive yet equally available through bonding. The complementary principle expressed in our development is that we are both states and both are available when conditions are met.

Like intuition, the particles of Bell's theorem communicate outside time and space. Time and space, which create the vast universe about us, prove to be but surface displays of a far vaster underlying continuum. But two questions remain: From where does that initial wave form, of 10^{-34} centimeters, come? And how is it that the wave "collapses" to the same configuration each time to create a stable universe? For instance, excepting heart and possibly brain cells, my body replaces every cell in it, including those in my bones, about every seven years, and replaces every atom within those cells within a year's time. Yet my overall physical form remains essentially the same—more or less (that is, more wrinkles, less hair, and so on). So how do the waves underlying my particles collapse into this more or less same localized form, so that I persist as this body (as long as I do)?

First, if each particle resonated out of its own private little wave, which private wave reduced down to its own private little final point of compaction, that source of Planck's Constant, then Bell's theorem would not hold and we would have only chaos, a random profusion of non-relating particles. The logic of the quantum movement of energy impels the conclusion that the phenomenon of wave fields manifests from a single source. Planck's Constant of a wave only 10^{-34} centimeters marks not the final point, but the first appearance, of creative energy. The point of origin must obviously lie beyond that first manifestation; and that point of origin is the mutual state inherent within all manifestations, and the point from which all bonding springs—the common reference point establishing the relations of all eventual appearances in restricted forms.

Ancient sages had clear models of this creative process, and physicists have recently become intrigued with the striking parallels between these oldest and newest systems. Yogic cosmology represented creation as springing from a single point of consciousness to produce a manifold universe. The yogis said that this single pulsation displayed as four "worlds": (1) the initial unmoving point from which all action springs; (2) a causal world of pure potential energy; (3) a subtle world that was the immediate precursor to, and mirrored back into, the physical world, as a kind of mental double; and (4) the final physical world. The yogis said that each of the worlds was represented in us as a body. Within the physical body is a subtle body; within that subtle body a causal body; and within the causal a supra-causal body, which is that unmoving state from which everything springs.

Furthermore, the yogis expressed these body-worlds as four states of consciousness: a waking state, associated with the physical body and world; a dream state associated with the subtle body and world; a deep-sleep state associated with the causal body and world. Beyond all these was our silent-witness state, the initial unmoving point from which the other modes were simply observed. They called this fourth state the seat of the *Self*. The Self is a single, indivisible unit of consciousness that expresses itself through these three modes of action. From the weakest, the physical, to the all-encompassing power of the final non-moving point of awareness, the Self, there is only a single, flowing action of creative energy. This energy is a single impulse of consciousness and so cannot divide, yet a series of contractions creates the illusion of infinite divisions, or separations, and the Self explores the play, or unfolding out, of its singularity. So, in spite of Maya, or the great play of illusion, there is only the one Self, and each of us, of logical necessity, is equally that Self, at the core of our beings.[5]

Even the most cursory glance at this yogic outline shows clear parallels with both brain structure and the development of intelligence. In Chapter 2 I discussed how the waking state and physical world are translated into our awareness through our primary brains, particularly the reptilian. We must establish this state in our earliest period of life. The dream state and subtle world are translated through our mid-brains and established in early childhood. The "deep sleep" causal world is translated through our new brains and we explore causality from age seven on.

The deeper one goes into a study and practice of yogic thought, the more evident these parallels become. And physicists will miss the implications of the relations between yogic cosmology and physics unless they recognize all the parallels. The physical universe, with its galaxies of stars, bodies, and brains, is the scientist's continual focus, point of departure, *and* destination; it is a self-encapsulated trap. The only viable focus or point of view, and the only point from which the human can mature, is that single point of consciousness beyond all universes, and from which they all spring.

David Bohm, theoretical physicist at the University of London, has grasped the totality involved here. Creation, Bohm observes, takes place as a single, indivisible movement of energy he calls the Holomovement.[6] This movement is expressed outwardly in endless variations through what Bohm calls the mathematical interweaving of this single energy; rather as you could take a single thread and, without breaking that thread, weave a huge, elaborate tapestry from it.

In this process of weaving we can observe four general categories, or orders of energy, through which the creative process moves. The weakest expression of energy is our physical universe. Bohm calls it the Explicate Order, that which is made explicit or manifested physically. (Obviously this is the order which is translated through the old brain.) This Explicate Order resonates out of a field Bohm calls the Implicate Order. In this Implicate Order, physical form is implied but not yet expressed. The Implicate Order is a subtle energy where the wave assumes its impulse toward actual configuration as a particle energy state, or as Explicate Energy. This Implicate mode has an inevitable intent toward specific expression and is a far more powerful energy than its final expression as matter. The Implicate Order acts as the blueprint whose implications are filled with Explicate Order content. (The mid-brain is the translating medium for this subtle energy.)

Implicate energy resonates from a yet more powerful field of pure potential energy, which in itself manifests as an intent toward creation in general. This potential order of energy is the intent to become implicate energy, so to speak, the intent to display as a functional blueprint of possibility. This potential is a kind of precursor to all form, a causal energy. (This is translated through the new brain; and the eight basic geometric families underlying our visual process, and all configurations of matter, are the imagery of this mode.) This causal energy is not quantifiable in any meaningful way, and is far more powerful than the Implicate Order it underlies (just as the new brain is the most powerful system within the triune brain, and the means for both concrete and formal operational thought).

This potential energy resonates in turn out of—or is the initial expression of—that hypothetical state beyond all energy as movement, that fourth state from which everything springs. We can add all possible energies of the first three orders and never accumulate anything suggestive of the fourth state, Bohm says, for it lies, of necessity, beyond and superior to any of its expressions. This fourth state encompasses all its possible expressions, from its own point of logic, but is not made up of any or all possible forms of its expressions. The fourth state is infinite energy and the genesis of creation itself. (Naturally enough, this state has no equivalent brain organ. The brain, mind, and body are its instruments or means of expression. The fourth state has been expressed as seated in the heart.)

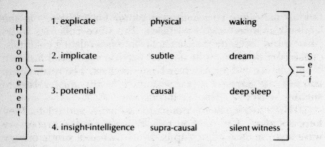

Bohm calls this final state the realm of insight-intelligence.
In so doing, he breaks with the mechanistic, dualistic, and
behavioristic thought dominant in our time. Recall that Newton first suggested that matter and energy were interchangeable, a notion rethought by Poincaré and refined by Einstein.
Bohm goes the next logical and inevitable step and points out
that energy also equals consciousness. Bohm says consciousness can "display itself" as either energy or matter. And at
that point, Bell's theorem and several hundred other major
paradoxes of contemporary science are immediately resolvable,
provided we will make the shift of logic involved; and from
that point of shift we can move into the true universe, the
one within. For, as Bohm puts it, this physical universe of
stars and galaxies is but the merest ripple on the surface of
the Holomovement.

   To say that consciousness can display itself as energy or
matter is not to restate Arthur Eddington's proposal that the
universe is one great thought. Consciousness is not thought.
Thought is a constricted, limited form of consciousness. Nor
is the physical universe, to which Eddington referred, the
same as Bohm's Holomovement. Bohm is one of the first
major scientists (hardly the last) to break from the fixation on
and limitation of our thought to a physical mode. Only by
looking beyond the physical, as Bohm has, can we grasp our
true dimensions.

   How, then, is form established and maintained in a flow
of conscious energy? Rupert Sheldrake, biologist at Cambridge University, has an interesting answer: through habit.[7]
Much as we get repetitive patterns of thought going in our
heads that become difficult to stop, consciousness as energy

follows patterns. The hydrogen atom, for instance, is the simplest combination of particles. The wave collapses to its particle and the particle either splits into two relating polarities, or the particle chances on another particle in its brief instance of appearance and forms a pair-bond, in effect. The relationship sustains the particle. (Any separated entity must relate to another separated entity to be sustained.)

When two particles come into contiguity and relate, they form a system. The relation reflects back into the precursory wave state since relationship is, by its nature, a subtle energy process, a wave phenomenon, not a particle function. So the wave field producing the particle is influenced in turn by the relation the particle establishes. This relation then enters into the flow of the wave field, which replicates the action. We form a kind of tape loop between possibility and actuality through this subtle effect of relationship. (Thus, isolated particles tend to disintegrate, or revert to wave status, since they do not participate in the subtle wave field producing them; they elicit no sustaining wave-collapse pattern.)

So the simplest atom immediately becomes a model for further movements of energy, an attractor or influence within the wave field. With an established entity as a model attractor, repetition of that pattern becomes increasingly more likely until virtually inevitable. The relational patterns reflecting back into the wave field become increasingly powerful, and the model factor is strengthened at each repetition as well. Profusion results because the model as stimulus feeds back into the wave field, setting up within the overall wave field a sub-set of appropriateness among the field's variable possibilities, and the appropriate variables tend toward expression. An implicate field is set up. Implications of the direction or tendency of particle expression are manifested within the now-specialized field within the overall wave field.

At the same time, the profusion of relating particles (the atoms) sets up its own particle field from which a further possibility opens: Combinations of the paired relationships form other, more complex relations, other atoms, not just pair-bonds of particles, but multiple bonds. Each new combination achieved acts as a possible model for the flow of consciousness. Each repetition strengthens the model relation, which acts back into the relational field and influences variations in the precursory flow. Each type of new wave-particle relation sets up a corresponding type of precursory response in the wave field. Different wave lengths articulate within the continuum of possible energy and tend to become self-sustaining spheres of influence on the course of events. Each sphere becomes a continuum of appropriate variables—the variables appropriate to the particular configuration intended by that implicate field.[8]

From the field of varied atoms arise fields of possibility—combinations such as stars, planets, chemicals, molecules, proteins, cells, bodies, brains, what have you. The longer a particular form repeats, the more stable and more likely its repetition. The entire play is consciousness unfolding as a separation out from itself, thereby establishing new relationships and possibilities. The rise of *Self* consciousness follows inevitably on combinations of increasing complexity, a tracing of which is far beyond our scope here. Suffice it to say that the more complex the conscious organization, the greater the power and possibility available, since there exists a wider number of causal fields to draw on. And the wider the fields available for expression, the more critical the role of the model.

Whether or not this particle, wave, or atomic model is a final "truth" is debatable and beside the point. The model partakes of our own nature and reflects back to us our self in some way, as all our models do. We can view our history from any angle and end with our own self as starting point. No matter our genesis, by the time evolution arrives at the human being we have *Self* consciousness, a complexity that reflects throughout the spectrum of possibility. As with all formations, this Self consciousness moves immediately toward replication and preservation. Each of us is driven to preserve his or her Self consciousness in the face of inevitable physical death. And the possibility of such sustenance could lie only through alignment with and relation to that source from which we arise. This is no simple procedure, and the role of the model by which such possibility as transcendence opens becomes critical. The narrower the field of possibility, the more casual, less critical, the model factor. The wider the possibility, the more specific that model must be. The characteristics demanded of a model of transcendency are both difficult and explicit.

We have no universe except as it is translated through our three-fold system. Rather than the brain being a micro-hologram of the macro-hologram universe, a full universe lies infinitely beyond the physical one, and is enfolded within us. But to consider that the four- or five-pound blob of gray-and-white matter in our heads might be the source of the power and possibility we can manifest would be naive and ridiculous. Vast amounts of information can be translated through a microchip in one of our new computers, for instance, but to attribute the source of that information to the chip would be equally naive and ridiculous.

In the same way, the brain/mind does not generate, but rather translates power and possibility. The brain/mind is the median, the interface between possibility and its expression. Our outer field is limited and restricted, but contains specific models that give the direction our inner fields can take to shape our experience. The progression of power is within, finally residing in that realm of the heart. Since this energy is a single movement, any expression of a particular order of that energy contains the whole of that order, according to Bohm. And any order of energy must contain the whole movement of creative energy itself. In looking at the physical world, even at our bodies, everything resonates out of that single center of creation. When the physicist refers to the empty space of his super vacuum, he does not mean space as in space travel to the stars. The space is that within us, beyond the world of subatomic particles, beyond existence. This inner realm is no miniaturized version of the physical world. Time, space, and measurement are left behind to enter this fluid state of power. The logic drawn out of our outer world of separated experience will not fit the reversibil-ity of this inner journey.

We must stand on our physical basis, however, in order to move in the opposite direction, away from the physical toward that state beyond existence, that point from which existence springs. With our identity established in that final state, we can then withdraw identity and awareness from our physical system, with all its supporting wave fields. Since that physical expression is in constant dissolution and reformation, it is not a satisfactory point of identity. The dissolution always outstrips the reformation, and our instrument of interaction gets shoveled six feet under all too soon. Identified only with such a weak and temporary system, despair is the only reasonable state of mind. Identified with the creative point from which all life springs, ecstasy, joy, and power are reasonable expectations. The problem lies in that shift of logic from existence to non-existence, or locality to non-locality. But this, too, is a matter of development, a development which is also built in, ready to unfold when given the proper teacher or model, and frame of reference.

David Bohm says all physical matter is enfolded within any part of physical matter, within a grain of sand or cell of our body. All time is enfolded within a single instant of time, all space enfolded within any cubic centimeter of space. The opening lines of William Blake's *Auguries of Innocence* anticipate and summarize the Holomovement:

> To see a World in a Grain of Sand
> And a Heaven in a Wild Flower,
> Hold Infinity in the palm of your Hand
> And Eternity in an hour.

Finally, of equal necessity, Bohm says the entire Holomovement is enfolded within every single human psyche. This too has been said by William Blake and the great sages down through the ages. Beneath the appearances of infinite diversity, each of us is that single unity, the core of the play of consciousness. *Tat Tvam Asi*. Thou art That. Each of us is the Self. This Self and our individual selves are complementary. On one level of logic they are mutually exclusive: We display as one or the other. Both are needed to fully explain our being, however, and the power of the bond is the arc across the gap of the complementary paradox. The bond is the means by which the individual, discrete self can identify with—and be as—the Self. And as usual, the bonding principle must display for us as a concrete model, out there in our ordinary world, if we are to establish the bond within our own state. And, as usual, the concrete, tangible, flesh-and-blood model can only be one bonded with that Self, one who is the actual arc across that gap of paradox; one who is in union with the Self while still displaying as a discrete, individual being. That is the way the play has functioned from the beginning, in the appearance of the first simple atom on. The formula remains the same.

11

Subtle
System

In *The Bond of Power* I reported a series of experiences I had
in the winter of 1979–80. A group of us was wintering at
Miami Beach with my meditation teacher, Baba Muktananda.
One day Baba told me to spend the second half of my
morning meditation lying flat on my back. So the next morning I sat for half my time, then lay flat down. Immediately
upon lying down, I went, as it is called, "out of my body." I
underwent no transition of consciousness, no preliminaries.
Some essential part of myself rose up, as a unit and all at
once, from my physical body. I rose no more than three or
four inches above my physical body, just hanging there. I
could hear my body breathing below me, but I, as me, was
quite clearly above it. When this happened I thought that I
was in for a great astral trip into other realms. I was familiar
with Robert Monroe's writings on out-of-the-body experiences[1]
and with Muktananda's own report of traveling in his subtle
body into subtle worlds.[2] But on this occasion I went no-
where at all. This event occurred for five straight mornings,
in the same way, and never did I go anywhere. I could open
my eyes and look around the room, but was afraid to roll over
and look at my physical body. After these five repetitions the
events ceased, with no great astral trip ever having occurred.

Some evenings later, when I was still stewing over what
the experience could have meant, Baba was talking at the
regular evening program. He interrupted his talk, looked at
me, and said, in effect: "You can't travel in your subtle body.
It hasn't enough power to break from the physical to go

anywhere. Only by incorporating the subtle body into the causal body can you travel."

I finally got the message. Experiencing an intriguing out-of-body experience was not the issue. I was being given a clear, concise, and valuable lesson. My Self, my teacher, had been telling me in those morning ventures: "You are not your body. Don't identify with it. Your body is your instrument for interacting with your physical world. Break your attachment to it." From that point at least some of my lifelong anxiety about my body and its mortality began to fade. I knew that there was more to my being.

The lack of content for the experiences was important for the lesson to be learned. It was given me to experience my subtle body as an independent state. Had I traveled places or experienced phenomena other than my ordinary morning meditation time Self, I would have rationalized the experience as a lucid or hypnagogic dream, and my attention would have centered on the content of the event. The lack of content allowed me to analyze the state as an independent phenomenon.

My subtle body felt identical to my physical body, and my personality, memory, and responses seemed ordinary. (This is not the case in hypnagogic or lucid dreaming, nor in ordinary out-of-body astral experiences.) I was experiencing my esthetic sensory system and ordinary ego as a phenomenon itself, separate from my physical body. Yet my senses were sensing as usual, without the intermediary of my physical system.

I realized that the subtle body is identical to the physical, point for point, but only as a feeling state. I could move my subtle body in the same way I moved my physical body and the impression was the same. I knew that my physical body was on automatic pilot, was well cared for, but that it sensed nothing since I, ego-awareness, was withdrawn from it. Thus, I discovered that my sensory system is a subtle energy that sparks and gives conscious awareness to the physical system, but which can be withdrawn and can operate independently. Yogis, Sufis, and Zen masters have been found who can arbitrarily withdraw their sensory systems from their bodies.[3] Their bodies are then anesthetized and do not register sensory phenomena.

The subtle system takes its content from its experience in the physical body and is always the sum total of our physical experience. But subtle energy is more powerful than physical energy, and, once set in motion, tends to persist even when no longer being stimulated by the physical body. The subtle system is either directly related to memory in general, or is, in effect, the memory of our physical body.

Though our ego becomes identified with the subtle system as the receptor of physical experience, ego is still not simply the subtle system. My favorite story illustrating this comes from Wilder Penfield, one of our century's great brain surgeons. He sawed the skulls off some 1500 patients in his career, and probed around in their brains with electrodes. Since the brain has no feeling, the patients did not have to be anesthetized (other than an initial local anesthetic), and would lie there awake, open-eyed, often talking with Penfield for hours as he probed.

Penfield would come across certain microscopic spots in the brain which, when activated by an electrode, would produce a complete memory or memory sequence from the patient's past. The memory would play into the patient's sensory awareness as a full-fledged event, in three dimensions, with all five senses involved as in the original experience. The patient would then report the event in detail as it unfolded, and the event played itself out so long as the electrodes were intact. Yet the patient was open-eyed, looking at Penfield, fully aware of the doctor and the hospital surroundings. Two complete yet separate events were playing on the screen of mind without mixup or interference.

The patients all reported the memory events equal in reality to the hospital setting, yet knew, arbitrarily, that only the hospital setting could be real, that the other event was only a memory. Penfield would ask, "But where are you, as your own self?" To which the patients would answer, "Just watching both events." From hundreds of such cases, Penfield drew the conclusion that mind was a separate entity, dependent on brain for its input, yet independent of brain in some way.[4] Yet if we consider the work of Ernest Hilgard of Stanford University, and his research into a "hidden observer," or silent witness to all events, even when we are asleep or hypnotized, we realize that mind is only an instrument, the

screen on which reality plays, but in some way not the end of
the perceptual process.[5]

Since only a tiny spot on the brain would give the
memory replay when stimulated, we might conclude that
memory was stored in tiny packets within the physical brain.
Yet Penfield often had to cut out huge chunks of the cortex
that were abscessed or cancerous, and found the patient's
memory not nearly as damaged as one would presume.[6]
Rupert Sheldrake proposes that memory might not be stored
in the brain at all but in a causal realm outside physical
processes, and that the brain may translate from such fields
into our awareness as called on.

Consider phantom limb pain, long a medical puzzle. A
leg, for instance, may be injured and after an agonizing time
have to be amputated. The patient may continue to suffer the
pain of the injury for months after the limb is gone. Where
does the pain come from? The answer is from, or through,
the subtle body. The subtle body is more powerful than the
physical body. It is the emotional body and persists in whatever state it is in, including the emotions involved, for an
indefinite time after the physical system is destroyed and can
no longer send information to the subtle. The memory of a
missing limb can persist after all signals from that limb are
gone. If the last signals from that limb were traumatic, the
trauma alone may persist and feed into our awareness as
though the limb were still there. Between the subtle body
and physical body is the same reflecting, tape-loop effect
found between the implicate and explicate orders of David
Bohm's quantum movement. In turn, this is reflected in the
constant playback and mutual support found between old and
mid-brain systems. Our subtle system feeds back into the
physical and on into the implicate causal realms of creative
energy that bring about physical reality itself. So the subtle
system is connected with the mid-brain, which is the medium
between the causal new brain and the physical old brain.

Earlier we explored how the mid-brain gives shape and
meaning to the information from the old brain, as we find the
implicate order of Bohm's model shaping the explicate order.
Our neat dichotomies help our understanding of the action,
but in actuality the interplay between the two is complementary. Both systems are necessary to describe completely the action shaping our experience. Our subtle system,

and our subtle body, however, are results of this interplay of emotional, esthetic response to physical experience, and are intricately connected with the slow growth of an independent ego structure. We could not have much of a subtle system at birth, nor for the first year of life, but the subtle body builds automatically as we esthetically experience ourselves as a physical body.

The construction of our subtle system goes into high gear after the object-constancy stage, when the locus of ego shifts into the mid-brain in parallel with the old brain. As development continues, the locus in the mid-brain begins to operate more and more independently of its physical brain's inputs until, around age four, the subtle body, along with language, worldview, and ego, is largely functional. Then, when the locus of ego shifts into the even more powerful new brain for that development, we can become aware of the subtle body as an independent system. This is our esthetic dreaming body, but with guidance and development we can utilize it in our ordinary waking state as well.

When I was about five years old, on going to bed at night and relaxing, I often would feel parts of my body expand and stretch beyond where they should be. I would feel my leg with my hand and find my leg in its right place, but that leg would feel itself a couple of feet longer, or off to one side. In nature's agenda, some separation of subtle from physical should begin during this period, as we anticipate the big separation of ego at age seven.

I have an educated, normal friend who, born on a farm, discovered in his fifth year that after sitting for a while on the farm's large gasoline storage tank (he liked the smell of the vapors), he would apparently leave his ordinary body and fly. For a while he could visit only local places in this flying body of his, but as time went on he developed the ability to go into ever more remote realms. He had no name for his venture, had never heard mention of anything similar, and did not until grown. He kept quiet about his travels, sensing intuitively that his family would have put a quick stop to his long hours spent "daydreaming on that old tank." During his twelfth year, his family moved to the city; he got caught up in the ordinary world, and his ability faded.

My friend and neighbor Robert Monroe (who wrote the book *Journeys Out of the Body*[7]) had, by 1976, received over

15,000 letters from all over the world, from people telling of their own experiences out of the body, and expressing relief that they were not necessarily psychotic. (Near-death experiences, of such current interest, obviously take place through the same general psychic machinery.) We do well, however, not to make errors of logic concerning subtle experience. We often assume that our ordinary, physical-state logic applies to the subtle, or vice versa. Subtle experiences are never direct perceptions of the same logical order as physical perceptions, even when we apparently view ordinary physical reality while in the subtle state. When we seem to perceive our ordinary surroundings in our subtle state, we may be perceiving out of our memory of those surroundings.

I have a friend who went out of his body one afternoon and wandered about his apartment, fascinated with the experience. Everything seemed normal until he noticed that each of his clocks—he had one in each room—told a different time, and that none of the windows was exactly the right height from the floor, and that around the place were other minor dislocations of the norm. In the same way, time and again I go into my subtle body during my morning meditation, experience various states, and apparently awaken from the experience. I get up to prepare for the day, when suddenly I notice that the windows are incorrect, or some other commonplace item is askew, and I realize that I have awakened within a dream or memory state. I then awaken to my ordinary waking state.

Because our subtle system is dependent on the physical system for the input of experience, when that physical system breaks down and the dynamic between subtle and physical is broken, our subtle system will, of necessity, slowly wind down and dissipate, if our identity remains largely locked into our physical body. Like phantom limb pain the ego must slowly dissipate as a subtle system, though that slow unwinding plays out the memory, expectancies, and archetypally shared images as found in near-death experiences. The subtle system must be integrated into the causal system for more permanence. Our subtle system is our own personal intermediary between the universal, generic blueprint out of which our awareness and our personal experience grow on the physical level. Even identification with the causal system does not give permanence, though, since the causal is, in turn, only the medium, or interface, between the Self, the source of creation, and our subtle-physical fields of experience. A final, true autonomy is found only through integration into that Self, the grounds from which everything springs.

Since the subtle system grows out of the mid-brain's operations and interactions with the old brain's experience of our world, all mammals must have some form of subtle system. Without a fully developed causal system, which requires a fully developed new brain, animals have no *awareness* of having a subtle system—they simply *are* that subtle-physical system. Our new brain gives us a locus from which we can separate enough from our subtle system to be aware of it objectively, as distinct from body. Our subtle system is what we have always called psyche, or soul (thus animals have souls). And, as should be evident, having a soul is no guarantee at all of having some sort of immortality. Only integration of the soul into higher integral structures can sustain personal awareness. And this integration must take place while in the body, that is, in this life, since only such integration can shift our identity *from* the body and provide us with another source of input and orientation.

With the addition of each brain, nature has added a new dimension to conscious awareness. The reptilian brain is aware only as the stimulus which brings about its awareness. Awareness and stimulus are the same. Remove the stimulus and awareness disappears. (Reptiles don't sleep in any sense as mammals do.) Through addition of the mammalian brain, we can stand apart from the direct reptilian experience as stimulus and be esthetically aware of, rather than just as, the event of stimulus. With the new brain we can stand apart from and so be aware of the esthetic system itself, and be aware of the event of stimulus as something different from ourselves entirely. We can then come into possession of our esthetic-physical system as an instrument at our disposal. Consciousness of self as distinct, separate, and different from all sensory experience can then be developed.

These additions of possibility bring with them a need for physical models to follow if they are to be realized. Consider again our blueprint for language, which was discussed in Chapter 5. Language is an open-ended blueprint in that we can imprint or adapt to any language using our basic phonemes. But this open possibility can exist only as a specific and limited language. We cannot speak an infinitely open language; only a very finite, limited one. This means that we must be given a specific actual language (or, perhaps, two at the most) as a model, in order to construct any language at all.

Through developing a specific language, though, we end with language ability, and *ability* is nature's goal. Through that language ability we can act back on our language, play with it, mutate it, transform it, create with it, adapt it continually to new circumstances, and so on. Thus, our language blueprint is expressed in us as an intent toward language, an open capacity for language, and an instinctual drive to cue in on and imprint to whatever stable language model we are given. No specific language is pre-wired into our circuitry, for if it were then no ability would be required. Ability is developmental. As a result, we must be given a model *of language* in order for language of any sort to form. What language is formed, out of that open possibility, depends on the kind of model given.

A closed or specific language could be built in ahead of time, I suppose, much as with bird calls, animal calls, and so on (though even with these modeling is needed). But then no language ability would develop. Speech, rather than being a dynamic process, would be as static as a dog's bark. We could not then move from concrete to metaphoric language and on to abstract, semantic language. For all these developments are due to the open nature of language as a possibility. As with language, so with all intelligence. At a certain point of complexity and richness of possibility, nature's agenda achieves open-endedness, a kind of random chance, infinite openness where anything and everything can and will happen. For that kind of possibility to be utilized, we must develop the ability for such utilization. And at that point the role of a model given us from our world, around which such development can take place, becomes critical, the central point of creation.

No such model is needed by plants and simple animals since a straightforward instinctive response to physical experience can be built in. Mama snake lays her eggs in a prescribed manner and goes off and forgets about them. A sufficient number of her eggs hatch; the little snakes go through equally prescribed actions and reactions, and a sufficient number survive to maintain the species. Little snake does not need to observe Mama snake to see how to go about the matter of living a fine reptilian life. (Birds are more advanced than reptiles and must have modeling.) A snake's circuitry is pretty well laid out and functional ahead of time for a certain statistical stability within the species, given a certain statistical stability in the environment.

The minute we add a mammalian brain to this simplicity, conscious awareness not only expands by a light-year leap; more important, awareness polarizes between sensory activity and the qualitative evaluation or esthetic experience of that sensory activity. We take possession of our senses at that point. We integrate those senses into a more complex structure, into another order of energy, and we can sit in judgment on our own experience. The mid-brain esthetic awareness, able to possess itself, stand back from its own content, and respond positively or negatively, gives flexibility and adaptivity. This enhances an individual survival, rather than just a statistical, species survival. (And, of course, individual survival then becomes an issue.)

A blueprint for such adaptive openness cannot be prewired as an instinct. Instinct means a closure of response along certain prescribed lines. In order to provide for open-endedness, nature must do two things. First, it must provide a non-specific general category of possibility, an open blueprint from which we must then construct a particular response. We can do this only by being given a physical model *for* that particular kind of response. Second, nature must build into us a corresponding instinctive compulsion to *follow that model* and construct accordingly. Thus we have no choice about following our models; we do so instinctively below the level of awareness. Nor, in the last analysis, do we really select our models. We automatically follow and imprint to the closest approximation of our blueprint's intent that we can find.

The greater the expanse and flexibility of the blueprint, the more critical the need for specific modeling. A frog's brain sees a restricted world, limited to shapes and movement indicating food or threat. Human vision is open, a field of possibility. So nature builds into infant vision one pre-set pattern, that of a human face. In the open possibility of all things possible *to* see, this face pattern acts as an anchor on which all selectivity is going to be based. That is why the newborn spends eighty percent of his visual time locked in on that face, and refers all other visual action back to this given model. A human face becomes the cornerstone on which the visual world and reality are based. Continual reference back to a face is needed to stabilize the open possibility of things to see.

When nature added our new brains, she upped the ante by many more light-years of possibility. And, correspondingly, the need for models to articulate something specific from this infinite potential grew ever more critical. When she added mind, she added the possibility of detaching awareness even from the causal properties underlying creation, the ability to look at causality itself objectively. This moves our awareness into randomness and chance, into creation itself,[8] and the need of model increases yet again.

Evolution takes our experience into ever greater fields of randomness and chance, less closure, more power, and a corresponding increase of instability and risk. The reptilian brain is the most stable, the most closed, the least available to change, and the weakest of our system. As we move up the evolutionary ladder in our growth of intelligence, the more critically dependent we are on the model function.[9] The model is not nature's afterthought, but the way in which bonding between a sensory system and the possibility for its sensing takes place. Without the model and the bonding afforded through the model, disintegration or fragmentation of ego takes place. Our human venture is thus a tightrope between ecstasy and terror. In a random chance system designed for such a precise and specific goal as union with the creative system itself, that tightrope is traversable only by following the guide, the model, one who has *actually traversed* that thin line to the goal.

12

Abstract
to Concrete

Yogic psychology considered the state of deep sleep the *causal* process, which relates to the new brain. They referred to our dream state as our subtle system, which relates to our mid-brain, and our waking state as our physical process, which, we have found, translates through the old brain. The new brain uses geometric patterns such as cone, grid, snowflake, cobweb, and so on, infinitely variable within their sets and capable of endless syntheses between classes of pattern. These are the precursors to all other types of imagery.[1] The images of movement and light or dark contrasts of our old brain, and the fluid, colorful images of our dreaming brain, are composed out of those geometric families of the new brain. Our new brains participate in the construction of our infinitely variable sensory systems, and, as such, give us a far richer worldview than that of the lower animals. More important, this new brain gives us a medium through which we can participate in that construction going on in the primary brains, as we found in operational thinking. At the time of adolescence our locus of awareness is shifted from brain to mind, and from that objective standpoint we can stand outside our causal system, in effect, and, using those basic patterns, manipulate the imagery of all the systems.

The three brains represent the three states that make up all possibilities of creation, as they represent three of the four orders of energy David Bohm proposes for quantum mechanics. Mind, though it stands outside brain action, is not the seat of creation, the Self of yogic psychology; nor is it the fourth order of energy, the realm of insight-intelligence in David Bohm's model.

H O L O M O V E M E N T	Explicate	Weak Reptilian	Physical	Wake	S E L F
	Implicate	Strong Old Mammalian	Subtle	Dream	
	Potential	Strongest Neo Cortex	Causal	Deep Sleep	

→ (Mature Mind is Interface Between) ←

Insight-Intelligence (Source) Supra-Causal Silent-Witness

A mature mind is the medium between brain and Self, between the translating instrument for reality and the genesis of that reality. A mature mind is objective, free of the subjectivity of the child and adolescent, free of direct influence from the primary brains. Once we have developed this objectivity, our awareness is free to shift, to some extent, from brain to Self. That is, mind can begin to function as the consciously aware medium between Creator and creation. We can enter as participants, directly or indirectly, in creation itself. The indirect way is most common and follows a general pattern exercised equally in scientific, artistic, philosophical, or spiritual pursuits.

A scientist, for instance, may grow dissatisfied with some part of his accepted belief system, his science's body of knowledge. He finds a hole in the fabric of this system's logic and plunges into that hole. He sees implications of a new possibility and is seized by the image of this new seeing. He gathers all content that relates to his new idea, researches everything relevant to it. Yet, though he puts all of it together in every way to support his idea, he finds his work to no avail. He has not the strength of mind to pull it together. His mass of data will not yield the final result. In a moment of despair, mental bankruptcy, or fatigue, he quits, if only for a moment.

At his moment of quitting, that elusive answer arrives of

its own volition in a single instant's flash; at that moment it is full-blown in the brain, complete and perfect. Aha! Eureka! Now he has it. He finds, however, that he must translate that "Eureka!" into the language of his brotherhood. His answer arrives as an obscure image that makes little sense in the light of day. The reason for this requirement for translation into the common domain is a key to creative action.

My favorite example is the chemist, August Kekulé,[2] who was seized with the notion of a certain possible molecular combination not then extant. He pursued his new possibility with characteristic zeal and passion. He exhausted all resources; the answer eluded him. One day he sat down before his fireplace to get his mind off his obsession and drifted into reverie. And there before him, in a single second, appeared a ring of snakes with their tails in their mouths, forming a peculiar configuration. Eureka! He had his answer.

Chemists, however, cannot make much use of a ring of snakes with their tails in their mouths. Kekulé had to take this dreamlike metaphoric animal image and translate it into the language of chemistry. This gave the world, for good or ill, the benzene ring, that hexagonal molecular basis of all twentieth-century chemistry. We could say that a hexagonal possibility gave rise to a ring of snakes that gave rise to a questionable world of "better things for better living through chemistry." In an address to a scientific convention, Kekulé said: "Gentlemen, we must do more dreaming." Hans Selye, in a study of scientific process, speaks of scientific discovery as a movement from dream to reality.[3]

The five steps of creative pursuit are easy to see in Kekulé's story: (1) seizure *of* and then *by* a passionate idea of a new possibility; (2) gathering of materials needed for that possibility to be realized; (3) a gestation period, or plateau, when all materials seem to have been explored to no avail; (4) recognition of inability to think it through, and a cessation of thinking, at which point the answer arrives; and (5) translation of the answer into the public domain.

An idea is generated in our causal minds as an inarticulate hunch. The supportive mind, with its emotional power and fluid imagery, fills in the hunch with appropriate images. (By "appropriate" I mean an inner picture that can transfer the initial abstract hunch into concrete imagery suitable to spur the search for content.) Our supportive mind also provides the driving passion of will, the determination to persist in the face of obstacles; and emotion, the excitement and intent of the pursuit. A functional blueprint, sustained in these interactions of mind, bursts into bloom.

The second phase, the pursuit of materials, requires intellectual discrimination of appropriate, relevant materials. Appropriateness means that the content selected must match the general nature of the inner blueprint of idea. To match the original abstraction, the concrete content must be capable of being transferred into that abstract imagery. This will depend, in turn, on the power of the analogical language system, the imagery of symbol and metaphor built up through play in the pre-logical years. Imagination thus comes into its own.

The passionate search is an intellectual activity of the three brains and of mind. And all intellect can do is put together and synthesize, scramble and rework, add and subtract, the relevant materials. Intellect can only self-replicate, can only feed back on its own system. And, if that system already contained the synthesis or material sought, the scientist would simply engage in discovery; he would stumble across something that had always been there within his materials, or the material of his field, the significance of which had been missed. But if genuine creative discovery is involved, those materials will not contain the goal.

At some point, when intellect has done all it can, exhausted all possibilities, a plateau is reached. Stagnation sets in, and frustration. The materials may hit a critical point in that collective work (and may not). If they do, true gestation takes place. At some point of final frustration, the person quits, and the moment of insight arises. Insight, as in Bohm's "realm of insight-intelligence," arises out of the seat of creation. It arrives at a moment out of mind because the fusion takes place not in the brain's circuitry, which can only ruminate over its own information, but in the realm of insight itself. The answer cannot arrive when one is passionately pursuing it or thinking about it precisely because of this self-replicating tape-loop circuitry problem. Intellect ties up the circuitry of brain, locks up the analogical imagery in support of its abstract ruminations, so that nothing is available either to receive or transfer the imagery of insight, since the imagery of insight will arrive through the highest mode of thought found in the new brain/mind interaction. Not until a cessation of intellect and its thinking occurs can the answer arrive.

We note that the great answer, when it comes, seems to appear in some dreamlike imagery. The reason is simple: This is the metaphoric imagery that can be transferred into both the abstract geometric patterning of the new brain and the concrete language of the primary brains. Thus the necessity of the translation step. Margharita Laski proposed that many an awesome "Eureka!" may never reach the light of day because of an inability to transfer the dream into reality, or transfer the imagery. So the image that gives insight must be one capable of being transferred both ways, into concrete and the abstract; and that means a mid-brain, right-hemisphere, analogic function, and a sharp enough intellect to make the translation.

Biologist Rupert Sheldrake once asked physicist David Bohm where, in Bohm's Holomovement theory, there was provision for the dynamic between explicate and implicate orders, between us here on this earth and that creative process in the realm of insight-intelligence. Bohm's theory gives a model for creation in the sense of God creating the world, but what about our human action, frail though it is? We bring things into our realm that were not there before, for better or worse. God's creation did not provide us with computers, dioxins, knowledge of the double helix, or algebra.

The answer to Sheldrake's query seems to be that the creative process works always in only one direction, and that is from the realm of the Self. But we can elicit from that realm of insight a response in keeping with the nature of some desire, provided we invest the necessary passion and will, follow the rule, and have the sense to stand back at the appropriate time and let the answer manifest itself. The process must follow the pattern of the Holomovement's expression since that is the way creation works. Effort on our part acts like the stimulus of the small ground charge found in lightning, which elicits a response from the far greater cloud charge of electricity and brings about that exchange we call a thunderbolt. Without sincere, prolonged, and intense effort on our part, no corresponding charge answers. Even little bits of the creative process are not bought cheaply. This holds even though our effort is completely dwarfed and is essentially peripheral in the overall effect.

A genuinely creative act opens a new category of possibility; we fill in that category through discovery. Since the beginning of this century we have been filling in Kekulé's creation. Once his model was in the common domain, that domain was different and we could discover the possibilities of this difference. Creativity gives the common domain something that was not there before. A truly creative act is not quantitatively derivable from what exists, and is always given gratuitously from the realm of insight-intelligence. We must set up the conditions for the creative gift, however, and the conditions we set up will determine the general nature of the answer received. We enter into the process as a determinate, and the answer, when it occurs, will be in keeping with the nature of what we have set up, and beyond the sum total of all our input.

Sustained passion and will are what elicit the corresponding charge, for all creation is an act of will. Consider too that the more strenuously we work for our answer, the greater the preparation we have undergone for reception of that answer, and making its translation. When my five-year-old son delivered to me the perfect essay on the creative process and our relation to God, I had not the strength of mind to receive, retain, or translate that soliloquy. The materials we gather in our pursuit of our answer may be almost incidental in the final analysis. We must gather all of them, perhaps, only to find that the answer is not quantitatively derivable from our materials; it is not the cumulative result of them. Though those materials enter into the nature of the final answer, they may only point out the general direction that creation takes. Our materials and passions enter into the overall model of stimulus evoking the creative response, but the response is qualitatively different from, and quantitatively beyond, the model stimulus. We again have complementarity, with an apparent radical break of either-or which is arced by will and passion. Bankruptcy of intellect is necessary to get intellect out of the way, since the system operates on this either-or process, and shows that only the realm of insight can make real the blueprint of idea we have earlier created.

The key to the movement from our position to insight and back again is imagery. Everything is imagery: The Creation is imagery. Imagination is that elusive quality we should have built up between ages four and seven: the capacity to see castles in the clouds, tigers in the bushes, or beautiful pictures when mama, daddy, or the radio tells a story; the internal imagery that can see the truck in the matchbox, road-roller in the spool; that sees all the world as conscious, alive, filled with personality and infinite possibility; where a certain molecular possibility can, through the metaphoric play of a ring of snakes, arc the gap between the possibility inherent in mind's eye and the world out there.

No creation exists except through imagination, and also no intellect, no logic, no abstraction, semantic language. From somewhere comes the image of something not now extant, and creative possibility leaps into the gap to bring about newness. That may be nature's use of our ceaseless (generally useless) thinking: Our thought can range freely over the universe of our knowing, pushing at the fabric of our reality, looking for the holes through which imagination might leap to create a new image of possibility. In the same way our Spirits are always pushing at the fabric of our minds, looking for the holes in our resistance to that great transformation that awaits us. Fundamental change can only be generated by the Self, but it is generated only in keeping with the passion and will of our unregenerate state here in our flesh and bones longing for that realm of the heart. Will and passion are the issues.

The making of a saint follows the same general pattern found in our creative discovery experience. Often the future saint, as a child, hears of a state of fundamental transformation, a state giving a completely different worldview and permanence to self-awareness. The young person is seized by that notion, and passionately desires such a state above all things. (Almost always he is so seized because he has come into contact with a person who has actually been fundamentally transformed in this way.) Seized by the passionate desire to achieve such a state of awareness, the young person abandons his family and home and sets off in pursuit of his goal. He devours all literature related to his search; follows every discipline that might in any way relate; hones his instruments of mind and body through austerity and rigors of discipline. And he holds in there, year after year, plugging away with fanatical will, through plateaus, deserts, and dry places of mind, when all but the strongest and most persistent would fall away.

Finally, he has done all that can be found to do; stripped his bones clean, given up his life not once, but over and over. He continues because nothing else is worthwhile, and he may enter the dark night of the soul, where he has lost both worlds; he exists in a kind of no-man's land. All his *doing* is undone and he finally really quits. He stops doing, and in that moment of not-doing the answer arrives. The fundamental transformation takes place. He then has but one goal, to translate that answer into the common domain, which can only be done by living that answer out, moment by moment, in every fiber of his being. Inadvertently, he *becomes* the answer. In that ongoing translation he becomes the model, the exemplar, and the guide for any other who might come into contact with him and be sparked by such a desire.

The scientist or artist is seized by an idea for a specific aspect of his world, a possibility for some new effect in his outer reality. He deals with something in the outside world, the explicate order, other to his own self. Nearly always some part of his driving will is the need to enhance his ego position in that outside world (a Nobel, a Pulitzer). And, if he holds in there long enough, and does all the right things, follows the rules, he generates from the creative source within him a response to that single point of his passion.

The saint, however, does not seek some specific effect or part of that creative core of Self, some particular aspect of newness out there in his reality. He seeks union with that creative core of his own being, the wholeness of the Holo-movement and nothing less. William Blake wrote: "More! More! is the cry of a mistaken soul. Less than All can never satisfy." The artist and scientist (and most of us) spend our lives seeking more and more, and are never satisfied. The saint seeks All and becomes one with it. He is then lifted up and draws all men to him. And in the secret core of our being, that is what each of us wants.

David Bohm said that insight could simply reach into the brain and shove its matter around to remove dysfunctions and make it functional. When insight arrives for the scientist, some new neural pathways must be emblazoned in his structures of knowledge to allow him to grasp the nature of the new image. The arrival of that image, in that moment out of mind, is the moment of insight's shuffling the materials of mind around to include that new seeing, enough so that the scientist might then intellectually battle his way through to a translation of the given imagery.

The saint, however, has every neural pathway rearranged into its opposite: oriented not to the explicate order that radiates out into an infinitely regressing universe; but oriented within to the realm of the Self from which all universes spring. He or she is then *in* our world but literally not *of* it. Only now is his threefold brain structure integrated into its proper realm. Now his mind is the two-way mirror designed by our nature: With his left eye he sees within to the realm of God; with the right eye he sees the outer world of fragmentation and folly. Now his new brain will be utilized in its entirety, for seeing within is what the new brain was designed to do. It was not intended for lowly servitude to a reptilian brain's small world (a task that uses only a fraction of the real power).

The saint is the model, the guide, the means for our getting to that state and becoming whole. For again, the Self is not quantitatively derivable; it is not the result of the cumulative effects we pile up here in our explicate domain. No international spiritual networking can amass the necessary ingredients; no accumulation of laboratory research can bridge that gap. Our Self lies beyond all its ingredients, and only will and passion make us available to that state. Our will and passion cannot take that kingdom by storm. Operation bootstrap always fails us, not by moral imperative, but by logical necessity. Our will and passion can set up the conditions where we may be taken *by* that storm. The quantum leap is made by the Self within us in response to our leap of faith.

The usual developmental procedures built into us from the time of birth work for our spiritual unfolding. But the formula found throughout still holds: Blueprint plus model equals desired structure. The blueprint is given from within, but it must be given *its* model from without. The progression is always from the concrete to the abstract, and our concrete model is one who has made real his or her blueprint, realized the Self within, and represents it for us in concrete form, in flesh and blood. The journey to the Self begins there, in that model, and only there, just as have all our previous developmental journeys.

I undertook many false starts on my journey, all intellectual bootstrap affairs, and my real journey began during my half-century mark when I met one who had realized the Self. More happened simply from the encounter with my teacher, Muktananda, than had happened in the previous fifty years. In Ganeshpuri, India, on New Year's Day, 1983, I took an "intensive," a meditation workshop, with Muktananda's successor Gurumayi. As usual in an intensive, young Gurumayi gave what in Sanskrit is called Shaktipat, a laying on of hands to transmit spiritual power (as referred to in earliest Christian writings). When she placed her hand on my head, my left hemisphere seemed to explode, my skull "opened," and my consciousness seemed to spiral out into a void. For days afterward I had the feeling that her hands were inside my skull, kneading my brain like dough. I underwent sensory shifts, feeling that the left side of my face would be pushed two to three inches beyond the right side, that my eyes would be pushed deep within and go out of synch. (I was sure at one point that I was losing my sight, though of course everything worked out splendidly.) Three nights later I awoke at 12:30 A.M. with a sharp, white hot pain in what I was sure was my cerebellum. I thought this the onset of meningitis and began to say the mantra of Gurumayi's lineage, Om Namah Shivaya ("I honor my inner Self"), thinking my end was near. This pain lasted some twenty-four hours and ceased. (Sir John Eccles, in what I think an accurate hunch, thinks our largely unknown cerebellum is the seat of consciousness within us. I think it may be the seat of mind.)

Following this period of pain, in my morning meditations, when I lay down after my usual sitting period, I underwent a complete collapse of my body's muscular system, an enforced relaxation of my total motor response. And at that point my arms and legs levitated; they simply floated in air. This was quite different from an out-of-body experience. (I think my body was kept grounded and only my limbs floated to make the contrast sharp and clear, lest I misinterpret the experience as being out-of-body.) It was as though the space within my limbs and the space surrounding them had become one; it was as if gravity had ceased and my limbs were floating in the void. Each time, though, I would become self-conscious over the event, indulge in the experience, as Carlos Castaneda would say (that is, try to possess or attach to the phenomenon, tape-loop it between my three brains, run over it for analysis, speculation, and a general dwelling on it), at which point my limbs would thump to the floor, the grace withdrawn.

I experienced this for three consecutive mornings and have been interpreting the meaning of it ever since. Each interpretation proves incomplete, for the levels of that lesson keep unfolding. Following that experience I entered into some two months of the most productive work I have ever known, as well as having the most extraordinary meditation experiences of my life. Suffice it to say here that the event was a lesson in causation and the causal mode within me. Recall David Bohm's comment that insight can reach in and push the matter of the brain around, remove dysfunction and make it functional. The left hemisphere seems to be the translating mode for the causal process, and my left hemisphere bore the brunt of this particular episode. Since I have so scant a subtle understanding, I was given this graphic, physical demonstration of how causation can be suspended or changed. I was shown how none of the mechanisms of our physical world binds us when we surrender our physical being to our Self. I found this causal bypass available to us only as we make ourselves available to it, through a state of profound surrender (hardly a popular notion in this day of self-assertion).

My experience symbolized how, for spiritual development, the biological must be surrendered to the non-biological, the flesh must give over to Spirit. For only in spirit do we find our true autonomy. And by the very mechanics of the developmental system within us, this integration into spirit must be put into motion, must be at least established, while we are in this all-too-frail flesh. If we cannot make the total shift to that Self while here on earth, as our saint-models have, then at least we must thoroughly secure our bonds with that goal before we get shifted out of this physical realm. Then, if the model through whom our bonds are established is genuine, those bonds will be reconfirmed after the big shift of identity and modality takes place, when this frail form gets shoveled six feet under.

13

Cultural Counterfeit

Bonding holds the life process together. Our development is designed to unfold through a series of bondings, from the most immediate concrete bonds to the final bonds with the creative function. At birth we bond to the mother, and then to family. Around age four we bond to the earth, at seven to society, at eleven to our society's body of knowledge. Later, male-female bonding is followed by our bonding with our own offspring, and over all of these processes looms our spiritual bonding.

Our instinct for social bonding is built into us, begins in our pre-logical years, and becomes fully active with the appearance of the social ego at about age seven. We must, of course, have a society to bond with, and, as usual, if bonding fails, attachment behavior is the remainder. There can be, however, no attachment to society. Society is the result of a people bonded together. If this bonding does not take place, we get an effect called *culture*. That is, in this book I use the word *culture* for the attachment-behavior form of our instinct for social bonding.

As the attachment-behavior form of social bonding, culture takes on the natural power that the blueprint of social bonding carries within it. Culture becomes a counterfeit blueprint shaping our lives even before our conception. All development is designed to lead us beyond our biologically oriented ego to the Self, and this takes place through our bonding with the models for that development. The model is the concrete manifestation of the higher integral structure toward which we are impelled to move. Culture, as a counterfeit model of development, points us back to the physical, sensory-motor realm as our only possibility, as in all attachment behavior. Since we are driven instinctively to follow our models, we have no choice but to respond to the counterfeits presented to us.

Cultural counterfeits cover every facet of our life. Consider, for instance, the newborn's need for the mother's heartbeat to confirm uterine bonding after delivery. Medical people recently discovered that piping a recorded heartbeat into the hospital nursery, where the newly delivered infants lie in sensory isolation, markedly reduces crying in those unbirthed creatures. We now market Rock-A-By Teddy Bear with an electronically produced heartbeat for use in home cribs, so that this electronic nurturing may be maintained. Consider, too, how medicine men analyzed mother's milk and found it nutritionally poor. They advertised widely for forty years the superiority of their drugstore milk, and made breast-feeding not just unfashionable but a cultural embarrassment.

Love is a bond of power which, like a gift, can be offered and accepted but not manipulated or possessed. Its cultural counterfeit is the opposite: that which can be possessed or used in domination. Culture's main activity is to manufacture lovable objects that can be possessed, at a price. Objects of attachment decay; attachments to people decay. Beneath every attachment we make is that little heart-wrench that knows instinctively that our object of love is, at best, only temporary. Attachment behavior to and the inevitable loss of the love object underlies our poetry, song, drama, news, and entertainment. "This time it's forever!" screams the frenzied pop singer into the mike, since everyone knows this great love of ours is always short-lived, again and again.

Self-pity, the cloying precursor of death, is our pity for our selves over our continual loss of those objects we love. Even as we are in the act of possession and attachment to our love object, its temporary nature haunts us. So sentiment, that saccharine substitute for love, equates love with loss and death, and its pathos runs like a rich bed of treacle beneath all cultural process. "My *mother* loved me, but she died," sentiment laments, and indeed culture offers sentiment as a substitute for the great bond that carries us beyond all death.

Rage, the anger of impotence, is the twin of sentiment.

Everything we grasp turns to dust and ashes, particularly relationships, and we cannot, as social creatures, survive alone. Love is the bond that centers us and provides our needs, but not only has love as attachment become equated with sex, sentiment, and self-pity; sex has been equated with rage and violence. The testimony of a Vietnam veteran on trial for the gang rape-murder of a teenage Vietnamese girl sums it up: "Well, we stood and took turns making love to her; after Jim made love to her, Jack made love to her, then I made love to her, and then Sam, when he finished making love to her, he pulled out his pistol and shot her in the head." [1]

Every cultural product is a counterfeit of something real, perhaps, but culture is itself a counterfeit, a pseudo-causal field. [2] Culture has no head, no governing body. No one is in charge since culture, like any blueprint, does not really exist. Culture exists only as a response to its own blueprint effect. We follow the models given us, as we must, and, without exception, our models turn us back into the physical mode in attachment behavior, forcing our new brain to turn back into attendance on the old brain. [3] Our real blueprint pushes us for a genuine ongoing development that we sense all our lives as a kind of nameless longing, while we roam in the deadlock of our self-encapsulated ego; tape-looped brain/mind feeds the thoughts of the new brain into the old brain, which the old brain interprets as shaping forces in the world out there because the new brain's imagery is causal and more powerful than the old brain's; and the new brain interprets as accurate the old brain's reportage of events shaped by the warping ideas of the new brain.

Through attachment behavior, we become like Freud's three figures in mortal combat: an old brain *id* struggling to protect its weak physical dominion; a mid-brain *ego* enslaved by its childish emotions, addictions, compulsions, and rages; and a *super ego* intellect fretting over its unruly support systems in its drives to escape anxiety and guilt. Culture expresses itself through power systems that battle for ersatz ways to fulfill our longing for wholeness. These power structures capture our energy by promising to alleviate those very compulsive desires that culture instills in us and encourages, and by promising us our missing stability and integrity through offering manipulative stratagems for power over our neighbors.

All cultural models, including our parents (and ourselves as parents), assure that our development is fragmented; that our thrust toward wholeness is given only those consumer items that counterfeit the real development and instead sustain culture. Our models must make sure that from birth our constructions of self and world meet the standards of the cultural model, which model creates in us the perpetual need for the products culture furnishes.

Were no language as model given to our language blueprint as children, that blueprint would atrophy. In the same way, if no content were given to our cultural blueprint, culture would atrophy. But a self-identity once enculturated is an identity that sustains culture, fills culture's empty category with content. My culture exists only as I *respond* to my culture. Culture exists only by the energy of my participation in it. Were we to withdraw the energy of our response, culture would disappear. We cannot stop responding to and thus sustaining culture, though, since our structures of knowledge of self, world, and their interrelations were formed according to cultural models. To "get rid of culture" would be to get rid of the only identity we have. In the same way, any real change of culture would mean a change of the only identity we have. My drive for integrity of self sustains the fabric of culture—by default.

Follow the sequence: Our knowledge of self and world must mirror our cultural models. These models turn our identity back into the physical sensory system at each stage, through failure to bond and the substitution of attachment behavior. We are driven instinctively to maintain the unity, such as it is, of our ego structure, which means we are driven to maintain and so protect our state of dysfunction, which dysfunction is culture itself. Nature cannot, as we have seen, program for failure. Driven to maintain our dysfunctional egos, functional wholeness threatens our integrity. Wholeness would entail a complete restructuring of our dysfunctional structures. Even should we really accept the notion of transcendent development, our survival drive will intellectualize a resistance beneath the surface of our awareness, and we will never recognize the nature of our rationalizations of resistance.[4] Maintenance of the fragmentation of ego is hailed as self-reliance, fortitude, courage; and is morally, ethically, and culturally acceptable, since this maintains the cultural fabric. We are born and brought up on slogans such as "Stand on your own feet," "Be an individual," "Assert yourself, get ahead in the world, be somebody." The irony is that the ways for implementing these noble gestures are all bought at the expense of a true social body. Any move toward development of spirit, on the other hand, which alone brings about community, is interpreted as selfish, anti-social, pathological, suspect, and a source of cultural embarrassment. (A common comment about spending some three hours each morning in meditation, chanting, and "inner work" is that this is such a selfish waste of time; we should devote that time to helping the world. My experience has been that since beginning such inner work my outer work is far more effective.)

Our enculturation forces from us a perpetual response to culture, since culture as an effect creates an impossible situation within us, one we will do anything to rid ourselves of, and indeed we spend our lives trying to escape: anxiety. Recall that the failure of bonding at birth brings on a continual production of the adrenal hormones connected with stress or anxiety. Failure of bonding to the center of our lives at adolescence results in a new set of attachment behaviors brought on by enculturation and ongoing anxiety. Anxiety is a free-floating fear—that is, fear without an object or reason. Anxiety is actually nature's danger signal that the brain/mind is not processing its information properly. As a result, anxiety is the one condition intolerable to us; we will do anything to escape it, since its signal comes from within to overlay all issues.

Our brains, though, are designed to process their information and project it onto our screens of mind. When locked into attachment, this projection is always reflected onto the outer world. That is, through enculturation, we interpret anxiety, nature's danger signal of malfunction, as coming from external causes. Under enculturation, "out there" is the only legitimate source of information, which leaves objects for attachment our sole concern. So anxiety acts in us like an empty category, projected on our world to be filled with content. Filling the nameless fear with content from the world around us gives us *something* to fear, which is more tolerable than the intolerable empty category itself. Since external events then cause our internal anxiety, we rush onto our world stage to change things, to rid ourselves of the cause of our anxiety. And it is this move that our enculturation must ensure, for culture's existence hinges on this single compulsion.

Our enculturation is the drive to change culture. Changing culture is, ironically, the energy investment that sustains culture. We recognize that our discord, unhappiness, and fear are caused by culture, but we recognize this in projected form. That is, we see our dysfunction as an external phenomenon happening to us. We see all those people, events, forces that are preventing us from being what we really are. We see the world as the cause of our anxiety and so are impelled to try and change that world. And that world is culture, and on our impulse to change it, culture is sustained. Without this driving passion on our part to *change* culture, culture would disappear.

Our desire for survival impels us to make culture work properly. Whether our energy paid to culture is positive or negative is of no consequence. Any move we make in response to culture generates culture as a power. Every act of cognizance we give culture gives it our energy. As an empty category culture is filled in by any idea, scheme, plan, or "ism" without regard, just as the blueprint of language cares not a whit whether the content or model is French, German, or Swahili.

The greatest, perhaps the only, sin against culture is not to try to change it, not to try to make it better. We fill its empty category with our constant changing of it, and each time we think, "This time Utopia, this time real freedom, this time happiness." Only later do we notice that the formal structure of our dysfunction and anxiety is unchanged. We hear of the "future shock" of out-of-control change. The change we witness, however, is a consumer-produced novelty within a form function that never changes. The change we think we experience is the novelty of our constant attempts to change the function of culture by changing its content. But culture has no content except that which we lend it in our attempts to change it. The only thing that changes is the growing strength of culture as a form function and our growing collapse of personal power.

There is always a priesthood of culture: the vultures who reap where they do not sow and sow a terror that all must reap. But the irony is that this priesthood is not in charge. No one is. Culture is the result of a breakdown of bonding and the ensuing truncation of development. The priesthood of culture succeeds by maintaining in us a high resolve to set the system right, bring things to balance, make our culture function. All of this enriches the priests' harvest, impoverishes the nation of incompetents the priesthood produces, and maintains culture. "Ask not what your country can do for you, but what you can do for your country" intones the high priest in pious tones, an outlandish perversion of Jesus' statement that the Sabbath was made for man, not man for the Sabbath. Culture, the antipathy of spirit, produces dogma and law, and hangs its prophets high.

If a television set is miswired in its construction, the resulting picture shown on its screen must, of necessity, reflect that miswiring. The dysfunction will underlie every image the set produces. Our brain/mind is like that miswired set. Brought up in a dysfunctional system, we automatically reflect the dysfunctions of our model at the very core of our brain/mind circuitry. And every product of our dysfunctional brain/mind, every thought, idea, brave-new-world plan, will have that dysfunction at its core. As the architect Bergman put it: "Each and every problem we face today is the direct and inevitable result of yesterday's brilliant solutions."

Cut off from our post-biological development, our screen of mind can only reflect according to the brain translating our data. So every attempt to bail ourselves out of our despair contains at its core the cause of that despair, and can only replicate and enlarge upon that which we would escape. Our dysfunctions grow with every attempt we make to correct our dysfunction. Every move we make toward freedom ensnares us more. We moved from a handful of nuclear warheads thirty years ago to 50,000 today, and will hit 100,000 by decade's end at our present rate of increase. The dysfunctional system can only self-replicate. Each solution achieved is only a recasting and enhancement of the problem we would solve.

So, my drive for integrity sustains my dysfunction. I project my dysfunction out onto my world. I am then driven to change my world—a drive that maintains culture, the source of my dysfunction. Any move toward wholeness must center within as a change of one's own being and will be interpreted by culture as pathological. Further, the world around us becomes too terrifying to turn our backs on to make the turning within. To the enculturated, the threat of freedom and wholeness is more threatening than the anxiety that freedom would replace.

Time and again in my life I grew disenchanted with cultural attainments, found myself lacking in meaning or purpose, and sensed a spiritual impoverishment. This led me into the greatest trap of all, as, true to my enculturation, I thought of spirit as the missing thread in my life-fabric, and so unconsciously tried to incorporate spirit into my enculturated ego, in typical attachment behavior. This is, of course, the reverse of true development and why the last stronghold, the most impenetrable defense of the enculturated and embattled ego, often is the spiritual trip. The hardest to attain, spirit is the easiest to counterfeit, for where are the criteria that define spirit or its attainment? These are nearly always given by some aspect of culture, some religious institution which produces an enculturated spirit.

In our spiritual seeking, we search for a system or path compatible with our esthetics. We research a path for its symbols, guiding lights, teachings, and necessary rule. Our will to survive that operates beneath awareness will manipulate those images in whatever way needed to simulate or counterfeit a spiritual journey in a way by which the attached ego can be enhanced, strengthened, and in no way changed. Thus attachment behavior manifests: We incorporate the spiritual system into our ego system. And culture provides a rich choice of corporate counterfeits. The act of incorporation of a pseudo-spirit gives religious sanction to our fragmented ego; gives us the warm security of spiritual delusion wherein nothing can again threaten to change our ego. Often a temporary relief from anxiety takes place when we incorporate a spiritual path into our attachment behavior. Ego finds itself strengthened, enhanced, euphoric, sanctified. If God be with us, who can be against us, the ego asks, while *Kaiser und Gott* strangely produce more bombs and cannon.

The cultural counterfeit of faith is belief: ideas that can be entertained by intellect. The child does not develop through belief or dogma but through faith in the models he follows. Faith means trust, however, and eventually the child is conditioned to trust only consensus prescriptions for action. When we turn within to the Self, we discover the same instinctive naturalness of response to the model we knew in childhood;

in this way our inner development unfolds in the same natural way our outer development did.

Our outer actions reflect this inner growth automatically, and so my spiritual teachers insist that the inner journey be made while we live squarely in the world, acting out our destined roles in ordinary life. For the person turned toward the Self takes his criteria from that Self, not from his world; and on that shift of criteria hinges the tale. As soon as his criteria are from within, culture is no longer his criterion and changing culture is not his focus. This means that the massive problems of the world are not his source of materials to work with. So, on the one hand he no longer replicates the problems of the world automatically, as the enculturated mind must. More important, he is, even unwittingly, the source for actual solutions—that is, possibilities from outside cultural self-replication. Jesus said: "Behold I make all things new," and the person turned within to the Self is a source of actual newness, a crack in our cosmic egg.

Great things were afoot within us when our spiritual energies awoke at adolescence. The good news is that that development, while ideally stage-specific to that period, is always functional and available. Jesus said the laborer coming to the vineyard at the eleventh hour receives the same wage as the one coming at the first hour. Nature has this ace up her sleeve through which we can always play a winning hand in the game of autonomy. If we missed our model and development at that most optimal time, our spirit still lies there, dormant within us. But to awaken that spirit constructively, and move beyond culture and its spiritual counterfeits, is no small task. And, since nature's blueprint must be given its model, we cannot accomplish this task on our own.

14

Autonomy
and Integrity

The goal of development is the creation of an autonomous ego, self-awareness sufficient to itself, dependent on nothing other than its own state. Since existence means to be set apart, awareness first must be set apart from a general field of consciousness. For this setting apart of an ego to be successful, it must immediately relate to other egos or collapse again into the general field (as we find, perhaps, in severe autism or cases of extreme deprivation). Since ego is drawn out and stabilized by relationships, ego identifies with that to which it relates. So ongoing development must both expand the field of relations and identifications—to expand awareness, and, in turn, maintain the integrity or unity of the ego—then separate identity from those relations with which it automatically identifies. Were we properly bonded throughout development, these drives of integrity and autonomy would work as a unit and produce an integrated, semi-autonomous ego by mid-adolescence, ready for the move to full autonomy. Since attachment behavior takes place instead, our autonomy and integrity work at cross purposes.

We start life as a single cell and our subsequent growth takes place through constant separation. Five of the seven steps of biological development are actually divisive and the other two are inherently so. Through this division, however, we clarify our sense of being unique individuals. Ultimately, we identify with mind, objectively separated from all our experience. From this rarefied state, we consider our body, brain, thoughts, and feelings as only possessions, even as we are totally dependent on those possessions for sustaining our awareness.

Post-biological, or spiritual, development has as its goal an absolute self-sufficiency beyond all such dependency. To achieve this, our spirits must first unite our awareness with that from which we had to separate in order to achieve our state of unique awareness in the first place. That ego which was set apart from everything must be united with everything to realize its union with the Self. At age four, for instance, we sense a separation that becomes full and active at age seven. This separation is only an internal play of the brain/mind, an illusion, but the illusion acts to construct for us a completely separate ego. Spiritual development unfolds the illusion as our own play, shows the unity of all things, yet retains the integrity of ego.

In physical development, if our egos become integrated into each higher structure through bonding, as designed, we unconsciously encompass greater possibility and power. Our integrity is not only maintained, but enhanced at each stage. The same holds for our post-biological development. Consider how particles of energy sustain themselves by being united into atoms, molecules, proteins, cells, and so on. Each new integration maintains the integrity of the particle, yet each new structure gives a richer possibility of relationship, in which each particle, atom, cell, and so on finds its fulfillment. Fulfillment, or maturation, comes by integration into ever more complex relationships, whereas an isolated particle tends to disintegrate. In the same way, union of ego does not dissolve our egos back into some amorphous field of unconsciousness, but maintains our integrity by integration into greater realms of consciousness, power, and possibility.

We filled in our physical blueprint by choosing from its infinite openness according to the nature of the specific models we were given. Our spirit unites our psyche and fulfills it by reversing this procedure and developing in us an awareness of, and ability to sustain ourselves as, those blueprints from which our original experience began. Our spiritual growth is from the specific to the generic; from the physical to the subtle, and on to the causal. From there we can then move into final autonomy, our union with our Self.

Recent studies show that our self-awareness is but a small fraction of a huge play of consciousness going on in our brains at all times. Some research people have recently claimed that ninety-nine percent of all brain action takes place below our awareness.[1] The seven-year-old, able to measure his world since now separated from it, is not aware that a separation of brain functions has taken place. Like six-year molars coming in on schedule, his seven-year-old awareness simply arrives without effort of self-consciousness, giving a more flexible, logical power. Development shifts our identity unbeknown to us. Our awareness resonates out of the condition each shift generates. We are the end result of work we have little to do with.

When confronted with the foolish responses of my pre-logical me, my seven-year-old me, now operating in concrete logic, thinks: "Of course, I know now how things really are, I was just too young back then," a few months ago. But the way things are with the seven-year-old is not the way they were. The new logic is the way it is because that is the stage into which nature has shifted him. Our awareness is always shifting, yet each state is simply presented to us. We have little to do with the process except accept and respond, though the process takes place only through our acceptance and response.

Enlightened people, those who have developed spiritually, tell us that we, too, are perfect and enlightened if we would but realize it. This realization is a tall order, however, as developmental as any other. To be perfect in potentiality is not quite the same as in actuality. A great oak tree is inherent within every seed the oak produces, but I cannot build much of a house with a sawed-up acorn. Our teachers cannot model for us piecemeal, however, since learning does not take place that way. They must present the finished product, since that is the model our blueprint within recognizes and imprints to. So the great teacher on the one hand insists *Tat Tvam Asi*— Thou art That!—immediately; and demands we assume such a posture. Then the teacher articulates the development to make our assumption the case, and models for us the goal we are after.

Each stage of development, as we have seen, is perfect in itself and yet only preparatory for what comes next. To accept the nature of our transcendent development we must accept the transience and impermanence of each step along the way, and keep our eyes solely on the goal. This requires bonding, since attachment behavior automatically looks back and locks in on whatever tangible identification it has already made. Attachment behavior reverses integration of ego into a higher structure and tries to incorporate the higher structure into our present state of awareness, which means our identity with our early, physical-sensory self. Instead of an effortless integration, taking place beneath our awareness, automatically giving greater power and possibility, we try, through enormous effort, to incorporate the new possibility back into the service of the primitive physical ego—an impossible attempt, but one which creates and sustains culture.

Paul MacLean implied that the sparsity of neural connections between mid- and new brains might be an evolutionary deficiency.[2] This is questionable in the light of new studies showing that nature can very rapidly bring about any kind of change needed. Gray and LaVoilette agree with MacLean that our current cultural breakdown is between our new, thinking brain and our older, animal brains. Intellect without emotion, empathy, and social bonding is destructive. They assume that the needed empathy and bonding which intellect lacks should come from our emotional mid-brain, and that the sparse neural connections between mid-brain and new brain are thus at fault.

Researchers continually remark on how little of our new brains we use. There are large, silent areas of our new brains that are either used for purposes unknown or not used at all. Research also indicates that the new brain seems to be totally preoccupied with the affairs of the outer world, which means that whatever small bit of the new brain we use is devoted to activities reported by the two primary brains, a perfect example of attachment behavior turning us back on our traces into primitive forms of awareness.

Well over ninety percent of conscious activity *should* be beneath personal awareness. Thank God I do not have to exercise my intellect or divert personal awareness to make my liver work correctly or my pituitary do its thing properly. Who says we should be able to control our heartbeat, glandular output, and so on, through essentially intellectually achieved and controlled processes? These are aspirations of the embattled, fragmented ego, trying to enhance its shaky position with assumptions of personal power. We have a brilliant automatic pilot within us designed to take over almost everything in our physical life, including our ordinary survival, precisely to free our awareness for its evolutionary thrust beyond the physical. The whole thrust of the new sports psychology, as found in Tim Gallwey's *Inner Game of Tennis*, for instance, is to get our anxious ego to stop its intellectual meddling and let our automatic pilot take over.[3]

The new brain is *supposed* to be able to operate free from the impinging emotions of the primary system and the tunnel vision of the reptilian. Nature knew precisely what she was doing in making few neural connections between the animal brains and the new brain, particularly the left hemisphere. Enough connections are there to draw on those primary systems as needed and withdraw from them as needed. No abstract, creative thought can develop until detachment from the early stages takes place. All the spiritual teachings emphasize that our likes and dislikes polarizing our thought must be left behind, as well as our preoccupations with physical process, once these biological developments have been stabilized. Only then can we move on in our development.

The large silent areas of the brain are not utilized since they are intended for post-biological development—as is most of the new brain—which virtually never happens. Instead, the new brain is occupied with concerns about our position in our world of culture. And this is the breakdown of the system. The new brain was not intended for such primary action, and such activity does not, could not possibly occupy more than a small percentage of that remarkable organ. The new brain was meant to process information from the other side of mind, the realm of the Self, the worlds within. When this powerful instrument gets turned around and focused on old brain information and mid-brain's childlike emotional reactions, we create the self-replicating madness we see about us. Every thought, every product of the brain, once so inverted and diverted from its purpose, is self-replicative, tape-looped back and forth between three brains cut off from the intelligence of the life process. And this self-replication only aggravates every problem it creates.

Intelligence is the means by which the life process brings its divergent parts into functional, symbiotic relationship; the process that ensures the well-being and success of its species. All species display a characteristic intelligence that works for their well-being; no species, except the human being, will work against its own well-being.

Intellect, on the other hand, is a tool of intelligence, a specific process designed to operate free of inputs, in a logical, analytical, non-judgmental, and unbiased way. Like all functions, however, this process of computation is developed only to be integrated into a higher integral structure, namely, intelligence. This integration of intellect into intelligence takes place in spiritual development. When enculturation takes place instead, intellect is developed as a tool of the lower brain functions, those concerned with the body, the world, and other people. Since body and world are in a constant state of dissolution, anxiety is endemic to enculturation, since no development beyond a body takes place.

Self-replication of a limited mental process results. The intellect is more powerful and dominates the lower brains, warping their reportage with its anxiety and accepting the warped imagery as the reality it must deal with. Our final attachment to physical systems is cemented over at the adolescent period, during which we are also finally separated from all physical functions in order to be identified with that objective state called mind. Not only does this lock us into a double bind, but we are lost in a hall of mirrors. Everything we do becomes self-replicative as we feed responses back and forth among our three disparate brains. The problems we fret over are problems created within our self-encapsulated system. Every answer we achieve reflects the problem we set out to solve. Every solution is the same problem in a new guise.

By mid-adolescence the physical universe should be an object separate from our ego, leaving us ready for integration into higher structures of organization that come not from the physical but from the fields of consciousness from which the physical arises. The logic of life leads to the creative process underlying all life. The blueprint opening at adolescence leads our awareness into those blueprints out of which our awareness has emerged. The new brain is the primary translating medium for this development.

Spiritual development is the only avenue leading to personal autonomy. The physical world and our body are given us as the means to move beyond the physical. No part of the physical realm is the goal of our life; to identify with the vehicle and take that as the goal is disaster.

God tells Moses that "I Am" is his name. "I Am that I Am" is ego, and ego simply *is*. Ego is Latin for I, self-awareness. This beingness requires no antecedent, consequence, apology, explanation, or meaning. And in no way are we called on, nor is it possible for us, to abolish our ego. The entire creative process is designed to produce ego. Ego is awareness, consciousness that has become aware of itself. The logic of the Creation is to create and then maintain the integrity of ego as ego searches out the infinite possibilities of being aware.

Some spiritual writers claim that our egos must be abolished, obliterated, our sense of personal being annihilated, if we are to be integrated into the Self. But we are always integrated in God; it is impossible for us not to be. The issue is, of what are we aware? How far have we developed awareness? What is our ego identified with?

Throughout development the child is moved in logical stages through shifts of awareness, a natural unfolding that carries the child along in what should be a wonderful adventure. The nine-year-old is certainly different from the six-year-old, but for a successful shift to operational logic at age seven that six-year-old's ego was not annihilated. Nor would it encourage the tyke were we to tell him that he faced ego destruction on his seventh birthday.

Why, then, should we think that this natural unfolding should suddenly cease at adolescence with no further development? Why should not the pattern of development, clearly evident from the beginning, hold throughout? My teacher Gurumayi states the case clearly when she insists that yoga, our union with God, is a perfectly natural process of growth and development. Contrary to much spiritual belief, Muktananada said: "I didn't demolish my ego; I expanded it until it encompassed everything; until I was one with God." As does every great teacher, he urged that we identify ourselves with that God within us and move unhesitatingly toward realizing that identity, which is the way all development takes place.

Under attachment behavior my ego is fragmented into various identifications. Whatever momentary integrity I achieve is through arbitrary domination by one of these fragments over another. My inner life is a constant struggle, an endless chatter of these arguments. My drive for autonomy and integrity cannot program for the failure of having no integrated ego to maintain or develop. So my attached and fragmented ego automatically views true integration as a threat, since each of my fragmented identities would have to give over dominance. Marilyn Ferguson's *Brain/Mind Bulletin* reports an "epidemic increase of multiple personality cases." These are the extremes, when the civil war among our three brains makes even cultural survival difficult. We are all multiple personalities to some extent so long as we are subject to attachment behavior.

The shift at adolescence begins a different type of awareness than that known in the first fifteen years, even though the same pattern of unfolding is followed. There is a qualitative shift of model and content. The shift requires a genuine rebirth; we must become again like little children in highly qualified, specific, and sophisticated terms. As infants and children we had no developed structures of knowledge, only the instinct to follow our models and so make such structures. We enter the post-biological stage only by surrendering our hard-earned knowledge and giving those structures over to a transformation we cannot make ourselves any more than we did those biological structures. We enter a development that involves relinquishing development to that point, and allowing that development to be used as a tool for further development. As Carlos Castaneda's Don Juan said, we must take the power gained and invest it in the path of power, and investment means risk. In the New Testament the parable of the talents states precisely the same case.

Victims of attachment as we are, identified with our primary system, we cannot leave our biological wombs for this rebirth. Our will, our drive for integrity, and even our drive for autonomy converge to resist the integration. We interpret leaving our biological womb as a threat of death. Will becomes at least partly volitional at adolescence, and we exert all our will to maintain our identity with our sensory-motor, physical system. Once will becomes volitional, we must be willing, we must use that will, to go along with further development, to enter the next stage. We must use our new volitional will as a tool for further development; we must enter the venture of our own accord, even though the development within that venture is not in our hands.

We must surrender the semi-autonomy achieved at adolescence and follow a model for post-biological development as we followed our parents from birth. Such a willingness is assured if bonding has taken place; that is, if we have had interactions with the proper role model for the new development ahead of time, and have the role model as guide at the adolescent juncture, the point of separation. Then the issue of willingness hardly enters the picture. Our whole blueprint is geared to move on in development and we do so naturally, just as the infant is designed to bond and move on in development after leaving the mother's womb.

Unbonded, the infant leaving the womb cannot respond to the blueprint and move on in development. He clings to whatever physical moorings are available and identifies with them. Not bonded to the proper role model at adolescence, the newly autonomous self cannot respond to the new blueprint and move on in development. He will cling to the physical moorings and the identity he already has. Just as the attached child clings to that tattered security blanket or tattered teddy bear to which he bonded, the adolescent will cling to his identity, to body, childish emotions, rages. This attachment behavior is intensified by the emergence of sexuality at puberty.

If no bonding has taken place, the only possible result is another play of attachment for the adolescent. As adolescents, we have no choice but to use our semi-autonomous wills, such as they are, to try to maintain our integrity and our position in a hostile world as best we can. We will try to incorporate all further development into our sensory-motor identification, and we do this as a survival move, even though it shuts us off from our only true avenue toward survival itself.

Post-biological development leads to the power to survive as a person. This personal power leads to our identity with the Self. Historical figures like Jesus, Saint John of the Cross, Eckhart, Ramakrishna, Ramana Maharashi, Yogananda, Muktananda, my Gurumayi of Ganeshpuri—all have incredible personal power, and they leave no pollution, no wasted, broken world. Technology appears when personal power disappears.

Throughout my enculturation I was taught that our machinery extends and enhances our human power. Our telescopes and microscopes give greater vision, our machines greater energy, our instruments greater accuracy and capacity for measurement, our medicines greater health and wellbeing. These manipulations, while on the surface appearing to enhance our capacities, at base erode and finally rob us of every capacity they were initially supposed to extend. And, at each point of erosion of our personal power, several things happen. First, an intuitive sense of despair grows, a despair whose source we cannot recognize. Our despair arises over loss of and subsequent failure to develop personal power, the only way by which we can move beyond our physical realm when the time comes. As Jesus said of personal power: To him who has it is given more and more, and from him who has not (this power) it is taken away, even that little he had. Second, our despair over our vulnerability drives us to develop more and better tools and gadgetry as substitutes for our continually eroding power. Finally, we become critically dependent on our technological devices, for we have no power left to deal with life as it is, and so retreat to an arbitrary and artificial existence over which our machinery can give us some modicum of control, so long as the machinery holds. So we then live in anxiety over the possible loss of the comfort and ease our devices seem to offer, and are ready to war on anyone at the slightest sign of encroachment. We identify with our created product and are lost.

Technology marks the cessation of evolution (that ceaseless movement from the concrete to the abstract). Technology has locked human consciousness into the lowest common denominator of our primary brain system.[4] On every side it produces massive pollution, destruction, and despair, cloaked by a rabid consumerism and demand for more technological goods. The strange apocalyptic air that moves across our globe is recognition that a day of reckoning must come, that we simply cannot continue as we are doing. And yet our current mental set avoids the truth of the law of action and reaction, the law that we must reap what we sow. Instead, we scrabble for scientific technological breakthroughs by which we think we might avoid the consequences of our fully.

Armaments, in the final analysis, are the life support, impetus, and foundation of scientific technology. Our scientific community decries the stupid warlords and politicians, but were war-making support withdrawn, academia and science as known today would fade away, and everyone involved knows this to be the case. Again, all look for ways to avoid the consequences of their actions. Willingness for the change necessary to avoid the mounting catastrophe seems non-existent and improbable.

The mechanists and behaviorists deny soul, mind, and finally even consciousness itself, and are then offended that the culture this denial produces reflects the insanity of that denial. As Suzanne Langer once said, the average person in the street has no choice but to accept the opinion of those he assumes know about these things. I have no notion that this sad process we have set in motion can be reversed. In an infinitely open universe everything that can happen will happen. John Anthony West feels that the ship of state has already gone down. Perhaps not even lifeboats are practical any longer. But we have, directly within us, our own personal life vest that will hold under every condition, if we will but shift our attention to it, learn of it, and follow the proper model to develop it. We grasp at external straws that systematically fail us, and leave untouched the magnificence of the power within.

1

Kundalini
and Sexuality

Shakti (pronounced as in "shock") is one of the most descriptive words I know. It is the ancient Sanskrit word for the creative energy behind our universe. Yogic psychology personified this power as a goddess, much as Carl Jung spoke of anima and animus to describe certain psychological functions. According to yogic theory, creation springs from a polarity of conscious energy: a non-moving point, called Shiva, from which all springs, and the creative energy emanating from Shiva, called Shakti. Shiva and Shakti are complementary—a single, indivisible consciousness, a Holomovement, in effect—but assume division in order to enact the play of consciousness. Shakti displays her energy as the three bodies, worlds, and states of consciousness associated with creativity. Shiva represents the fourth state, the silent witness who watches Shakti's display. The parallels with Bohm's Holomovement are obvious, and the general model has striking parallels with physics and psychology in general. I will use the personified form of this model in this discussion, since these are entirely internal, personal functions.

Shakti expresses herself in two forms: one physical, the other subtle (as in particle and wave forms). Our physical Shakti is the intelligence and energy that builds our bodies and brains, and keeps all in coordinated movement with our world. Her plan creates and nurtures our ego to its physical maturity, at which point the other expression of Shakti takes over, the subtle aspect, to nurture our spiritual development. The Sanskrit name for this subtle power is Kundalini Shakti.

She, too, has a clearly designed plan for nurturing our ego to its spiritual maturity.

I first heard of Kundalini through my friend Lee Sannella, then a medical doctor at Kaiser Oakland Hospital in California. Lee had found that many persons in their mid-thirties who came down with inexplicable epileptic or schizophrenic seizures were victims of spontaneous Kundalini "awakening," as it is called. Since the effect is surprisingly widespread, systematic research into this area is not surprising. A department of Kundalini research, in fact, has been opened by associates of the Salk Institute in La Jolla, California.

I would hardly have taken the notion seriously, however, had I not had a Kundalini awakening myself—and had I not found that the extensive Sanskrit literature on the subject of the development of Kundalini showed a far more striking parallel with child development than does yogic psychology with physics. While the subject sounds esoteric, knowledge of Kundalini goes back many millennia, a history beyond our scope here, but I will outline the general characteristics of Kundalini as a developmental process.

First, Kundalini remains in a dormant stage until puberty, along with sexuality. (We do well to remember that our sexual apparatus is largely complete at birth, and is simply held in waiting for its appropriate appearance. Kundalini is an aspect of this same potential.) Kundalini and sexuality develop at the same time. Sexuality is the highest, most subtle expression of our physical Shakti and the lowest, or most physical, aspect of our spiritual-creative energy. Sexuality is a pivotal, transitional energy on which we swing from biological to post-biological development. As the most subtle of our physical drives and the most physical of our creative-spiritual drive, sexuality gives us the most physical form of our creative possibilities, *pro*-creation, the re-creation of our own kind. Sexuality completes and rounds out our physical development, sparks it from then on, and reproduces our system, so this energy is primarily recapitulative. It is circular, turning our energies and attentions back into our bodies and to the world. This Shakti never lets us forget our connection with and dependence on body and world.

Kundalini, sexuality's subtle twin, has the exact opposite as her goal: the realm of insight-intelligence, the Self. Kundalini's job is to wean us away from our attachment to the body and the world, and direct us toward our true goal, the spirit. These two energies, our sexual Shakti and Kundalini Shakti, unfolding within us for development at the same time, form a kind of double helix, interdependent, calling on each other but aimed in opposite directions. They are designed to cooperate through bonding, and if that cooperation takes place, we have the best of both inner and outer worlds.

The Sufi saint in Irina Tweedie's diary, *The Chasm of Fire*,[1] claimed that the impotent person, one without sexual energy, could never realize the Self. For sexual energy is part of the fuel Kundalini must use in its work. It is this fact that gives our sexuality a far greater impetus and importance than in animals.[2] For humans are far more sexual than other animals. We hear people refer to our sexuality as our animal nature, but no self-respecting animal would behave sexually as we humans do.

In nature's economy, our physical Shakti's sexual energy is the basis of our subtle Kundalini Shakti. Just as our subtle sensory system must have a physical system for expression, Kundalini must have its physical counterpart. Through development, however, our subtle system develops its own "body" and can eventually break free of the physical body. In the same way, at a certain point in its development, Kundalini breaks free of her initial dependence on her twin, sexuality.

Kundalini is said to lie dormant at the base of the spine until its proper time for development. We should remember here that the spine is a vital part of the reptilian brain system. Kundalini unfolds in seven developmental stages, which are represented as points along the spine and our head, with the final stage at the top of the skull. The development of Kundalini involves a reorganization of our total brain systems from bottom to top, following the same evolutionary stages of biological development but shifting us from that biological orientation to a non-biological, or spiritual, one. These points along the spine are called *chakras*, from the Sanskrit word for wheel. The chakras are major energy centers or nerve plexes, ranging from the lowest, most physical energies on up to the highest point of consciousness, our union with the Self. The chakras are the subtle counterparts of actual physical neural centers of the spine, governing and controlling the various parts of our body. The chakras represent the rungs of our spiritual development and are subtle systems which, though they lie in the body, are not of it. They are, in effect, the wave complements underlying their physical counterparts.

Each chakra is like a resistance point in electricity and must be pierced by a development of that aspect of subtle energy in order for the Kundalini power to move us on to the next stage of development. Under ideal conditions, where a proper bonding and guidance are provided, the chakras unfold in sequential order. Based on evidence of post-adolescent brain shifts that continue past the adolescent period, the chakras are designed to unfold on the same three-and-a-half-to-four-year cycle found in child development.

The series of chakras and the Kundalini power by which we ascend the chakras give the blueprint for post-biological development. The chakras are chain-linked, as in earlier development. Theoretically, when a person develops the capacities inherent in one stage, the accumulated energy breaks through and he or she is moved on to the next stage, the next chakra. As in physical development, preliminary bonding back and forth takes place as each chakra sparks the previous one while it also prepares for the opening of the next. In actuality, at least when a Kundalini reawakening occurs later in life, a great deal of skipping about takes place, and simultaneous work on all centers might go on.

Kundalini is the subtle equivalent of the same intelligent force found driving us from the time of physical birth. As with that first, physical Shakti, which is modeled by the mother, Kundalini can only be developed when awakened and guided by the proper stimulus and nurturing, which means a teacher who has developed his or her own Kundalini under proper guidance. If awakened without proper guidance, which does sometimes happen, and with no nurturing by discipline or following the proper model, the power can be destructive, as we find in recent medical studies. A passage in the Gnostic Gospels states: "If that which is within you is brought out of you, it will save you. If it is not brought out of you, it will destroy you." Unguided, or guided by a misguided teacher, the power can cause grief. Lee Sannella found specific psychological and biological disorientations from unguided Kundalini. Without a model acting as stimulus the power is unorganized, the circuitry of stimulus-response is incomplete, and the energy upsets the physical neural circuitry. As with all development, our post-biological development is totally dependent on its role model. The now-familiar formula still holds: Blueprint within plus model without equals functional structure.

Using the simplest, most commonly available descriptions, the seven chakras are, in order: (1) physical, (2) sexual, (3) will and volition, (4) emotion, (5) time-space creation, (6) intelligence, (7) realization, or enlightenment, full maturation. In our body these subtle energy points are located along the spine successively: (1) physical, at the base of the spine, (2) sexual, right above the genitals, (3) will, slightly below the navel, (4) emotion, on the right side of our physical heart, (5) time-space, in the throat area, (6) intelligence, between the eyebrows, (7) intuition-realization, at the crown of the skull.[3]

The first two chakras are physically oriented and translate into our awareness through the reptilian brain. The next two are relational and translate through our mammalian brain. The next two are related to intellect and intelligence, and translate through the new brain. The final chakra, enlightenment, stands alone and has no correlation in any particular brain part. One must, in effect, break out of the system and leave the biological in order to be integrated into that final state.

Kundalini emerges out of the physical chakra when that chakra is completed. Completion of the physical chakra takes place in the general period of puberty. The physical chakra represents, in effect, the entire biological development taking place in the first fifteen years or so. Kundalini and its sexual twin await the completion of this physical stage for their emergence on the scene. As Kundalini leaves the physical chakra, she animates, fills with life, the second chakra, sexuality, which then sparks and drives that physical chakra on which both energies rest. The physical system is then the support system for sexuality, and sexuality the support system for further development of Kundalini. On its awakening, sexual energy links with will and volition, the third chakra, which in turn sparks sexuality. Will and volition, the most physical aspects of the subtle fourth chakra of emotion, bring that fourth chakra into play. This central, fourth chakra, the heart chakra, is literally the heart of our spiritual system, as the physical heart and mid-brain connection was the heart of biological life. The power of the heart chakra radiates out in both directions, on up into the higher chakras, to lead us on to final maturation, and back down into the lower chakras, to bring about union and bonding with all aspects of our physical life, including pair-bonding of male and female, family bonding, further social bonding, and so on. The heart chakra is the center of relationship and coordinates, balances, unites, and gives purposeful cohesiveness to the first three stages, the immediate post-biological, while preparing the ego to move on beyond the biological entirely.

If we substitute the term sensual for the term sexual, in that second chakra, we have exactly the stages of development of child intelligence from birth to adolescence. The chakras exactly parallel the stages of child development, since each stage of child development is the basis for its corresponding subtle chakra. The entire physical part of our biological plan, unfolding in those first fifteen years, is but the vehicle, the instrument and the basis, for the far more powerful and open-ended development that Kundalini holds in store. The stages of child development up to puberty are grouped in those three phases: physical, emotional, and intellectual. These, as discussed earlier, are related to our triune brain system. Kundalini's job is to lead us beyond the brain/mind, in its physically oriented adolescent form, but Kundalini must use the brain/mind as developed *in order* to get beyond it.

We have a far more powerful sexual drive than other creatures since sexuality must play a dual role in our lives, as the physical twin and support of our spiritual development. Sexuality can be used for procreation (and recreation), but *must* be used by Kundalini if spiritual life is to unfold. Further, sexual energy must be used by Kundalini in Kundalini's own way. The physical must become supportive of the subtle if development is to continue past adolescence. Sexuality must both complete and round out physical life and, at the same time, support Kundalini. Kundalini, as the more unrestricted and powerful energy, achieves this goal without "civil war" by means of will, the third chakra of our subtle system. Kundalini uses will to unite the ego, in its new sexual identity, with the fourth chakra, the heart chakra, the bond of love. The bond of the heart balances all energies, completes the physical, and supports the Kundalini. Under the bonding power of the fourth chakra and will, its instrument, sexuality is a balanced affair; both aspects of its job are met. Sexuality leads naturally into a male-female pair bond when within the bond of the heart of our spiritual system. The heart center moves in both directions at all times, down into the lower chakras for bonding of family, society, and world in a perfect immanence, and up into the higher chakras in a constant transcendence.

The love found in the heart chakra is the power to unite all things. It cannot be possessed or contained—it can only be experienced and passed on to others. A child's version of love comes from having its needs met. Adult love comes from meeting needs. And our greatest need is to identify with and be in that bond of the heart. So the driving power of the relationship between bonded people is that each desires to gratify, to meet the needs of the other. This gratification both meets our needs and completes our self-development. Our early, physical stage of development was acquisitional, of necessity. We had to acquire, bring in and assimilate experience. The post-biological growth must free us of acquisitions and attachments, teach us to give away, if we are to open to the power of love and intelligence, and move toward autonomy.

The fourth chakra is the pivotal point between the human and the divine, as the third chakra is the pivotal point between the animal and the human. The fourth chakra pulls things together from the animal-human level by uniting us with the divine. Union always means integration of diverse parts into a greater whole (rather than the attachment behavior of an intellect trying to make a whole out of diverse parts). Love starts with the union of the pair bond; spreads with the pair bond's union with child, family, society and world; and completes in union with the creative process itself.

Under the bonding power of the fourth chakra, pair-bond love is a manifestation of that love that sparked creation in the first place. True pair-bond love is a physical expression of the love of Shiva for Shakti, of God for his creation, the concretized form of love as an abstract, non-localized form. The pair re-create the creation and enter into the initial impulse that consciousness makes in its separation venture. The universal play of creating matter only to separate from it completes itself in the pair's union. They are the twin sides of God who plays at separating Self in order to explore the possibilities inherent in relating the separated parts. They are the pull toward reunion and the joy of merging.

Young lovers, even when under attachment behavior, are never stirred first in the groin, but in the heart. And the heartache of love is not on the left side where old thumper carries on, but on the right side, where the subtle fourth chakra, the seat of the Self, resides. Love begins in the subtle heart, and its power transforms the young man and woman into God and Goddess. The fourth chakra rounds out the biological by pointing beyond all biologies. We fall in love with love itself as projected on the other. Love is a blueprint within searching for its content without. Each person of the pair bond finds in the other the content filling his blueprint. When they are within the bond of the fourth chakra, the couple finds God in each other—and this is no sentimental metaphor. Pair-bond love is the concrete expression of the love of God. Following its steady formula, development will extract this love out of its concrete moorings and move it on into its subtle form, the love of God. In A. E. Housman's "A Shropshire Lad," we read:

> Oh, when I was in love with you,
>   Then I was clean and brave,
> And miles around the wonder grew
>   How well did I behave.

> And now the fancy passes by,
>   And nothing will remain,
> And miles around they'll say that I
>   Am quite myself again.

We think the state of intoxication should be sustained "forever and ever," but all development is transitional and leads beyond its own stage. Were the pair bond stabilized within the bond of the heart, the early bond would last, but within a far greater discovery that would be made. Finding God in the other is the essence of love. Finding that each other is God is the first stage of finding God within one's own self. The lover wants to give his person completely to that Self sensed in the other. Each wants, in effect, to disappear into the object of love. This is the concretized form of the separated ego longing for absorption into its final identity beyond the biological.

Through surrender of identity to the other in this physical pair bond, we prepare for the abstract form of the same function when we surrender our ego to the Self within us. When we reverse the outward display of love and turn within, we discover the blueprint from which love itself springs. In giving ourselves up to each other in the pair bond we find ourselves completed; we are, in effect, given back to ourselves enlarged. The more we give ourselves away, the more we are returned enhanced. In this way the pair-bond experience extends the ego and prepares it for the great integration within. When within the bond of the heart, sexual love can prepare for and lead to the bond of ego and Self, beyond male-female, beyond humanity itself.

To the lover, love is spiritual. Each worships the other precisely as a devotee worships God, and rightly so. And in the earliest stage of this love there is only worship, awe, and wonder at the feet of an astonishing, shaking power. The power, whether recognized for what it is or not, is the power of the fourth chakra. Young lovers are nearly always offended at the crass jokes of jaded elders (who have sex but no love) that their motives are crude rutting. Often the final sexual aspect of love is delayed by the lovers in that initial period of awe and wonder, that concretized worship of God as the other.

Were this state sustained and allowed to mature as it should (which is possible only through bonding), the specific, or physical, would be led to the generic, or subtle. At the appropriate stage the two lovers would shift into the heart chakra. Bonded with their own hearts, their outer bonds would reflect this inner power and give the stability needed for a successful family life. If this turn within and discovery of the source of love does not take place, the early stage fades, as expressed in Housman's poem, but has nothing to replace it, no mature form of the relationship. Under attachment behavior we try to sustain and possess the early period of breathtaking awe and wonder, which is impossible. So each eventually "disappoints" the other, and a new relation is sought, to try to rediscover some aspect of that initial period (which, like all stage-specific processes, never comes again).

The antecedent of genital sexuality and the love of the

mature pair bond is found in "puppy love," the crushes of the pre-adolescent. These occasions are far more poignant and powerful than is culturally acknowledged. They are not sexual but preliminary exercises of the heart. Genital sex is a stunning embarrassment at this age since it is out of balance with nature's design. The heart always takes precedence over the groin, and always the love that is trying to be expressed is generated within the person, implicit, but expressed through discovery of the other person. The maturation process should always have the same goal, the eventual reversal of directions: discovery of that inner source, which is independent of any outer stimuli, and never fades.

Male-female love is the specific form of the generic category of love itself. And maturation is, as usual, the reversal of the concretized aspect, and discovery of the inner source. Kundalini Shakti is the power of this reversal development, but is subject to the formula of development: A model of Kundalini development must be given from out in our world, and the model is one who has gone through the maneuver of reversibility and united with the inner Self. The model must form a bond with us in our early stage of development, since all bonds must be established before the stage needing that bond. The bond must then be confirmed at the appropriate period, namely, puberty. Then Kundalini, which automatically arises along with its twin, sexuality, will be activated within the bond of the heart. Since the bond with the heart can only be established by interaction with a proper model, one bonded with that fourth chakra, the individual at puberty is automatically bonded to that fourth chakra as well, even though this bond is established long ahead of time and, like puberty, awaits its manifestation.

This pre-established bond with the model is what establishes Kundalini as the dominant energy over its twin, sexuality, from the beginning. This assures a proper balance between the two Shaktis, Kundalini and sexuality; a balance between immanence and transcendence, between body and spirit. Then a powerful sexual drive can unfold, a drive that is in balance with all needs, since sexuality will itself be bonded, pulled on into transcendence by that heart chakra. The young person will search primarily for love (as all do) and through love express sexuality. Then the sexual chakra will be pierced, fulfilled, and gone beyond, in due course of time.

Were the bonds with the heart chakra established in their proper order, before sexual experience begins, then sexual experience and the Kundalini experience could (theoretically) be the same. (William Blake alludes to this, and some of the true Tantra disciplines of yoga work for this end.) Were development functional in our first fifteen years, and our ego integrated by early adulthood, which would mean a true bonding at every point and a transcendentally oriented society, Kundalini might be stimulated anew at each sexual encounter in the early years.

There is no way to account for the power, exuberance, ecstasy, and longing of our middle and late adolescent period except through Kundalini. (Recall Thomas Wolfe's writing of the "grape bursting in the throat" of the adolescent.) This is the power of God trying to awaken within us to be expressed as our own Self. This is the fourth chakra, the center of creation, which awakens, activates all the lower chakras and draws them upward, preparatory to moving ego on beyond all biological life.

The model that can establish the needed bond in our pre-puberty stage and confirm it at puberty has its closest equivalent in mother-infant bonding. For if we are not given this model, and thus miss the bonding involved in puberty, the result is the same as at birth: Instead of the balance of the bond from the fourth chakra, we will get attachment behavior. This will mean reversion, a turning back into the lowest chakra, of the new energies then opening, *including Kundalini*, as found in all attachment behavior. The phenomenon of Kundalini in attachment behavior results in a mounting, pyramidal, and escalating series of disasters.

Our era has dismissed the great longing, energy, and emotion of the early pair bond in the same way that we

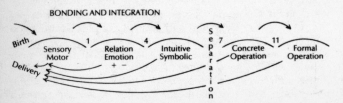

BONDING AND INTEGRATION

ATTACHMENT INCORPORATES AND FRAGMENTS

dismiss the "grape bursting in the throat" of the adolescent, as "misplaced sexual energy" or "sexual repression." This is contemptible nonsense. The exact opposite is the case. Our imbalanced, morbid, and unsatisfactory preoccupation with sex is a sign of a misplaced, dysfunctional, and misguided Kundalini. What has happened to us, in our unbonded and attached culture, is the unleashing of an unbonded Kundalini which must, of sheer logical necessity, revert to attachment behavior. Kundalini is expressed in early sexual activity even when sexuality is repressed and not allowed overt expression. But since Kundalini is activated with no understanding of what is taking place, with no cultural support at all, without social models of spiritual development, and in a culture morbidly preoccupied with sexuality on a commercial, pornographic, and compulsive level, Kundalini energy gets equated *with* its twin energy and sexual energy then proves the only possible outlet or expression of Kundalini.

Recall that attachment behavior is the attempt to incorporate a higher integral structure into a lower one, rather than allowing integration of the lower into the higher. Kundalini is a far more unrestricted and greater power than sexuality. Under the impetus of attachment behavior, Kundalini, when even partially incorporated into sexuality, seriously overstimulates sexual energy without any of the necessary balance that only the power of the fourth chakra can bring about. Sooner or later this leads to a sexual excess that dissipates the Kundalini energy itself. Kundalini slowly atrophies, and the transcendent, ecstatic waves of expectancy fade away, generally by our early twenties, leaving us with a growing despair and over-stimulated sexuality. When this happens, sexuality, which is now equated unconsciously with its twin, Kundalini, becomes equated with that now-missing transcendent quality

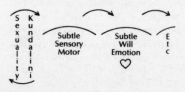

that the bonded Kundalini is designed to give. Each of us feels that something tremendously important is supposed to happen with sexuality, and this is acutely so at adolescence. For a time the sheer excitement of the sexual venture holds us, but, stripped of its transcendent aspect, its bond with the fourth chakra, nothing beyond physical sensation happens. (Every once in a while, some suggestion of the transcendent power manifests, as Hemingway described in *For Whom the Bell Tolls*, when the young couple "left the earth" in that sleeping bag. The old gypsy woman said that if people experience that even once in their lives they are lucky. There is something pathetic in her observation, since this "rush" of ecstasy occurs quite commonly in meditation. Again, that which we seek from without is always manifested from within.)

So we fill libraries with books on how to enhance this physical sensation, and we enter into a perpetual excess of rutting, searching for something that is supposed to happen and does not. The psychologist writes knowingly of the "post-coital blues" as though they were as natural as the "post-partum blues" of the violated and unbonded mother.

We look for the spiritual in the sexual with no notion of what we are looking for. And we do this under the compulsion of attachment behavior: We unconsciously treat our sexual partners as objects to be possessed (if only temporarily), on the one hand; and unconsciously expect from them a transcendent element they cannot possibly deliver, on the other. And, of course, the opposite is always the case: The other treats us as an object of attachment behavior, attempts to possess love through us, and looks for a transcendent experience that we cannot deliver, either. The result is almost invariable—each member of the encounter sooner or later disappoints the other. The disappointment is intangible, and so all the more frustrating. Since we automatically project this frustration onto the other, we express betrayal and rage.

Consider now that the awakening and activating of each chakra stimulates to some extent, as it should prepare for, the opening of the next chakra. Activation of the second chakra, sexuality, to some extent activates the third chakra, will. Will, when activated by the Kundalini, is pushed from below and pulled from above by the power of the heart. The third chakra, will, unites the second chakra with the fourth, unites sexuality with love, when within the bond of Kundalini and the heart. The third chakra is not the conscious, volitional will that unfolds with us at adolescence. Our personal, volitional will must be surrendered *to* that third chakra, integrated into it, under the stimulus of the bond. Under attachment behavior, however (which always attempts to incorporate the new power into the previous identity), ego attempts to incorporate the power of the third chakra into the service of the second, sexuality, and our sexual tie with our physical system. Will, designed to overcome obstacles and lead us to our fourth chakra, is inverted at this point, and some aspect of it turned back into the lower chakras, into our fragmented ego identities. This breeds a will-to-power centered on some form of sexual domination, which spills out onto the whole society and world.

This will-to-power breeds domination of the sexual partner, rather than the surrender to each found in the pair bond. Each of the attachment pair struggles to maintain his or her integrity in the face of the will of the other, a maintenance that demands a counter-domination of the other as the only way to maintain integrity. Which ego is going to devour the other emerges as the survival issue, following the initial flurry of sexual activity. Thus we undergo a constant changing of sexual partners, since at each new encounter there is a modified rush of at least a quasi-Kundalini effect: This time might be it! And generally there is some simulation of "it" on the first encounters, a simulation that rapidly wears thin. Then the disappointment factor enters and begins its work. Promiscuity is an attachment-behavior necessity, and the reason why the "sexual revolution" of our unbonded culture left us with dust and ashes.

The ramifications of attachment behavior and sexuality would fill volumes, and are literally a life-or-death issue. I will conclude this chapter with an interesting aspect of the physical-subtle energies involved. The job of the physical Shakti is to maintain the physical system. Eventually most of the body's machinery should be assumed by this automatic pilot of ours. This frees consciousness for further development. When bonding takes place, this physical Shakti assumes her rightful place as the support system for the emerging Kundalini. The physical is the launching pad for the subtle venture.

If a failure of bonding occurs, the physical Shakti cannot

fully take over the physical system and free the ego. For in the cascade of disasters, our intellect reverts back to the physical realm; the actions of the new brain lock in on the information from the animal brains and their reportage of the world without. In our anxiety we try to assume conscious control of many of the jobs our physical Shakti is designed to assume. Much of the findings in sports psychology, and the new extensions of the martial arts, as found by Ralph Strauch, have to do with getting the ego and its intellect to relinquish false dominion and attempts to control everything, and surrender the body to that physical Shakti, who loves to do her thing when allowed, and does it so miraculously.

The job of this physical Shakti is also to maintain the integrity of the physical-emotional unity of the two primary brains, which gives us the basis for our life. Early in this book I mentioned a ninety-minute wake-dream—deep sleep cycle during which consciousness shifted weight from brain to brain. One of the observations of our sleep cycle is that "genital engorgement" takes place when we enter the dream state. Any male knows this; it may be more subtle in females. Male penile erection on a regular cyclic basis has been observed even in the late uterine male (using new scanning devices). The same effect is found in higher mammals' dream cycles. When we dream, we shift to our subtle system and largely suspend the physical. And nature enacts a little fail-safe device: We go into genital engorgement. Usually this brings on some form of sexual arousal, which then brings about at least some activation of our physical brain and body. Nature does this, perhaps, to prevent our "wandering" in our dream state. Theoretically our soul might simply leave our body and fragment out into some astral wasteland of the psyche—so nature fires her safety device into effect. We "go on the horn," as the male euphemism expresses it, to some extent, perhaps just by having our dreams take a sexual turn. Robert Monroe writes that on each occasion of leaving his body he was drawn back by intense and unreasonable sexual desire. He had to learn to override this effect in order to explore the worlds that opened. (Perhaps he did this by simply proving to his system that he could always get back.)

My teacher Muktananda told me to spend half my meditation time sitting in the conventional cross-legged style, and the other time lying flat on my back. All of my meditation experiences, sensory ventures into other states, take place during this lying-down period. And without fail, any experiences during this time bring on serious sexual arousal. (Actually, meditation itself does this, but the effect becomes evident and disturbing while lying down.) During meditation I am often given a series of creative experiences designed to teach me a point, or to expand my awareness. This is part of the general reversibility maneuver of the Kundalini development. I experience states well beyond the biological, and nature's instinctual fail-safe sexual maneuver may fire in to hook me with desire and bring me back to my subtle physical interconnections.

Meditation stimulates the Kundalini Shakti, since that energy alone leads us to the Self. And Kundalini stokes the sexual fires since Kundalini uses that energy to move us beyond sexuality and the body. I was told by my teacher to meditate between three and six in the morning, traditionally the most auspicious time for this discipline. A recent study showed that the human male is at his most sexually potent between three and six in the morning. This is odd, since three in the morning is also the lowest point of our whole physical life; we are closest to death at that time and more natural deaths occur then than at any other time. Thus our Kundalini is designed to develop our capacity to move beyond the biological system—and our physical Shakti, with its highest and most subtle servant, sexuality, is designed to maintain our physical life. A neat little tug-of-war unfolds, and the yogis of history have always utilized these early hours for meditation to take advantage of this fact. Our physical Shakti is at the lowest ebb and activates her fail-safe sexual response. The yogi activating the Kundalini at this time, through mediation, then has a flood of sexual energy (needed by Kundalini), and the lowest point of resistance by the gravity of our physical system.

Consider, now, the attachment-versus-bonding problem in a larger light. When we are faced with our physical death, nature fires in her last-ditch sexual procedure to try and hold us in pattern, hold the mammalian and reptilian brains in synchrony. According to all spiritual traditions, at physical death itself, our sexual desire, activated for attempted survival and holding its pattern in the subtle body system, tries to keep us united with the body. Failing that, we are left with a subtle body stuck with the heaviest of all physical desires and no way to expend it. Our sexual desire remains with us like a phantom limb pain long after its member is removed. This sexual desire is expressed in our subtle state as an irresistible compulsion to attain a body and fulfill the desire. This brings on either some form of reincarnation, if there is anything to that questionable notion, or to our becoming stuck on some subtle-astral level where sexuality finds some form of expression.

(The giant mastodons found frozen in Siberia are believed to have died a very sudden death followed by flash-freezing. Fresh grass was found in their stomachs and mouths. Autopsies show they almost surely died of suffocation. Among the effects of suffocation of a mammal is genital engorgement; the male mastodons had penile erections.)

Sexual desire, then, grounds us in the physical system, or, at best, in a subtle state that in some way simulates the physical, where sexual desire might be expressed. Maturation moves us beyond all expressions, into the realm of the Self, from which all springs. And sexuality proves the biggest single stumbling block to that movement. This may be one of the reasons that we humans, in spite of our revolutions and freedoms, have always been uncomfortable with our sexuality. We have never known quite what to do with it or about it, seem unable to live with or without it too successfully. Sexuality has always, without clear reason, been the scapegoat and taboo factor of most spiritual paths. Spiritual systems that try to incorporate sexuality as an activity generally end as rather shoddy affairs.

Attachment behavior locks the identity into the physical-sensory system. When sexuality opens in the attached state, with its energy of desire, sexuality seals the identity into this primary stage of awareness. Locked into the sexual-physical system, our Kundalini atrophies. We end, as William Butler Yeats described us: a raging bundle of desires in a dying animal. The solution lies in rediscovering the bonding process. Identified with the power of the heart, we move beyond the sexual-physical; the Kundalini can stoke those fires and all will be in balance, all will be fulfilled, we will have the best of all worlds and move on in development. Further, when bonded, and the sexual chakra transcended, no fail-safe device activates at death since the physical Shakti and her sexual servant are integrated into the higher chakras as proper support systems. The developed psyche freely leaves the biological sphere behind.

All spiritual disciplines urge some form of celibacy, which is a most threatening word to an attached culture. And a paradox ensues, since the more we meditate, the more likely our sexual desire. We cannot *will* ourselves out of the paradox, since will is linked with the sexual chakra in attachment behavior. Further, Kundalini uses will to activate the sexual chakra and draw it to the fourth. So our solution lies in simply willing that we might open to the fourth chakra. There alone are our needs met and balance achieved.

(Let there be no welshing on the point, however; sooner or later actual celibacy must be undertaken for a completion of our spiritual journey. We cannot serve two masters, nor remain split between allegiance to the body and spirit. Sexuality must be transcended, yet retained as an energy available solely to Kundalini.[4] So this move must be made while we are still sexually active.)

Under the guidance of the teacher, the model who has completed the spiritual journey, these developments unfold in due course, in a natural and joyful way. The problem lies in finding that model and guide. I look back on the only model of the spiritual venture I could find in my first few decades of life: the symbol of the cross, which, on the one hand, empty, shows the teacher disappeared from our cultural scene, on the other hand, occupied, a mauled "suffering savior," brutalized and removed from action. Either way, the symbol is of a culture that has rejected the model-function of the teacher principle underlying all life, and which model alone can move us beyond the biological and its inevitable death. The Gnostic image depicted Jesus dancing on the head of the corpse on the cross, saying, in effect: "They cannot get me; bodies are expendable. Here I am, always among you." The bishops of the early Church threw the Gnostics out, and with them the idea of the ever-recurring teacher, leaving us with only a mythical symbol.

The great Sphinx of Giza, in Egypt, is another intriguing symbol. Recent evidence indicates that this monolith may be between thirty and forty thousand years old.[5] The late German archeologist Schwaller de Lubicz found Egyptian hieroglyphics stating that the Sphinx was there before the Egyptians were. The Sphinx represents the integration of our animal and human natures and the integration of our human with divine nature. The statue is a human head on the body of a lion (which represented dominion over the earth). The head of the Sphinx is adorned with what looks like a peculiar headdress, but which represents a sunburst, the sun at sunrise illuminating the head. The halo of Christian and Hindu usage is a similar symbol, using the full-blown sun. In every case this halo represented a final maturation of human nature, our union with God.

Eighteenth-century drawings of the Sphinx, made by European scholars and travelers, depict the Sphinx in its intact state, with the head complete. For in the early Napoleonic wars a scraggly army of Mamelukes came up the Nile and used the Sphinx as a target for cannon practice. From the crown of the skull of the original, intact Sphinx, there emerged a large hooded snake, which curled over the forehead, resting its head between the eyebrows. Throughout tradition, in Europe and the East, spiritual development has been represented by a coiled serpent lying at the base of the spine and eventually emerging from the top of the skull, when spiritual development is complete. This "serpent power" was the Kundalini, whose successful journey up the chakras, emerging finally free of all physical process, gave enlightenment, represented by the sunburst. The enlightenment, or realization of our union with God, gave intuition, which curled over from the top of the skull onto the sixth chakra, the chakra of intelligence, situated between the eyebrows. This sixth chakra has always been called the Guru chakra, that is, the chakra of the teacher.

With prophetic precision the Mameluke cannonballs blew away the bridge of the nose, that sixth chakra, the seat of the teacher; seriously damaged both eyes (the left eye of the teacher looks within to the heart of God, the right eye looks out on the world); and completely destroyed the symbol of the great Kundalini coming out of the top of that head. All but a thin ridge, just a trace of the serpent, is gone. This was truly an act of the enlightened age: War had grown to mature size; the dark and dismal mills of England were mushrooming over the world; cesspool cities burgeoned and over-population appeared; science and technology bloomed forth, sowing the seeds of a final destruction; medicine men began to take over childbirth, using surgical instruments with which they carved cadavers at night, and "childbed fever" raged into the world.

For upwards of thirty to forty thousand years the Sphinx had sat as a symbol of development and wholeness. And in a few short moments the Mamelukes turned it into a symbol of coming events: an intellect stripped of its intelligence, locked into its identity with an animal body and damaging the inner vision that knows God. The end result is what we see about us: a split intellect devoid of intelligence, devoid of spirit and power, destroying both Self and world.

These two symbolic acts, cross and sphinx, have left us with an engulfing nightmare in which we are losing the best of all worlds, the paradisaical good earth, the society of the human, and certainly the world beyond the human, the Self. We are now isolated in the void between, a no-man's land, a place of darkness and gnashing of teeth. And in this strange twilight time of waiting, we certainly find a massive genital engorgement hitting us from every angle: nature's fail-safe device outstripped, out-maneuvered, with nothing left but raging desire, the lust of impotent anger, the marriage of sex, violence, and death—"and then Sam made love to her, and pulled out his pistol, and shot her in the head."

16

Reversibility

Each stage of physical development has as its subtle counterpart the blueprint out of which that stage springs. Our job in post-biological development is to reverse the earlier biological process and go from our specific experience back into the generic realm. The known becomes the bridge to the unknown.

Kundalini gives the power and intelligence of this passage, when one is under the guidance of the proper teacher (one who has developed the Kundalini). As Kundalini moves us from our established physical orientation into that causal field from which we came, the real meaning and goal of the growth of intelligence from the concrete to the abstract unfold.

Nature sets aside our first fifteen years to establish our concrete base, the sum total of which furnishes the first rung of the ladder, the physical chakra, of the post-biological stage. This physical system, in its entirety, has its own equivalent subtle system. If we can open to this subtle, wave-form world which precedes our particle-form one, we can achieve a perfect rapport, unity, and harmony with our society and world.

That our physical body has its subtle energy equivalent seems self-evident. I have written here of my teacher's lesson for me, when I was taken out of my body for five straight mornings. I was then in my dream body with my waking consciousness intact. In all the subsequent lessons given me, this theme has been repeated on a broader scale: We are more than physical systems. Huge archetypal realms of possibility precede and go beyond this physical realm. All this is our heritage. We must develop the ability to enter them, however, while keeping our awareness intact, just as we had to do to enter each stage of our biological plan.

Unfolding the subtle counterparts of our physical experience involves much of the post-biological development. The second chakra of our subtle system is both sensory and sexual. Sexuality is the most subtle of our physical senses and sexuality also has its subtle counterpart. In *Bond of Power* I related a causal subtle experience of the pair-bond union between my Self and my anima, one of the most powerful experiences I have known.[1] Since sexuality is the pivot between physical and subtle energies, it can be consciously employed and physically enacted when we are in a subtle dream state (easily the most rewarding of all sexual experiences).

Each of our five senses also spins out of a category, a generic field of that sensation as an open possibility. Our Kundalini leads us into an unfolding of this causal realm as a creative possibility. Through meditation our Kundalini can lead us into each of these realms singly or, at times, in marvelous cross-indexed mixtures of all our sensory modes. Before I entered Siddha meditation I had had a number of visual experiences in the meditation state, but nothing like I have known since. The earlier ones were haphazard, confusing, and all too rare. Now they are frequent, rather systematic, and quite purposeful. Often in meditation, displays of imagery unfold in waves of interchanging pattern, three-dimensional, full of color, and breathtaking. The Shakti of creation dances before me, delighted to have a witness to her expertise. Geometric patterns and tapestries of exquisite movement occur one morning, unearthly and very beautiful scenery the next. Though I view these as a silent witness to Shakti's play, I have no feeling of incompleteness or of being alone.

Discovering the open category of visual process is exquisite, but so is the process of sound. Baba Muktananda used to say: "If you think the sounds you go to hear with your orchestras are great, you have no idea how great the inner sounds, the *Nada*, are." I have experienced the *Nada* on occasion, less frequently than I experience the open category of vision, perhaps because music has been a serious love of my life and I may tend to clutch at it. In *Nada*, the experience of the inner world of sound, I have on occasion melded with the Shakti in her creation. I have become the actual production of the music, not a passive witness as in the visual experiences, but the receiver and producer at once. It then becomes "my music" and follows my tiniest nuance of creative imagination in a direct perfection of form and content, with no intermediaries. We hear that in realizing any work of art the inner conception is always to some extent betrayed. The form in some way always betrays the content. In the *Nada* this is not the case. Creator and that created are a single impulse, where all is perfection.

These experiences are complete and perfect because they lack nothing; they do not need to be shared. My son once said that for a piece of music to be born into the world it must not only be written down and performed, but is complete only on being heard and shared by an audience. The audience completes the circuitry from composer to performer to listener. But this does not hold in the inner world of creation. I am all elements, in a sense, including audience. There is no separateness in that inner state, thus no aloneness. And it is this discovery—that the ego encompasses everything, that there is no divisiveness—that is the transformation. We say the ego dissolves into the absolute, but we can as well say that the absolute has integrated the ego. They are whole experiences, lacking nothing.

I am sure psychedelic drugs duplicate forms of this, and that may be why many people who have taken drugs never again quite buy into the behaviorist, mechanist worldview. But how much greater the experience when under the guidance of Kundalini, whose goal is to lead us to the Self and who uses these experiences to expand our conceptual capacity. Under Kundalini we enter into the realm of subtle experience as an integrating process, whereas the synthetic counterfeit produces disintegration.

Kundalini extends our visual capacity by playing with us, as we play with a child to extend its capacity and response. We have nothing to do with this creativity other than to accept it; and if we attempt to interfere, to indulge in the experience, Shakti instantly quits. (To indulge means to try to possess the experience in our ordinary attachment way, to try to feed the experience back into our reflective system for tape-looping and analysis.) Learning to accept, without clutching to possess, is necessary if we are to undo all our years of

enculturated attachment behavior. These creative gifts are
not our doing at this stage so much as our *not*-doing. We
must first learn to receive. (My teachers say the most difficult
job is to persuade people to accept grace, the gift freely
given.) To receive means to let the experience flow through
one unhindered by expectation or desire. That is what we did
as infants and children in following our early models, and
what we must learn to do on a whole new scale. Little by
little we learn to become a part of that power flowing through
us, and eventually we identify with it and can direct the
process by becoming that process.

The archetypal category of taste is spoken of as the
Amrit, a maddeningly familiar taste I knew as a child and
searched continually for. I used to dream of finding this taste
bottled up and felt I had entered paradise on hitting that
bottle. I have experienced this only twice in meditation,
though I have had many little hints and suggestions of it.

The sense of touch in its generic state is infinitely varied
and gives a powerful type of mystical experience in the classical sense. The most that can be said is that every cell of the
subtle body undergoes a stimulus that is similar to a rushing
wind; it translates as pure love. At times it is felt as a falling
through great spaces at the speed of light, a true ecstasy,
being taken outside one's ordinary self. My teacher Gurumayi,
one of Muktananda's two successors, has spoken of this wind
effect brushing every fiber of one's being, and how at times it
rushes not only through every cell but through the "cave of
the heart," that "realm wherein God lives." (This, apparently, is her state of natural repose, from which she issues
forth to tend the affairs of the world.)

Walt Whitman spoke of touch as a mystical experience,
and seems to have known an ongoing form of this subtle
experience in his everyday waking state.[2] In my limited
experience, this touch of the subtle and causal bodies is the
most powerful reportable experience I have had. Whatever is
said about it is flat and inadequate; suffice it to say that I
would cheerfully give my life in this world to enter that one
permanently. (Nevertheless, there is still a state beyond that,
beyond all sense, at which point reportage breaks down.)

Shakti leads us into these causal fields of open sensuality
by using the abilities we developed through our actual sensory experience. That is why the body is the only vehicle by

which we may attain identity with God, and why the nature
and character of our physical experience determine the nature and character of God that we can then experience.
Muktananda's experiences of *Nada*, for instance, centered
around flute music and variations of essentially Indian music.
My *Nada* are of pianos and orchestras, huge choral Masses,
with a doff of the hat to Bach, Beethoven, Brahms, and a
whole panoply of musical heroes in my life.

Having experienced the causal fields as our own being,
our actual, limited specific experience here in the physical
world seems pallid by comparison, yet enhanced as well. I
was offended on reading, a number of years ago, the advice of
the great woman saint Ananda Mayi Ma, to "eat without
tasting, look without seeing," and so on. Ignore the outer
world, this total renunciate taught, and concentrate totally on
the inner world. I read this at the height of my involvement
in the consciousness movement, with its emphasis on "total
awareness," which involved immersing oneself in sensory
experience, really tasting food, smelling air, seeing nature,
plumbing the depths of sensation. When the physical-sensory
is all we know, this seems sound enough advice. Through the
grace of my teachers, though, whose grace provides these
experiences of the inner world, I can only say that Ananda
Mayi Ma was right. The child must be weaned, and so must
the adult. The movement is always from the concrete to the
abstract, the particular to the generic, a continual giving up
of life for greater life.

Our Kundalini Shakti leads us into the third chakra, the
chakra of will, will as raw, uncommitted power. By uncommitted I mean a power that can flow down into sexuality and
the world, and up into the heart chakra, as opposed to one
that resides specifically in one area. Carlos Castaneda's Don
Juan, the Zen people, and the martial arts people all concentrate on this chakra, which is the pivotal point between
animal and human, and the center of gravity of physical life.

My third chakra (called the Kath or Chi by the martial
arts people) became active in my twenty-third year. I had no
idea what was happening, but discovered that by a suspension of all ordinary criteria, judgment, and, above all, fear or
concern over outcome, things out there in my world could be
altered. I experienced my immunity to fire at this period (see
Chapter 8), experienced a long, exhilarating reversal of gravi-

ty's ordinary dominion at the Palos Verdes cliffs outside Los Angeles, and experienced other paranormal phenomena. I became disturbed over the "tiger by the tail" situation, began to consider it possibly demonic, and shut it out. (The violations of natural process I had undergone, always with witnesses, led to my eventual book, *The Crack in the Cosmic Egg*.)

Of itself, the third chakra *can* be demonic, for it is the power of will, a power seldom developed. When Jesus made such seemingly outlandish statements as "If you had the faith of a grain of mustard seed, you could say to this mountain, move into the sea, and it would move," he referred to the power of this chakra. Faith and will overlap. Will can step out into nothing and find something there. When we are in the bond with the teacher, Kundalini incorporates this power within her developmental agenda, for her own ends. The third chakra becomes the will of our Kundalini, through which we can overcome all obstacles to development.

Twice in mediation I have stumbled on what I can only suppose was the causal field of this chakra as itself, the power in its raw form, and I ricocheted from it like a Ping-Pong ball. I had no notion that such power could exist, yet here it was within my own psychic structure. The experience offers little to report. I felt the usual roar in my ears during meditation, the rush of falling in space, and found myself in a loka, or state, of pure power. There was no imagery involved as such, but rather discovery of a state of consciousness within myself. I felt I had run head-on into a red-hot force without heat, like a field of solid electricity of incomputable wattage-voltage. I bounced off it subdued and a bit cowed, finding that I was, after all, but a babe in the woods of this inner world. (I had been getting into my third chakra in meditation rather willfully, exploring its outer fringes, and had had a bit of ego inflation.)

The third chakra is the more restricted form of the fourth chakra, the heart chakra, the seat of the Self. Our development hinges on how these two chakras, the third and the fourth, relate. We have seen that the fourth chakra, love, is the emotion of perfect unity or relationship, the bond of power which holds creativity in its diversified unity. In the agenda of development, will finds its true power and purpose by giving over to that fourth chakra. The formula holds: Each stage finds its completion and perfection by being integrated into the next stage and supporting that next stage. The high point of the will of the third chakra is the low point of the fourth, the will of God. The will of the heart is love. Will is the way this love of the heart is expressed, the way it moves down into the lower chakras to unite and bring them under the bond. At the same time, this empowers the lower chakras with further development. Will as love moves into the whole physical experience, as love of the other person, society, and world, as one's love of Self. My teachers insist that spiritual development gives the capacity to live fully in the world, and that the final test of spiritual power is one's capacity to so live. We should not meditate in caves, they say time and again, but in the middle of Main Street. We do this, though, as the higher form of will pulls us, with an insatiable longing, on in development, to move beyond humanity itself.

Development of this third chakra could give us volitional control over non-ordinary phenomena, ordinarily so quixotic and unpredictable. There are people who develop this chakra and opt for a premature autonomy. That is, they develop Kundalini to this extent but do not give over their will of that third chakra to the will of the heart. They can then turn that power of will back into the lower chakras willfully, without concern for relationship, and cause havoc. Castaneda's Don Juan warned of this danger, and Jesus' story of the Temptations in the Wilderness spells out this idea graphically.

Muktananda was a highly developed yogi when he submitted, in his fortieth year, to his final spiritual teacher, Bhagavan Nityananda. This great saint beat his disciple Muktananda with a stick for having *siddhis* (powers over material process possible to an advanced yogi through his will), and forced Muktananda to give up such practices. Once the yogi hits a high degree of attainment, these powers just naturally become manifest, and what one does with them is pivotal. Muktananda, at forty, was a highly evolved yogi and thought nothing of his paranormal powers and seldom used them. But his teacher had far higher goals for this pupil. Altering physical process was a sidetrack. The capacity to give *Shaktipat*, the transference of spiritual power from teacher to student, to awaken or restimulate the Kundalini, on a universal, broadcast scale, was his teacher's goal for Muktananda. This, as far as is known, had never been done before, and required extraordinary preparation. Bhagavan Nityananda made

Muktananda give up all minor sideshows that might siphon off energy from the great historic task in store.

India has many yogis who develop this third chakra to some extent and opt for ego aggrandizement and personal power. This stops their development and often such people become rather demonic. During the winter of 1983–84 I was, as usual, in Ganeshpuri, India, at my teachers' ashram, where I spend my winters with my family. On Shivaratri, an ancient day of celebration, a yogi typical of these magicians appeared, as usual, in front of the ashram. (He is not welcomed inside.) The yogi had long matted hair and beard, wild, fierce eyes, and carried a bow and arrow, a trident, several pouches, and various symbolic fetishes.

He stood in the middle of the wide road shouting, then pulled out a pair of wooden sandals with several sharp spikes driven through each, points up, and stood on those points. He then pulled out three metal skewers, like thick knitting needles. One of these he ran through his cheeks; his tongue extended way out of his mouth, showing that the skewer ran through it (which kept him quiet, at least!). One skewer he ran through his Adam's apple, and apparently through the back of his neck. The other he ran through his neck from right to left. Then he produced a large, live, and vicious-looking hooded snake (I don't know whether it was a cobra or not), which he wrapped about his shoulders, and, open-eyed, went into a catatonic trance, coming out of it some eight hours later. The snake kept watch the entire day, moving its head to keep a steady eye on anyone coming near.

This ascetic comes every year at this time, apparently to seek an audience. Why develop such powers unless one can show them off? The third chakra gives rise to the will-to-power sensed by Nietzsche and Schopenhauer. The Russian monk Rasputin seems to have had some bit of this kind of power. Such people often take on a religious or political cloak, and generally cause havoc. The truly developed third chakra is one given over to the fourth, of course. The fully developed human will is found only in the will of God. And it is this mature form of will, love, that gives true dominion over the earth.

The fourth chakra is the heart of creative power, which stands at the balance of the biological and the spiritual. When we give over our third chakra to the fourth, then we have but one will in our lives, and that is the will of God. (Kierkegaard wrote: "Purity of heart is to will one thing.") Love is the only relation that endures, since it is its own state and needs no object. Love is the state of unsupported awareness; from here ego can move into the biological or into the nonexistent beyond the biological. Love is the state of autonomy, the relation of self to Self.

The fifth chakra seems more available to random exposure and exploration than the fourth or third, at least in a limited way. For this chakra includes, of necessity, so-called astral or subtle states. Many people go out of their bodies and find their awareness in this randomly open continuum. Dreams seem to draw on this state at times; it seems a hodgepodge of general memory. So-called psychics draw on this state, generally in a haphazard, random fashion. "Near-death" experiences seem to tip into one of the myriad possibilities of awareness within this locus. To make this type of experience an end in itself can impoverish development, inflate the ego, and sidetrack us into dead ends, into cosmic wastelands. Castaneda's Don Juan warned that one could become isolated in this state.

Muktananda wrote briefly of his exploration of various lokas, or locations, in this realm. He saw that which was in keeping with, supportive of, and necessary to his own spiritual growth. Under the guidance of his teacher he went through the chakra and beyond. His accounts of some of the states encountered are quite beautiful, and some stunningly horrible.

Many of these states perceived in our subtle awareness are in themselves somehow existent. We re-create them as we perceive them. This is a step toward actually creating such states, wherein lies freedom. (Perhaps Charles Tart's couple in hypnotic dreaming touched on a preliminary form of this creative possibility, though they were merely recipients.) My friend Robert Monroe made the most systematic and intelligent exploration and reportage of this state ever recorded (so far as I know). One of Bob's critics leaped on the fact that years ago Bob had been a producer of radio fantasy shows (*The Shadow* was one of his more enduring enterprises). She dismissed Bob's ten years or more of out-of-body reportage as his own fantasizing. This error of logic is a failure to grasp the role imagination plays in any seeing. All our seeing is a re-creation from a standard stock of possibility. Other stockpiles of possibility abound.

The real issue was that Bob has an exceedingly strong, active, well-developed system of imagery transference. He had the capacity to transfer imagery over a wide spectrum, which means the capacity to perceive where ordinary, weak perceptual systems cannot. Monroe could enter a field of experience alien to our ordinary one because he had a strong and flexible imagination, images capable of transferring alien imagery into meaningful perception. His experience of these lokas was his own creative interpretation of them, to the nearest point of correspondence with his ordinary conceptual patterns. And this is true of all of us in our everyday world. I am sure that some of his reportage was only an approximation of what the states might have been to someone within those states. And he came across situations where no approximation of any sort was possible, where there were insufficient points of correspondence to make any transfer.

No experience in this fifth chakra is a mystical experience of God, though they be awesome and paradisaical. The fifth chakra and its possibilities must be conceptualized, and God is not a concept. They must be perceived, and God is not a perception. The experience of God is not perceiving in any sense. There is nothing to perceive since perception is a creative act and God is not and cannot be created. God is creation itself. Again, we do not perceive God, we perceive *as* God. I am God's perception of Self, from this particular perceptual point of the creation. The question is, What *do* we, and *can* we, perceive? A limited perception is a limited God, which is, after all, our starting point in life. So the task of post-biological development is, among many things, to expand our perception.

During his sadhana (his spiritual practice), Muktananda's Shakti gave him a visit to Siddha Loka, the abode of all the great saints and sages of history. The Loka formed for Baba according to his ability to conceptualize it, and he did so according to his cultural and spiritual tradition. Since such "lokas" form only as we form them by our entry into them, all the great masters sat beneath the wish-fulfilling tree (imagery from yogic tradition) in meditation. Whatever the saints imagined or wished for became their instant reality—rather as my small sample of the *Nada* became my very consciousness and experience. Imagination and reality are a dynamic. Everything is imagery, as Meister Eckhart claimed. Creation is a great metaphor, a play of images and transference of image.

The fifth chakra is the more restricted sensory form of the sixth, which is pure intelligence. In our Piagetian counterpart of child development, it is our isolated intellect that cuts itself off from all other considerations in order to analyze, dissect, recombine, and play with physical experience. But the intelligence of the sixth chakra is the intelligence of God, that power of creation that exists as the well-being of all creation, not to combine and play with a limited physical experience, but with the whole flow of creation as itself. Real maturation welds heart and head, unites the sixth chakra with the fourth. Insight, in the sense of David Bohm's realm of insight-intelligence, is the seventh chakra, a seeing-within, when our self sees as our Self in its entirety, unsupported, complete and perfect without expression, without existence, without experience. Locked into our physical awareness as we are, dependent on relationship for existence, we cannot grasp how we could be aware of awareness itself, rather than aware of thoughts or things. Only through the grace of the teacher, who can lend us that very experience because he stands in that state while in our world, can we get a glimpse of this state in meditation, and thus understand what the goal is.

Insight's intelligence, that unifying force that always moves on behalf of the creation, is intuition in its highest sense. When the seventh chakra—God as God, Shiva, the non-moving point—expresses itself, intelligence is the first aspect of that expression and is the unifying aspect, or the intuition, of all further expressions. Intelligence is the bond between creator and created. This is why the sixth chakra, intelligence, is called the Guru Chakra. The word *guru* is Sanskrit for dark-light, and means the teacher, the force or principle that models, bonds, and leads from the darkness of ignorance into the light of knowledge.

My teacher Gurumayi of Ganeshpuri, representative of this principle, urges us to concentrate on the fourth chakra, the heart of the system, that pivotal point between human and divine. Centered in that pivotal point, we are in the world but not of it, the union of biological and spiritual. Premature concentration on the seventh chakra might take us to the goal, but we would be less effective in the world of everyday affairs. Concentrated on the fourth chakra, the intelligence of the sixth chakra flows into the love at the center and directs our lives for a balanced fulness.

Concentrated in the heart chakra, we are both effective in the world and the bonds are made for our final shift beyond the world when our time to leave it comes. Our Shakti is always working on all our chakras, even as we settle our sights on the one in the heart. Concentrated on the heart, Kundalini does her work beneath awareness, as needed, so long as we make our response to the will of that heart, as guided by the teacher.

In spiritual development our awareness is moved into the causal fields out of which our three states of consciousness grew—physical, subtle, and causal—in order that we might then move into the fourth realm beyond all brains and states. We must, however, make this movement through the three brains in our skull; Kundalini must use the conceptual development of each brain as the basis for her movement into the open-ended blueprint of possibility. The best analogy is our little child abstracting out of her sensory-motor achievement of learning to open that door. She applies the essence or idea within that action on an ever-wider level, into the general category of all possible doors. This is the pattern throughout development. Our doors open to ever-wider vistas, finally into that state from which all springs, if we are willing. The saying "God becomes human that the human might become God" summarizes the blueprint of development we carry within us. The door to our development is the door to our hearts, and the models of that development are people who live in that heart. The blind cannot lead the blind.

17

Always Becoming

In the early 1930s, the German philosopher Eugen Herrigel spent six years with a Zen master in Japan who taught Zen through archery. When the Zen master prepared to shoot the bow, he waited until "it" breathed him. At that point, "it" shot the bow. The bow used in Zen archery requires the strength of the strongest man to bend it at all, and the bow is held above the head, arms almost straight up, making leverage difficult. When "it" breathes the master and bends the bow, however, the master's muscles remain loose and flaccid. (At night the master could sink the arrow into the bull's-eye at sixty paces in a darkened hall, and split that arrow with another.)[1]

An action that can move us from within, without our muscular input, is paradoxical and largely unbelievable. That such a force then fuses, in effect, the archer, his bow, the arrow, and target into a single, synchronous event is even more paradoxical. But paradox, as we have seen, is the threshold of truth, the boundary between logical sets. The boundary can only be crossed by a suspension of one logic and the adoption of another. In Chapter 10, I discussed the general principle of complementarity in quantum physics. We can observe either the wave aspects of an event, the non-localized form of energy, or the particle form of the event, the localized form of energy. Both are needed to explain the event completely, yet the states are mutually exclusive. David Bohm and yogic psychology consider both states an aspect of a single consciousness. Consciousness can display itself as localized or non-localized energy. Localized energy, as matter, is a restricted energy. Non-local energy is unrestricted. The issue is, What is the dynamic between? David Bohm and Rupert Sheldrake propose that non-localized energy has within it the implications of the form that will be assumed when the energy localizes. I presented a case for these modes of energy and causation as translations of our triune brain structure. Only from the realm of insight-intelligence, from which these energies spring, are they fused into their single unity. The bonding function is that overall unity.

The Zen master with whom Eugen Herrigel studied used to take a student's bow, hold it, wait for it to breathe him, and use the bow in this fashion for a time. And for a time thereafter the bow would respond for the student as it did for the teacher, without the student's muscular action. This gave the student some toehold, at least, in a logic quite outside our ordinary biological reference. The purpose of the teacher is to give us this experience of the bridge between localized and non-localized consciousness, that we may begin the construction of a new, non-localized logic. Leaping logical gaps is the function of bonding, and bonding is the function of the teacher. With the concrete experience of the bow bending without muscular action, the student can open to the abstract possibilities.

A perfect example of the model-and-bonding function is the mother at birth. A bond between mother and child is established in utero and re-established and reinforced at birth through the mother's physical and emotional nurturing. She provides the infant with the impetus for his own potential to unfold. She is, in effect, the bridge between localized and non-localized fields. Bonding is not an afterthought, like a rope thrown in to tie up a package. Bonding is the unifying force of creativity itself, which keeps nucleus and electron in their atomic pattern; holds Bohm's quantum energies in their unity; is the force of the stimulus-response function through which our blueprint for intelligence unfolds; and acts within us to assure infant, parent, family, earth, social, and spiritual union. Bonding cuts across and overrides all states of consciousness or energy fields. The bond, which exists in each of the stages through which we move, acts as the bridge spanning the logical threshold separating each stage. For the bond to manifest, however, it must be presented graphically, through a tangible, flesh-and-blood model, to act as the stimulus for our blueprint's response.

The goal of the post-biological period is to move beyond the biological, to free ourselves of dependency on it. As we move up in development, the paradox increases, the stakes are higher, the need for a model more critical. But to move beyond the biological is a paradox of major proportions, since we have only biological patterns of conception and perception to work with. As Herrigel found, all he had was his functional sensory-motor system, his muscles and bones, to bend that bow. Without the teacher who can represent both states at once, who can demonstrate the dynamic of leaping the paradox, we are largely helpless. Herrigel could have stood holding that bow for many a year to no avail. He continually tried intellectually to figure out and, in effect, synthesize the leap. Only the true teacher can break this evolutionary compulsion and lead us to that point of allowing integration into that non-localized realm through bonding.

Counterfeits of spiritual development abound, and beneath all counterfeits one finds a sub-stratum, a hidden agenda of concern over the biological system. The point of the spiritual venture is to get beyond the biological. The realm beyond the biological encompasses the biological but not the other way around. Winning the biological game has nothing to do with surpassing it. Perfecting ourselves physically and mentally, according to our intellectual notions of perfection, has nothing to do with the real goal. Nor has bringing about some paradisaical kingdom on earth.

Jesus commented that it was better to be crippled, blind, and maimed in body but in the Kingdom within, than be physically whole and outside that Kingdom. Referring to a famous man, he said: "Among men born of woman there is none greater than he, but the least of those in the Kingdom are greater." Perfection according to our cultural criteria plays no part in the ultimate game. The goal lies within ourselves and nothing in the entire visible world—other than another person who has achieved that goal—has anything to do with, or offers the slightest hint toward, that inner goal or its attainment. There are no grand strategies available to our intellect by which the ultimate goal is reached, though culture creates an endless stream of counterfeits, all promising an intellectual dominance over the spirit. Castaneda's Don

Juan warned that once you are on a path, it is difficult to get off. The more powerful the path (and some of the martial arts, for instance, are powerful paths), the more powerful this holding effect. For one is altered in brain/mind and changed by one's path, even when it is a path we are making. All paths are creative ventures, and in creating or re-creating a path we are conceptually restructured to some extent.

The positive aspect of all this is that we need no credentials to enter into the reversal procedure leading to spirit. As with Zen, no virtue, accomplishment, skill, or talent gained in the world of folly has anything to do with the path to the Self. The surprise turnabout of expectation is that the path unfolds only by a sole concentration on the goal. We have no access even to the game rules, for they are generated from that Self we would achieve. The Self we pursue instructs us in the only pursuit by which that Self can be attained.[2] Each movement along the path opens for us only as we make that movement, with our eyes on the goal.

"There are those who would take the Kingdom by storm," Jesus commented, and they do so by intellectually devised strategems. Perhaps they succeed at their game, but it is their game and the self they attain is but an enhancement of the intellectual ego, a counterfeit of the real, another subset to spin about in the orbit of cosmic junk. The move toward maturation begins when a willing student meets a true teacher, and the only requirement is the student's willingness. The only requirement of true teachers is that they have achieved that mature state.

One can enter the new development blind and crippled since no physical criteria apply. Nor does entry into the new development mean that physical and mental failings will necessarily be remedied. The higher integral structure integrates the lower, according to that higher logic. The highest integration can cut through all enculturation and restructure our system as needed. But what is needed? Nothing we can think of in our enculturated state. If we could think those needs out they would be available intellectually.

Therapy is a great illusion. Whatever patching up is needed will be done by the Kundalini Shakti, the intelligence that leads to the Self. Kundalini can skip grades. She employs a Knight's move, skipping over our logical syllogisms with ease and repairing whatever needs to be repaired to move us along on our path.

Few statements have been so puzzling as Jesus' command: "Be ye perfect as your Father in Heaven is perfect." We are perfect at any moment of our lives in which we are oriented toward the Self. Perfection *is* that orientation. No matter that our childhood has been horrible or our career a bust. All dysfunctions in our biological state may be meaningless in regard to the path. To stop and supposedly perfect some aspect of our system is to position that aspect as our goal—and at that point we lose perfection.

Lesser teachers busy themselves with elaborate schools through which they display their erudition and intellectual skills. Elaborate schema are laid out by which we engineer our paths. The egos of both teacher and student love this eclectic play, for these are endless delaying games, in which inflation of ego is interpreted as spiritual superiority. We come up with continual systems for perfecting ourselves, but the Self is already perfect. Until identified with that state, however, we can have no notion of what perfection means.

My teacher Muktananda came into the kitchen of the ashram one day to fry *dosas* (a kind of pancake in which various fillings are rolled, making the shape of a dosa important: The more perfectly round, or at least oval, the better). A whole bunch of dosas could be fried at once on the huge ashram griddle, and Muktananda took the pan of dosa mix and began to throw ladles full of batter out in grand fashion. The results were awful. No two dosas were anything alike; their shapes ran the gamut of ink-blot catastrophes. We cringed. Baba was a master cook, had taught his cooks to do dosas perfectly, yet at each monstrosity he threw out, he said, "Ah! Perfect, perfect."

Slowly his lesson registered on us. We were those dosas, the monstrosities and messes, the misshapen enculturated and insane figures which he was to somehow roll into a new shape and fill with new life. And what he was telling us was that he saw us as what we really were: perfect. The perfect dosa, the perfect human, is the creative process within us, the "Father in heaven," a blueprint of possibility for our beings. By filling in that blueprint with the content of our lives, an infinite number of shapes must unfold. And this infinite variety of shapes is precisely what the play of consciousness is all about.

The play of consciousness is *stochastic,* to use Gregory Bateson's term.[3] Nature makes available an infinite possibility, in which anything and everything can and is going to happen. She operates by profusion, and a certain random, chance element underlies everything. Nature has, however, within her random potential, a clear objective. (Jesus referred to a broad way that leads to destruction, and a narrow gate that leads to the Self.) The only requirement of the ultimate game, the movement to the Self, is the option itself; and, opting for that Self, I am immediately turned toward that path. I believe that the major limitation of my earlier book, *Magical Child,* was to propose that some hypothetically perfect upbringing would alone give a true maturation and full humanity, that we would then come into our true power. And I saw in various paranormal experience indications of that power.

Whose criteria should we use for the perfect Magical Child? Whose curriculum? No matter how we tried, at each stage we would leave out an untouched mass of potential, and be "imperfect." Any stage of development has meaning only as it is integrated into a higher structure of meaning and in turn supports that higher structure. The entire Piagetian stage of development has value only as the platform for the next stage, the spiritual journey. For the physical stage to be successful, it must be integrated into and support the spiritual. Any other use is an alignment with our inevitable physical death. The final goal is the only criterion: Development must be in line with our ultimate goal. With the ultimate goal as the criterion, each stage will unfold as needed for us to stay in line with that goal. The goal has its agenda, and creates that which is necessary to achieve that goal, and, in the stochastic play of consciousness, the goal never repeats itself. Each of us is our own curriculum.

The parent of that "perfect child" is one aligned with the path toward the Self. If the parent has, as his own personal model, the true teacher, the representative of that final state, then the child automatically has that ultimate model as the underlying structure on which that child's life and learning will be based. Within that framework anything can happen (everything always does happen), and the system will work perfectly. The content and information of our experience are always expendable, of use only as a means of developing ability. And the ability gained in our childhood and adolescence is the ability to enter onto the path of post-biological development. A life that mirrors the model of that teacher who is in that state of the Self is always unique and perfect.

Here the issue of bonding or attachment comes into focus. The attached ego cannot make itself available to the teacher but must, automatically, through the non-conscious survival drive within, try to incorporate the teaching into the ego system. The logic of this is unassailable, too, because we desire enlightenment; we set about incorporating it into our system as we have been trained to do. Yet this will not work because all the power, information, experience, and possibility ever available from the realm of our three brains and our minds can never add up to the fourth realm, the Self. We cannot incorporate the path to the goal, for that goal does not exist. The goal is not a commodity, information, practice, content, conceptual material, or a product to be thought about; it is an empty category for us until given content, and we give it content by our response to it. We cannot respond to an empty category, but only to something tangible, which leaves us in a double bind that only the teacher can break.

We naturally respond to the concept of having a goal; we conceptualize some image of the probabilities of what the goal should be; we convert our imagery into a blueprint of the goal and immediately set about filling in our blueprint with our own content. We thereby create a self-fulfilling tape-loop effect of real delusion. We create a novel synthesis of our folly, then wonder why our world crashes down on us in ever greater ruins.

I have already explored how we replicate culture and the double bind we face in the resulting dysfunctions. I have outlined how we are driven by our survival instincts to maintain the integrity of our egos; how, since nature cannot program for failure, our intellect rationalizes protection of our egos in its dysfunctional state. Only a force outside this tape-loop can break our deadlock. Should the Self within our hearts directly rise within us (as it does continually) to break through to us, its signals are incorporated into the tape-loop effect and selectively screened or interpreted to maintain integrity of our system as it is, and we will never be aware of

all this defensive action. We manipulate the imagery unconsciously, in spite of ourselves. Dysfunction lies in the identity
with the intellect as it is: a one-way mirror reflecting on its
own thought about its own material world, picked up and
echoed throughout the supportive systems of the brain. Once
this self-replicating tape-loop makes one error, the error itself
must then self-replicate. When this happens on a broad cultural level, the power of that error is immense.

The only way out of such dysfunction is to bypass the
dysfunctional system completely. Our survival system, interpreting this as tantamount to loss of integrity, will not allow
this, but will bring about a rationalization to avoid it. Our
intellectual minds are only a reflector and receptor of brain
function, yet we think our one-way mirror of mind can integrate our three facets of brain, our physical, emotional, and
intellectual modes, into a unit of wholeness. (The new-
consciousness movements centered on this fallacy.) We cannot take three separate physical objects, put them in front of
a mirror, and expect the mirror to fuse those three into a
single unit. The only possibility of integrating the fragmented
ego comes from the Self, presented to us in tangible form:
the teacher in flesh and blood who cannot be rationalized or
manipulated, but who forces the issue and compels a decision.

The biggest problem of spiritual development is to shift
us from attachment behavior to a bonded state. Once the
bond with the Self is firm, integration takes place as a natural, progressive development paralleling our earlier development in general outline. To wean us from attachment behavior
the teacher follows a fairly standard procedure. First, he
gives *Shaktipat*, an infusion into us of the creative power of
the Self. When the teacher gives Shaktipat he infuses into us
the Shakti from his own integration into the Self, and stimulates our own Shakti within us. The teacher arouses our
Kundalini by lending us his power much as the mother lends
the infant her power at birth until the infant can generate his
own.

The teacher's own power, infused into our system, bonds
us with the teacher and our Self, and immediately begins the
restructuring of our conceptual system. David Bohm said that
insight could push thought out of the way and remove dysfunctions in the brain. This is a major part of the teacher's
job. Once the Kundalini is awakened and active, by this

initial move of the teacher's, that power continues the job of transformation. Given the stimulus, the response is automatic and assured.

Originally I thought that Shaktipat was a once-for-all event, that once the Kundalini was awakened the job was done. Since my early days in Siddha yoga I have found that Shaktipat can be an ongoing procedure, a continued renewal of the stimulus. At birth the infant imprints to a face pattern if given that pattern at the required distance for the required period; we also found that the infant needed a continual return to and restimulus by that model if development was to be rapid and thorough. In *Bond of Power* I wrote of several Shaktipat experiences with Muktananda, both my own and others . Each experience of Shaktipat clears away more mental debris and widens our concepts, as the teacher guides the Kundalini.

Earlier in this book I mentioned the two particles of energy that, once part of a closed system, mirrored each other regardless of time and space. I used this example from Bell's theorem to demonstrate how bonding works. Once I had met my teacher, our bond held outside time and space. It did not matter that we were on opposite sides of the globe, because he was in constant contact, within the logic of the bonding process, with me. If I got seriously out of line with my goal (which I certainly did), he clobbered me on the spot in unmistakable ways. The gap between error and correction closes when we are in alignment with the teacher.

Another function of the teacher is to give the student a direct sensory experience of the goal, according to the student's capacity to conceptualize, or transfer the imagery involved. Just as the Zen master uses the student's bow in order to give the student the experience of what the bow does when "it" breathes the student, so the teacher gives the student an experience of the teacher's own state within whatever capacity the student has to receive.

In my four years with Muktananda I had many meditation and Shaktipat experiences—sensory, visual experiences of other states of consciousness. In each case these were teaching experiences and a particular lesson was involved (for example, in my being taken out of my body each morning those five consecutives times). The lesson of this was direct, clear, and unmistakable. Further, such a lesson expanded my conceptual framework. Even the most non-ordinary sort of perceptual experiences, such as the *Nada*, the *Amrit*, the breathtaking visual ventures, were clear lessons in the play of consciousness; each in turn expanded my consciousness. Many of the experiences, though subtle, related directly to my ordinary physical orientation and greatly enhanced it. My ordinary perceptions were being stretched into new dimensions, which changed my responses to my ordinary world, giving me more flexibility and freedom than I had known.

In each case, I thought these events were experiences of the Self. This was not correct but all right, for they were so exhilarating that they stirred me on in my spiritual practice. In 1983, under Muktananda's successor, Gurumayi, I had an ongoing series of experiences from her Shaktipat, which were essentially causal by nature, not subtle, as though my four years with Muktananda had been only preparatory to being able to handle straight causal function as itself. (Earlier I briefly described my various limbs levitating during meditation, following Gurumayi's Shaktipat.) These experiences also translated through my physical system or related to it in some way. So all my experiences in yoga to this point had been from the standpoint of my usual physical state extending out into unusual states. None of this was an experience of the Self within me from the vantage point of that Self.

A year later I again received Shaktipat from Baba's successor, Gurumayi. Following this I experienced, so far as I can tell in retrospect, an experience of that fourth realm itself, as itself. It was qualitatively discontinuous with anything in my life and without physical points of reference—and so non-reportable. I came out of that state realizing that everything in my experience up to that point had again been only preliminary, a clearing of debris and building of enough foundation that I could undergo a brief exposure to the goal. And it came as a surprise to me that possibly only then, from that point, was a path actually opening within me; only then was development (as opposed to mere remedial work) ready to begin. I had experienced a possibility of rebirth, but with the real gestation yet to take place. The notion of rebirth has suffered from a bit of casual misinterpretation and oversimplification. At rebirth one is born into a new conceptual system ready for a developmental process that is as long and involved as was our original development from our first infancy.

The state of the Self is creation itself. The experience of that state is an experience of creation. To receive the experience is to enter into the creation of it. Again, one does not perceive God; God is the *act* of perception. The entry we make into creation is contingent on the nature of our teacher (who is mother, father, and midwife to the new state), the teacher's lineage or tradition, and one's own history. The teacher gives us a concrete experience of that state of creation, but it is our state, not the teacher's. We are the dynamic between teacher as stimulus and our Self as response.

To try to patch up our background through therapy or other means is pointless since the Self cannot be brought about by additions to the three modes of our brain and mind. Our total concentration must be on the goal, and that means the teacher and teaching. With our attention on the goal, the Kundalini patches as needed for movement to that goal. The teacher's job is to wean us from our identification with our physical, emotional, and intellectual developments and re-identify with the universal or causal fields out of which these conceptual processes grew. The teacher must move us beyond our sensual natures; not because our sensual natures are bad (we can hardly do without them), but because they are limited. An archetypal field of sensuality, limitless and awesome, awaits us.

In the same way, we must be weaned from our childish emotions, our esthetics of like and dislike that were so vital to our early development and around which our structure of ego was built. Again, this process is necessary not because our esthetics are bad but because they are divisive and crippling to further development. (This is not easy. To treat all sensory experience as equal I tell my body that the hot shower and cold shower are just relative states, but I have a difficult time telling my soul that the strange wailing of a Hindu woman singing *bhajans* is equal to Bach's B Minor Mass. My esthetic snobbery dies hard.) The emotion of pure love awaits us beyond our primitive likes and dislikes, and an ecstatic esthetic experience lies ahead.

Our teacher must finally wean us from our intellects, the lifeblood of our egos. Then we can open to pure intelligence, and the power of not-doing, which is the subject of the last chapter of this book. And through all these weanings and experiences beyond the biological, we prepare for the final weaning, from our identity as a limited ego, a separated self, to the realization of being the Self, from which we were never really separated at all.

Without the teacher we sense the nature of such moves and unconsciously try to incorporate the movements back into our ego identity. Little by little the teacher tightens the bond and weakens our attachment. This teacher principle, this model function, is built into the life system. We have been subject to it from our very beginnings. At each stage of development we are subject to the character and nature of our models; life provides us—or tries to—with an ongoing series of teachers as needed by each stage. The society without the proper model of a teacher aligned to the Self is unnatural and illogical; it becomes psychotic and self-destructive. Intellect estranged from intelligence grows increasingly illogical and, finally, insane. Can you think of anything more illogical than one hundred thousand nuclear warheads when a mere one thousand will destroy life on earth?

Some fifteen centuries ago, Saint Augustine wrote that there was never a time in the history of man when that which is called the Christ was not among us. The teacher is an ongoing principle, a functional part of us, and the bond of the creative process. In the Christian Gospels Jesus is referred to as one of a long line of teachers (rabbis). He referred to himself that way, and continually pointed beyond himself to the teacher principle on which his life was based. "Before Abraham was, I am," he stated. He promised that after his death he would return to his followers within their own generation. He was even more explicit in the Gnostic Gospels, where he not only promised that soon after his death he would return in another form, as another teacher, but said, in the greatest statement ever made about this teacher principle: "I am always becoming what you have need of me to be."

The teacher appears, generation after generation, as we have need of him to be, in flesh-and-blood form. The teacher meets us where we are, as we are ready, able, and willing to be met. He or she appears on behalf of our post-biological development, since learning takes place from direct encounter. *Theophany*, an "appearance of the God," is an integral part of human experience; each true teacher is a theophany. Theophany is, as well, a way of initiating the role of the teacher where no model exists within a culture. Theophany takes place sporadically as our Shakti searches for chances to display the goal in tangible form. My favorite story of a theophany is contemporary, from the anthropologist Adolf Jensen. I used the example in my book *Exploring the Crack in the Cosmic Egg,* and do so again because I see it now in a richer light. Jensen's report comes from an Apinaye hunter of one of the Ge tribes of eastern Brazil. The hunter reported:

> I was hunting near the sources of the Botica Creek. All along the journey there I had been agitated and was constantly startled without knowing why.
>
> Suddenly I saw him standing under the drooping branches of a big steppe tree. He was standing there erect. His club was braced against the ground beside him, his hand he held on the hilt. He was tall and light-skinned, and his hair nearly descended to the ground behind him. His whole body was painted and on the outer side of his legs were broad red stripes. His eyes were exactly like two stars. He was very handsome.
>
> I recognized at once that it was he. Then I lost all my courage. My hair stood on end, and my knees were trembling. I put my gun aside, for I thought to myself that I should have to address him. But I could not utter a sound because he was looking at me unwaveringly. Then I lowered my head in order to get hold of myself and stood thus for a long time. When I had grown somewhat calmer, I raised my head. He was still standing and looking at me. Then I pulled myself together and walked several steps toward him, then I could not go any farther for my knees gave way. I again remained standing for a long time. Then I lowered my head, and tried again to regain composure. When I raised my eyes again, he had already turned away and was slowly walking through the steppes.
>
> Then I grew very sad.[4]

He always appears as we have need of him to be: to the hunter, as the perfect hunter. And he confronted the Apinaye with that perfection. He was, of course, the hunter's own projected Self, concretized and made real. The Apinaye was terrified, as we would be, for the address he knows he must make to the God will apparently mean his own end as he has known himself. The hunter speaks for each of us, since, though the God appears as we have need of him to be, we instinctively try to convert that God to what we want him to be. The biological will to survive paralyzes us, and we try to incorporate the spiritual into our physical state. Attachment behavior seems built in. I suspect that could the hunter have made the confrontation, he would have returned to his people inwardly transformed. Integrated into his Self, he would have then acted as the catalytic agent by which a new dimension of consciousness could have opened within his people. He would have become the Teacher.

The hunter's integration would have resulted in that society's movement toward transcendence, not toward our notions of civilization. They would not necessarily have built better guns for hunting or exploiting neighbors, nor created an abstract alphabet to read our enlightening newspapers. We do not get beyond the biological block into the freedom of spirit through our jetcraft, rocketry, sciences, algebras, or quantum physics, nor literacy competency tests and college degrees. The Self exists within us and has its own criteria. The Apinaye might have ended as a society based on certain dances around a fire through which a coiled serpent unfolded from their spine, moved up, and carried them into realms beyond all bombs and dioxins, bulldozers and asphalt. Evolution's statistical play of consciousness may have won in that remote sector, quietly and unannounced.

In a culture such as ours, with no tangible teachers, we remain in our spiritual natures like that twenty-two-year-old woman found tied in an attic: vegetable, mindless, and lost. People complain of a poor quality of leadership today, but from where do we draw our leaders? How can those in darkness bring light? When we look to the world of folly for our leaders we get only fools, and we deserve no better. We can, in the privacy of our own being, at least, look elsewhere for our own private leadership, and we will always find it.

Saint Simeon, in the eleventh century, wrote that the saints of history are "linked together and united by the bond of the Holy Spirit. . . . Those who appear from generation to generation, following the saints who preceded them . . . be-

come linked with their predecessors and . . . filled with the
same light. In such a sequence all of them together form a
kind of golden chain, each saint being a separate link in this
chain . . . which has its strength in God and can hardly be
broken."

Simeon goes on: "A man who does not express desire to
link himself to the latest of the saints in time in all love and
humility, owing to a certain distrust. . . will never be linked
with the preceding saints and will not be admitted to their
succession, even though he thinks he possesses all possible
faith and love for God and for all his saints. He will be cast
out of their midst, as one who refused to take humbly the
place allotted to him by God before all time, and to link
himself to that latest saint in time as God had disposed."[5]

Always the focus is on the flesh-and-blood model, the
representative of the Self here among us. In the West this
practical fact has long been lost to politics and enculturation,
but in some parts of the world this lineage has been maintained. In *Bond of Power* I pointed out that genius never
arises in a desert but out of conditions of great ferment and
activity. To a society of people who have power, power is
given, along every line.

India, in spite of its collapse into chaos following centuries of foreign domination, rape, and pillage, has somehow
maintained a deep stratum of genuine spiritual investment.
In the vast countryside, where foreign influence is less marked
than in those cesspool cities of which we hear so much, lies
an astonishing depth of spiritual power. The relation of God
and human runs to the core of the basic Indian village society. Even if much of it is empty formalism, this too has been
imprinted for thousands of years and is an unbroken heritage.
Enormous reserves of spiritual power remain, fed both by the
devotion of common people and by a surprisingly large number of fully realized individuals, people who have achieved
the highest state.

India produces a steady stream of these religious ge-
niuses, great beings who arise from her soil because they find
the proper nutrients for full spiritual growth. That India does
not match our technological standards is beside the point.
The heart of spiritual power on this globe is probably India,
today as always. India has always given us Siddhas, great
beings who have broken the deadlock of the biological block

and achieved the highest transcendence. And today, in a historic shift, perhaps a last-chance gambit by the spirit, teachers again beckon to us from India, again offer to bring us back to sanity. The wise men from the East have traditionally come to the West, and now that the chaos of the West is sweeping the East, a true crisis impends. "I am always becoming what you have need of me to be" was the promise made, and it is always being kept for those with ears to hear and eyes to see. Our need today is an exemplar, a model of who we really are. Such models are among us, and offer us our only avenue to that change we must undergo. I see small chance of the change necessary for us taking place on a broad enough scale to stem the tide. But each of us must work individually, in the inner privacy of our lives, to make ourselves available to the only change that counts.

18

Not Doing

When athletes suspend the interference of intellect and allow the body's own intelligence to take over, their muscles respond magnificently, as though of a mind of their own. The martial arts display an intriguing extension of this. George Leonard, in *The Silent Pulse*,[1] tells of thirty-five-year-old Richard taking his black-belt examination in Aikido. At a certain point Richard suspended not so much his intellectual interference as his whole ego dominance. At that point "it breathed him," as the Zen practitioners would say. He heard a phrase over and over: "I am not Richard," not that social persona so carefully nurtured all his life. His body became a single fluid action and a gold light suffused the hall, witnessed by all present.

Further extensions of this are found in Zen archery, as we saw in the last chapter. A force takes over and one's entire motor system is bypassed. Herrigel referred to this as "not-doing," a term picked up by Carlos Castaneda. I once spent a number of weeks with a self-taught yogi who was attempting to break through the acculturated shell of my mind. One evening we sat for long hours in straight-backed chairs beneath a bare lightbulb hanging from the ceiling. Toward midnight, "it" breathed the yogi. He was large and fat, but fell into a state of deep relaxation where his huge limbs floated in the air. His muscles were not involved. It was a numinous experience for him and he wept.[2] In yoga and Sufism there is a final application of this not-doing. The Sufi call it the divine hint and the yogis refer to the concept of doership. Just as Richard, in his black-belt exam, discovered that he was not-Richard, the yogis say we must discover that we are not the doer.

On either side of my teacher Muktananda's chair were two inscriptions. One read: "The guru is the root of all action." The other read: "Only he who obeys can command." Together they describe the divine hint and give the key to its development, for it is a central issue in spiritual growth. In the New Testament, Jesus spoke of doing the "Father's will," an action, and I always wondered what such doing might be. The idea of a will of God has been bandied about for millennia, the source of riotous bloodshed, political chicanery, and general fanaticism. The reason for this obscurity of meaning is that this will is only a hint. It is implied, a subtle phenomenon, and has no content; it takes on content by being enacted. It is a causal process, a blueprint of the instant moment that can be filled only by our corresponding response within that instant. To be enacted, the implicate order hint must use an explicate order actor who must be willing to be so used, someone whose will is in resonance with the will behind that hint.

This will is elusive because the process may act through one person on behalf of some other person without the actor's knowledge. The one through whom the will is translated into action may not be aware that this is taking place. So any action can be the vehicle by which the hint is given content, unbeknown to the one acting. This can occur, though, only when an individual's volitional will is centered on the notion of the divine hint and being open to it. So when we are actually *in* this will and doing it we need not know the particulars of how that will unfolds through us, since every act we make is then a possible channel for this divine hint to be expressed.

Since a play of consciousness is involved, the divine hint can be displayed in quite playful, light ways, within the flow of the moment. Siddha Yoga holds two-day meditation workshops called intensives, in which the teacher goes around and gives each person "the touch," a laying on of hands that transmits the teacher's Shakti to the recipient. A friend of mine attended an intensive, following an automobile accident in which her foot had been injured and failed to heal properly. When Muktananda came around giving the touch he stepped on her bad foot with his whole body weight and kept it there for a time before moving on. The pain was considerable for the woman but the foot quickly healed. Since she was quite new to Siddha Yoga, had never seen Muktananda before, and there were 1,250 people taking the intensive, she wondered how he knew about the foot. He knew not by some hocus-pocus or ESP; knowing in our sense was not part of his response. The teacher is one in a state of balance, a flow that is maintained only by making the appropriate response to each moment's unfolding. Stepping on that foot was simply an impulse that felt right and had no more meaning, and needed no more reason, than brushing a fly off one's nose.

The divine hint arises out of all possibilities inherent within each moment of encounter. Within all possible responses inherent within a moment's relation lies the right option, the intelligent move that meets the needs of that situation. When I first met Muktananda and recognized him as the source of a power I had never known, I wanted to ask him to bless (the word *bless* means bestowal of power) a talisman memento I wore around my neck. On approaching him with my request the foolishness of such a petty notion struck me and I could not say anything to him at all and turned to leave. He grabbed me, took my memento from around my neck, looked at it, rubbed it, and with a smile put it back. Again, there was no mind-reading as such. The issue of the encounter was the memento, and to that he responded simply because that was the appropriateness of the moment. Words were unnecessary. Recall the discussion of the bonded mothers and their diaperless infants "going to the bushes." Bonding brings about the appropriate response according to the needs of the situation, and words are superfluous. The communication takes place in the realm of non-locality and is enacted on location.

We can maintain the flow of intelligent harmony through this response of appropriateness; it arcs into the present as an intent toward action. To dwell on a possible action, to analyze it or reflect on it, is the job of intellect. We certainly need to employ intellect, but it is a very slow and primitive process in comparison with the divine hint, which is faster than lightning. Intellect must close the openness of any moment's context in order to tape-loop, play back over some specific possibility. This action immediately ties the three-fold brain system into self-replication. When we reflect, we are not in the context of the moment. And to lose our identity to our ensuing tape-loop, to get caught in its circuitry, is attachment behavior.

Carlos Castaneda spoke of *indulgence,* our attempt to take some grace being given us and tape-loop it into our brains for playback, in order to dwell on the transient event and give it some kind of permanence. This attachment behavior cuts us off from the flow of real events and locks us into a true illusion. If the brain/mind is involved in playback, the present moment is lost, and with it the divine hint, the action that maintains the balanced flow of all things.

Muktananda's spontaneous responses to the divine hint appear differently in the light of our mundane world. All my life I have entertained the covert notion of doing the will of God. But should I suddenly feel impelled to step on some woman's foot my intellect would rebel. I would demand good logical reasons for such a notion and would deem it necessary to discuss the issue with the person concerned. All my training and instincts are channeled to analyze, predict, and control incoming information, most of which I do very poorly by constant thinking. Reception of a divine hint is not possible until one is free of such biological blocks, since reception and acting out of the hint are a single, unbroken response. Time and again Muktananda was asked (as his two successors are now): "What do you think about when making the appropriate response?" To which he would counter: "What fool would be thinking at such a time?"

Our brains are designed for far more than thinking, or reprocessing information. In my meditation and mystical experiences I do not hash over the experience as it is being given, for that would immediately terminate the experience. Nor do I think. I perceive, I receive the gift. I can experience the reality given but I cannot compute on it at the same time. Thinking sets apart from the flow of reality those items to be thought about, at which point those items are not real but imaginary; they are images played back and forth within my system. Our huge new brain is designed, among other things, to respond to the divine hint, which manifests in "abstract" or non-localized terms and which we must give their locality through instant response. This action opens us to whole universes of non-computable reality, a reality where computa-

tion is trivial and useless. The new brain and mind are
designed to operate free of the primitive emotional and instinctive mediation our animal brains impose. The superior
energy of the new brain and mind can operate on the simpler
brains and use them as instruments without their emotional
clutter and instinctive concerns.

What do we do with our new brain? Again, research
estimates we use a scant ten percent of it, and use that for
attending to matters reported on by our primary brains.
Intellection is a primitive use of the new brain and can
employ only a bit of it. When the Zen master is breathed by
it, the bow bends, the arrow strikes the bull's-eye, and so on.
The relationship among archer, bow, arrow, and target shifts
from the ordinary world of divided parts, each in its orbit and
logic, to a single fused unit. At this point only the event, and
none of its component parts, exists. It is the totality of master, arrow, target, and so on. The moment of its "breathing"
the master is the opening of mind to its two-way function.
Now the new brain is employed as designed—at least in this
restricted, rather formal Zen way. This is the practice of the
will of God, the divine hint, within this Zen tradition; the will
integrates whatever parts of the physical realm the target of
integration requires. Training in Zen archery is rigorous because it must break down our insistence on using intellection
when it does not fit, and our resistance to giving over to
integration. Our evolutionary past must be bypassed, the
animal integrated into the human, and the human suspended
as needed to a process beyond the biological.

If we are going to suspend predictive control, we must
do so on behalf of a more integrated order. We do this by
starting on the most mundane level. Herrigel spent years of
frustration holding that bow and trying to get all the movements right by ordinary intellectual processing. He finally
bankrupted his intellect and it breathed him. To maintain his
newfound awareness he had to practice with his bow daily,
without fail.

In 1976 I had dropped out of the world, left no address,
and declared I would never again write a book or lecture in
public. I met Baba Muktananda and he informed me that
meditation was not in caves but in the middle of Main Street
and urged me to resume writing and lecturing. This was not
in keeping with my idea of a spiritual path and quite difficult

for me to do, but eventually I submitted and began the old grind. In October of 1982, when Muktananda died, Siddha Yoga suspended all activities and we spent some three weeks in meditation and chanting. I resumed activities in late October and flew to Chicago to take part in an intensive being given by one of Baba's monks.

The thrust of my two talks at that intensive was the divine hint, which had been uppermost in my mind for many months, particularly in the four weeks since Baba's death. To make my points about the divine hint I had to refer to Muktananda time and again since he was the only model I had for how the hint operated, and his death was too recent, my emotional edge too raw. I was quite likely to burst into tears simply on hearing his name. Yet my passion for the divine hint and explaining it was greater. So I meditated with that problem in mind, asked Baba for strength, and entered the intensive quite confident. All went well with my first talk until a woman in the very front row, immediately to my right, burst into tears. Instantly my thin edge of control vanished and a sympathetic anguish welled up within me. Just as quickly, though, the impending tears converted to serious anger. I *did* want to make my point about the divine hint and this silly hysteric was about to ruin everything!

I was seated slightly to the left of a large, illuminated portrait of Muktananda which had been placed in his chair. Instantly I was on my feet in a burst of anger. I pointed down at the woman and dramatically exclaimed, "You shouldn't do that sort of thing!" As soon as I had done this, I was both embarrassed at my action (I had never done anything like that before) and relieved; she had glanced up at me with a startled look and slumped into a heap, head down to the floor, silent. "Thank God. Took care of *that* problem."

My own emotional state now stable, I continued my talk, in full control. Break time came and I went over to the woman, still balled up and motionless, put my arms around her, and asked her forgiveness. "I don't know what got into me," I said. "Go away," she mumbled without looking up, "I'll explain later." We came back from the break and she was still there in that slump, and remained that way through the whole meditation period, moving finally during the lunch break. At the end of the day her story came out: Right before Muktananda left the United States to return to India for the last time, this woman had begged him for an experience of the Self, an experience of God, which thousands have from contact with the teacher. Though she had been a devotee for years, and other people had had the experience, she had not. Baba *promised* her that he would give her that experience of the Self.

She never saw him again. In October news came of his death and she was doubly forsaken. Now she would never have an experience of the Self. She had signed up in September for the early November intensive but debated coming because at any mention of Baba she wept. But she came, I started talking about Baba, her grief and loss overcame her, and she burst into tears. At this point she heard a voice saying loudly and imperiously: "You shouldn't do that sort of thing," which she interpreted as Baba telling her that she should never *doubt* him. She glanced up on hearing the words: I was standing directly in front of Baba's illumined photograph, my arm pointing toward her. She, however, saw only *his* picture and this arm pointing at her. And from that pointing finger came a bolt of brilliant light that entered her heart, illuminated it in a great explosion, and she went into a vivid, prolonged experience of the Self. Baba had kept his word.

Note that I was acting out of my own self-interests, centered on the job I had flown to Chicago to do, which was my *seva*, or service to my guru. I was determined to fill my post, and my attention was centered on the subject of my talk, the divine hint and the issue of surrender to the will of the guru within us. And, in this centered, selfish state, I unwittingly became an example of my subject; I became an instrument for my guru's action. Note, however, that it was not necessary that I know that my body movement gave the framework for that action. That I ever should know of such a result of my move was peripheral, beside the point, and none of my business. In fact, to find out that my action had been used in such a way could easily have caused self-consciousness and ego inflation. My actions were within my world, meeting my needs as related to my teacher. My actions within the woman's world and her needs and relations to our same teacher, however, were a different matter. The single action took place in two different worlds, so to speak, and met two different needs. It was not necessary, and is never necessary, that such overlaps be conscious to each of the parties involved for the effect to be played out.

If my anger seems the most unlikely channel for the "will of God," so are tears. The fact is that anything can be a channel for this bonding power. Our criteria do not apply to this non-localized function that brings synchrony to our localized and restricted beings. The divine hint arises out of each moment; every situation generates it whether we translate it or not. So the will of God two minutes from now does not exist, but exists only as it presses into our awareness moment by moment. It cannot be codified into commandments or laws since it does not exist; it cannot stand apart from the instant moment that generates it. Only our reception and enactment of it in this moment exist.

Muktananda's successor, Chidvilasananda, or Gurumayi (which means Guru-mother),[3] served as Baba's interpreter for a number of years. This task demanded an exact interpretation of what Baba said. She was still in her teens when Muktananda came to the West on his second world tour in the mid-seventies. Interaction with young Western people revealed that there were words and topics that were taboo in our more polite circles, and Gurmayi knew that Baba was liable to say anything without regard to our social niceties. Should she not, she wondered, perhaps at times transliterate, that is, substitute words when Baba touched on taboo territory, lest he inadvertently embarrass his audience and jeopardize his work to spread meditation? (And of course, peripherally, also spare herself embarrassment.) She realized, as instantly as this thought occurred, that to do so would be a serious breach of discipline. (She had not been brought up in the ashram under Baba's direct tutelage to no avail.) Whatever her guru said was precisely what she must translate as faithfully as was possible to her. (And Baba gave her ample tests of this fidelity!)

Consider, now, what this young woman had to do. She had to suspend her judgment, her rational, logical responses; suspend her mind-set of protectiveness that tries to predict and control. She had to suspend her social orientation, her esthetic responses, and such social concepts as "What will they think of me?" She had to suspend her self-image in the eyes of the world and concentrate solely on her teacher.

How easy to say this; how difficult to employ over and

over, day in and day out under every condition: radio, television, large audiences, and private meetings with important personages. She was being trained to listen not to her ego or super ego, but to those words of her teacher. This was one of many ways her teacher concretized the divine hint to prepare her for reception of the subtle aspects when she became the guru.

Gurumayi tells of other experiences with Baba. Time and again, she said, Baba would be giving a talk and suddenly stop, stuck for a particular word, phrase, or particular poem he wanted to quote. Baba would look at Gurumayi at that point, perplexed, then irritated, beckoning young Gurumayi to come up with the missing link. Usually there was no remote hint as to what Baba was after, but he would gesture insistently and Gurumayi would suddenly hear herself telling Baba what he wanted to hear. Baba would smile, pleased, and continue his talk. Gurumayi would be mystified about the source of her knowledge, since the quote or name was rarely known to her. (I was witness to this many times, though it was much later before I heard all the ramifications, and understood all that was taking place.)

Gurudev, like his sister Gurumayi, having been brought up in the ashram for this express purpose, was being trained to open to this subtle inner prompting that requires absolute openness and trust. After an elaborate and lengthy preparation for his successor to assume his role as guru (including a huge inaugural with thousands in attendance, lest there be the slightest doubt of his intent), Muktananda left this world. At that point his two young successors, without a moment's hesitation, immediately began to function as their teacher had done. They continued serving as they had always served, though now on the subtle level, their apprenticeship complete.

For a while the overlap between teacher and disciples was obvious, even though the teacher was no longer physically present. For instance, some three months before Muktananda died, a Western woman had a vision of him during her morning meditation. In the vision she asked him to please give her something to remember him by. He replied, in this visionary exchange, that if she would come to Ganeshpuri, India (Baba's main ashram), he had a gold necklace for her. She awoke from the vision in high euphoria, determined to travel to India and hold Baba to that promise. She was saving her money when she got news of his death. When she had the necessary air fare, she came to Ganeshpuri anyway, to visit Baba's shrine and pay respects to his successors. She met Gurumayi, and after they exchanged the usual formalities, the Western woman turned to leave. Gurumayi looked puzzled and said, "Wait a minute, I have something for you." She rummaged around and came up with a gold necklace which she put around the astonished woman's neck.

Each of us in Siddha Yoga has his or her own personal stock of cases like this, where the guru principle cuts across time and space to act on our behalf. And now I know why John of the Fourth Gospel said that if all the sayings and actions of Jesus were recorded, "all the books in the world could never hold them." Each student is himself a "book." When questioned about this kind of phenomenon, our two young teachers tell us: "He does it all; we just do as he says." He is, of course, Muktananda. Nothing has changed. Gurumayi still interprets for her guru. That which she learned on the concrete level she now practices on the subtle. Her development followed the only path development can.

One evening Gurumayi was recounting how in Baba's company those answers to Baba's questions would fall in her (Gurumayi's) head on request. (She found that Baba always had his quotes used in his talks written out in his notes, so the whole play was simply a teaching device.) "You think," Gurumayi said to us, "that you must think in order to get your answers or your information. But to get the perfect answer, the right information, that which is perfectly appropriate to the situation, you need not think as such, but go inside and open to your heart, center on the guru there within you, and that which you need will be given."

There is no suggestion of the idiot-savant here. These enlightened beings have an uncanny intelligence, are bright, informed, intensely aware. But they are aware on levels closed to our five senses and know when and when not to use the various modes of awareness available. Recall Jesus' statement that "when you are called before the judge to make your defense, you should take no thought about what you will say ahead of time. In the moment of your need, the right words will be given you." Over and over Muktananda would say: "My baba, my guru, the Shakti, God, will do this or that for you." Never did he (nor do our present teachers) point to himself as the doer; he points beyond himself to the principle of action moving within him. In the same way Jesus said: "Of my own self I can do nothing; the Father within me does these things." They point beyond themselves to the source of real action, to which they remain transparent.

Note that the will of God manifests in life in the most trivial or mundane ways: a woman's longing for an experience of the Self, or for a gold necklace; my desire for a trinket to be blest; a woman's injured foot. I recall Cecil B. deMille's 1956 movie in which God gives Moses the Ten Commandments. It was a spectacular show, high on a mountain with a stormy sky, symphony orchestra booming away, and God carving out those commandments with awesome blasts of lightning. Good theatrics but not very good theology. The truth of the matter is that each of us is equally God. As Baba said: God dwells within you as you. So each of us is equally the source and expression of the will of God, and each unfolding moment is the subject at hand.

How, then, does a person open to this power for appropriateness? A reporter asked Gurumayi how it was that Baba had passed on his power and responsibilities to such a young person. Without a second's hesitation Gurumayi said: "I paid him." "What?" the reporter exclaimed. "With my life," Gurumayi continued calmly, telling the reporter more than he may have grasped.

Newcomers were always struck by the fact that Baba kept a huge portrait of his own guru, Bhagavan Nityandanda (who died in 1961), right above his chair in the meditation hall. On coming into the hall, Baba always bowed to this picture before sitting in his chair. When questioned on this practice, Baba explained that he bowed both to the chair, as symbol of the office of guru, and to his own personal guru, Bhagavan. "But aren't *you* the guru?" these people would ask. And Baba would point up to the picture and say: "He is my guru." Now Muktananda's picture sits above that chair, and the two successors follow the same procedure and respond to the same question in the same way. Someday their portraits will hang there and others will occupy the chair.

The Guru Principle is always becoming what we have need of it to be: The next link of the golden chain always forms.

Throughout history we hear these refrains: "Not I, but the Father within," "The Guru does (this or that)," "The Shakti will take care of you," or, in a narrower, more specialized vein, "It breathes the Zen master." These saints are not being coy or playing humble in stating things this way. They are stating the facts, the way reality functions when it is allowed to function in its natural synchrony, a synchrony which gives freedom and from which everyone gains. The Guru or Christ Principle is the root of all true action, action as creation and newness, free of our self-replicating traps of intellect.

In January 1983, following an intensive in which Baba's successor Gurumayi gave me "the touch," or Shaktipat, for three straight mornings in my meditation my body lost all muscular tonus, collapsed completely, and my limbs levitated. Since all my thought had centered on the divine hint for months, I took this grace as an example of how it breathed one. I wondered if this had been how Baba and his successors operated when they were giving the touch, and so on. As usual, I took a simplistic, concrete explanation and missed the greater, subtle teaching. Our teachers in Siddha Yoga are not moved in this fashion. The superior state of the Sufi or Siddha (the realized master) is that he is the whole of the movement. Gurumayi does not suspend all action waiting for an unknown *it* to breathe her. She and that breath are one. She stands in both worlds equally and at once, as Baba did. They are always *in* that breath, translating the divine hint. Thus they furnish the bridge which can carry us across the gap of paradox.

The lesson I was given in that levitation did not have to do only with the profound relaxation of the Zen master's body when it breathed him, but with the profound state of surrender one must achieve in order to be moved into that state and become one with our own true breath, the God within our heart. We must surrender our wills and egos to our hearts, but we cannot do this unless we begin on the most concrete level, as our teachers did. We cannot surrender to the divine hint nor abstract mythical and shadowy images of ancient teachers or abstract concepts of God. All these abstractions are too amenable to the inevitable manipulations our intellect will make below our awareness. One cannot manipulate the flesh-and-blood teacher, at least for long. When the ego surrenders on the tangible level, though, there is tacit recognition of our inability to transform ourselves. Surrender to the living master snaps the biological deadlock.

Will is the key, the breakpoint between physical deadlock and spiritual freedom. Surrender on the outward, concrete level is surrender to one's own heart, God within us as our own being. But we cannot know this until we have made such a surrender. The true teacher is equally our own Self and so naturally we are tossed right back to ourselves once we have made the outward surrender. For total surrender is actually impossible. All we do at that point is break our enculturated delusion of intellectual doing. Then we are given back to ourselves open to our hearts and bonded to the Self. The outer move, in response to the outer model, opens us to the subtle inner state. That is the sum and substance of spiritual development, and the real meaning of intelligence as a move from concreteness to abstraction.

Consider creation as an unbroken wave that presents us with our moment-by-moment reality. At each point of this creative wave, intelligence displays as the perfect mutual response of all participants. This is the bond of power, the spirit of wholeness, the Christ or Guru Principle, the heart of the life system, and we must learn to translate it into our awareness. The Guru Chakra, the chakra of intelligence, traditionally located between the eyebrows, represents the integration of intellect into intelligence. When intellect is integrated into intelligence, we move into synchrony not just with our immediate ambient, as the bumblebee with purple clover, but with our individual lives and the Creation itself, the unbroken wave within us. This is why the new brain was constructed in such a way that it could operate as though removed from the two animal brains. Our synchrony is with Creation as a total process. Again, the breakdown of the human is not between new brain and animal brain but between human intellect and the intelligence of the creation.

The unbonded intellect is locked into information of its primary brains as its only source of information, which limits us to sensory information or memory feedback, tape-looping previous sensory information. This builds a kind of dam in the creative wave of reality, and limits us to variations on physical input. The vast world within is shut out and so our outer experience is itself restricted and replicative. Intellect feeds back on its sensory material in a continual computation, turning its limited data into a self-encapsulated stasis, an arena of intellectual ferment where no real action takes place. Intellect attempts to predict and control the outcome of its own resulting picture in the attempt to safeguard its untenable position.

The problem is that the variables of each instant are infinitely regressing and beyond any computation. The dammed-up material of our intellectual construct is overwhelmed each instant by the flow of the Holomovement that dwarfs our small dam. Intellect tries to screen out all but that information amenable to its computations through which it thinks to predict and control the flow of the wave. The attempt is doomed to failure from the outset, as the unpredictable grows within the tightly controlled boundaries of thought. So our intellect becomes absorbed in dealing with the problems cropping up in its predictive-control system. The focus of attention shifts to the errors and problems, at which point these errors and problems become the materials on which intellect feeds its tape-loops. Feeding back on its own error, the error becomes immediately self-replicating. Error becomes the tape-loop itself, and culture is born.

We are born into this tight little dam of delusion and enculturated to maintain the dam at all costs. Conditions within the dam are of necessity chaotic since error is the structure of thought on which it is based. The fact that things have gone wrong absorbs the psyche of this culture and all its participants; our enculturation is solely to improve these intolerable conditions. Overriding even this intolerable condition is the general fear that the dam itself might burst. Only by improving conditions within the dam can we even be assured of its preservation; bad as its conditions are, they are all we have. As Susanne Langer expressed it, our greatest fear is of a collapse into chaos should our idea systems fail us.

We know our artificial construct cannot last, that what we are currently doing is alien to the flow of life, but this knowledge of the heart is overridden by our enculturated intellect, which insists we can yet compute the answer, given enough time. The teacher comes along and says drop the computations, the dam is a delusion. But we have no conceptual machinery to grasp what the teacher means, and our intellect is offended. After all, we might yet outwit the system.

The teacher represents an intelligence to which our intellect should give over, and we are culturally embarrassed and offended. The teacher speaks of an action generated by intelligence that gives joy and power, and we wonder how these teachers can speak of joy when the world is in such a mess. The teacher speaks of intelligence which gives power through obedience to that intelligence. At the word "obedience" our enculturated mind closes shop and will hear no more. We are enculturated to be obedient to the crying needs of our culture and must work to improve its conditions. The teacher states that through obedience on a concrete level, the power of intelligence manifests within us as our power and intelligence. Culture immediately produces its counterfeits of the teacher in the likes of Jim Jones.

Culture's dictum is "Thou shalt have no other gods but me." We are urged by cultural counterfeits of the Guru Principle to turn without and devote our lives to hunger projects, financial revolutions, drives of every description to "bring the rascals down." All of this builds the dam walls higher, assures the pressure of madness and final point of destruction. Jesus' comment that "to him who has, it is given, more and more" referred to power. It can refer to negative power as well as positive, and our negative madness seems stronger every day. The other part of his comment was, "And from him who has not (power) even that little he has is taken away." This seems to be our personal power, our ability to enter into our destiny in a meaningful way.

Jesus also said that there would come a time when that which he told his inner core of Disciples in secret would be shouted from the housetops. And from the East this housetop address has been coming, over several generations now, always becoming what we have need of, heeded or not. At the turn of our century the pioneer Vivekananda came; then that gentlest of saints, Yogananda; then fiery Muktananda shouting from the housetops for a meditation revolution, the revolution of a people turning within to the heart. Huge forces mitigate against the teacher. The Judas factor operates at full steam. The power of the heart is behind the teacher, however, and this Guru-Christ Principle has its own agenda. My young teacher has doubled the power of her ancient lineage; to her much has been given, more is added daily, and we can participate in this legacy by linking ourselves to her golden chain.

The issue for each of us is not just eventual enlightenment but an immediate shift of criteria, an immediate giving over of our will to the will of the heart. Years ago, having read Castaneda's *Journey to Ixtlan* for the twelfth time, my longing for spirit hit a breaking point of anguish. I knew I did not have the strength for the necessary undertaking, that the only way out was through a Don Juan of some sort. And I realized, in a flash of honesty, that were I to come across an actual Don Juan, my arrogance, cultural defensiveness, intellectual snobbery, and spiritual pride would be put off by some dirty old Indian, for surely that is the way he would appear. I would never find Don Juan for I would never be able to see him. As William Blake said, Satan never sees, he always has to be shown. And who would there be to show me?

All my life a secret lover of that shadowy image of Jesus, I knew that were I a Jew back in early Palestine some two millennia ago, I would have been offended by some rabble-rouser who broke the laws, consorted with women of bad repute, was called a glutton and wine-bibber, stole grain out of people's wheatfields, would not stick to an honest job, and finally got his just deserts from the authorities. Yet the psychic distance of two thousand years lets me safely manipulate this image of the Guru Principle at its greatest into a sweet sentiment, a bumper-sticker slogan for inflating the ego, bolstered with bombs and rocketry.

Ten years ago I would have been offended to be told that I would, a decade later, give my life to a young person from India, and spend my days traveling and lecturing about the world, claiming that in my Gurumayi, God has become human that the human might become God. But my teacher has given me no room for psychic distance, that trump card played by the embattled ego. She has offered only the experience of God directly within us. She did not offer herself as an image for intellectual manipulation, but as the power to force the issue within us and compel us to decision.

There is offense in the rawness of this decision they represent, since it allows no buffering by intellect. The Guru-

Christ Principle stands at the other side of mind, at a paradoxical break with our biological structures. We cannot take anything with us if we wish to make this break for life, and, of course, we do not need anything if we do. Sadly, it is also true that we cannot take anything with us if we *do not* make this break, though we will need everything we then do not have.[4]

There are thousands of ways to say no to this decision for our spirit. Our culture furnishes us with them all and applauds our negation. There is, however, only one way to say yes and that way is given by our spirit, anew in each moment for the ongoing affirmation our lives must become. We can shout our no in the safe din of numbers; but our yes is said in the solitary silence of the heart.

Notes

Names mentioned refer to entries in the Bibliography, which follows this section.

CHAPTER ONE

1. See Bernard and Sontag; Condon and Sander.
2. See Condon and Sander.
3. Development of language and intelligence in general lends direct support to the thesis of Rupert Sheldrake.
4. Reuven Feuerstein has had success in remedial work with dysfunctional children, and questions the validity of Piaget's stages. Compensation is possible later, but a full function is probably stage-specific. Feuerstein shows how flexible development is, but this does not negate the validity of stages. See Chance.
5. Scott G. Williamson and Innes H. Pearse, physicians and cellular biologists, spent over thirty years in research into health as a state. They found no suitable words in our language to describe *function* as opposed to our ordinary state of *compensation* (patchwork) and our preoccupation with a breakdown of our compensatory capacity and dying. See Williamson and Pearse.
6. See Orville Schell, *Modern Meat* (Random House, 1984). Schell reports on the synthetic hormones by which we speed up marketability of our food animals and increase all production. These are essentially sexual hormones and are a principal source of our epidemic increase in premature sexuality in children.

CHAPTER TWO

1. Ontogeny is from the Greek *ontos*, being, and *genes*, producing (or beginnings): the history of an individual organism. Phylogeny is from the Greek *phylo*, race or species, and *genes*: the evolutionary development of a whole species. Our triune brain encompasses the brain forms developed throughout evolution.

2. See Barr.

3. From the earlier work of R. E. Gregory (see Bibliography) to the recent discoveries of melanin, evidence shows that our picture of the world is an internal production made, we can only assume, according to external stimuli. A more accurate appraisal is to say we place stimuli into the category external or internal according to logical necessity, the brain mechanisms involved in translation, and a general dynamic between possibility and realization. Consider the work of Hugo Zuccarelli. (See "Holophonic Sound . . . ," listed under Miscellaneous Articles.) The brain produces a steady sound vibration in the ear mechanism. Sound waves other than this steady state modulate our inner wave, and the brain places the sound in the outer world according to the modulations of the two wave forms. Zuccarelli synthesized electronically the wave-length the inner ear produces, and recorded ordinary sounds, music, voices, over this steady wave state. Played to a person through earphones the sound is not heard in the head, as in most earphone sound, but the brain places it outside, in the world in ways indistinguishable from ordinary "out-there" sound.

4. See Luce; MacLean.

5. William Gray and Paul LaVoilette (following Ludwig von Bertalanffy; see Bibliography) use feeling tone to cover subliminal effects. The term can be used for conscious qualitative responses as well.

6. See "Conversations Between Heart and Brain" (Miscellaneous Articles) and Muktananda, *Mystery of the Mind*, for yogic statements concerning heart and mind. The yogis refer to the subtle heart, but the subtle has its physical counterparts.

7. See Sperry. My information on the appearance and slow

growth of the corpus callosum came from private correspondence with Roger Sperry in 1974.

8. The nature of deep sleep dreaming and the abstract
imagery of thought results from a combination of research (see Cartwright; Kripke; Singh; Tart) plus yogic
psychology and personal experience.

9. See Luce. There is a point, when the body brain mechanism is at its lowest ebb, when brain waves appear that
are similar to ordinary, waking consciousness but without
any of the body supports necessary. I think this indicates
a brief sojourn of consciousness into the state of the Self
itself.

10. See Werntz.

11. Any left-hemisphere action requires support from the
right hemisphere. There are no specializations that do
not require integral brain action—a kind of complementarity is involved. We tend to oversimplify seriously this
division between hemispheric specialization, though at
times such modeling helps describe otherwise abstract
functions.

CHAPTER THREE

1. See Ainsworth; Geber.

2. See Kennell; Klaus.

3. Colin Turnbull (see Bibliography) gives examples of the
mother meeting the needs of the infant without the infant expressing those needs.

4. See "Conversations Between Heart and Brain," op. cit.

5. Live brain cells on a microscopic slide show an explosion
of new connecting links (dendrites, axons, and so on) the
instant ACTH is injected. See Epstein, "Phrenoblysis . . ."

6. See Ainsworth; Chamberlain; Hales.

7. Water is the infant's first habitat, and an extension of
this, in the new medium, affords a pleasant transition and
a relaxed bonding. For some references see Bibliography: Articles on Underwater Birthing.

8. See De Chateau; Kennell; Klaus; and Luria on the stage-
specific nature of bonding.

9. See J. D. French and Serrano. My references are sparse
on this rich subject.

10. See Wm. Gray; LaVoilette, "Thoughts . . ."; MacLean; Zaslow.
11. See Fantz.
12. For information on immunization in colostrum, see *Nutrition and Health* Vol. 1 (London: A. B. Academic Publishers, 1983). The report was given at the Oxford University conference on obstetrical practice and early child health where I also gave an address. See Pearce, "Nurturing Intelligence . . ."
13. See Jensen.
14. See Ringler. Justin Call, M.D., University of California at Irvine, has done long-term studies on the relationship between breast-feeding and intelligence.
15. See Montagu, *Touching*.
16. See Bertalanffy; Wm. Gray; LaVoilette.
17. During the crawling stage, the infant does not blink his eyes. The reptilian stare was one of Paul MacLean's clues in his research into brain anatomy. The early infant is limited to single entrainment, cannot distinguish subject self from object of interaction, and so on. The sensory-motor system must be established first to release consciousness into the higher brain centers for their specialized development.
18. The shift of object-constancy is made as early as six months by bonded children and as late as eighteen to twenty months by unbonded ones.
19. Again, see "Conversations Between Heart and Brain"; Mitchell.
20. I first read of the use of recorded heartbeats in one of the scientific journals, and in the *Brain/Mind Bulletin*. Then I saw one of the advertisements for the home version. Following the research of W. G. Whittlestone (see Bibliography). Kerry Callaghan, of Nairne, Australia, promoted a fine little treatise: "Creating Optimal Environments for Newborn Infants and Their Families." Both Whittlestone and Callaghan had recognized the role of the heartbeat in early infant development.
21. Obviously if the heart is a mass of melanin molecules, and melanin is an interface between consciousness and physical apparatus, and if two separated heart cells can leap a gap and communicate, surely two massive groups of cells do the same. So the link between mother and

infant on levels below awareness is established and continually reaffirmed through proximity of hearts themselves. Thus continual nursing keeps this link established in the early periods of growth.

22. See De Chateau; Geber; Kennell; and particularly Ringler, as well as the work of Justin Call at the University of California at Irvine.

23. Henry Massie's work shows a relation between lack of physical contact between mother and infant as one of the factors in infantile autism.

24. Western delivery practices, at home or hospital, have been far from ideal, and Western child-rearing itself has been monstrous. See De Mause.

25. Blurton Jones (see Bibliography), working under Nikos Tinbergen, reported that all drugs transfer to the infant in utero within some forty-five seconds. Also see Brackbill; Chamberlain.

26. See Towbin. Abraham Towbin, who discovered this damage, is a physician at Boston University.

27. In 1977 I was sent a report on delivery of ghetto babies in the United States. I had dropped out of all activities at that time and did not keep the report. Most charity cases are paid for by the state, at a nominal fee, and treatment is far below standard, at times barbaric. The breaking of the parent-infant bond at delivery is reflected in an ongoing breakdown of the extended-family bond, which was the strength of ghetto and minority people in times past.

28. Rene Spitz (see Bibliography), typical of the research mentality of his time, referred to the long period of unconsciousness of our hospital newborns as the norm for nature, and spoke of the "smiling syndrome," which appears between the tenth and twelfth week of life, as the first sign of consciousness in humans.

29. Rosemary Wiener has made one of the most thoroughly documented studies of circumcision and its effects on infants ever undertaken. She has devoted her life to trying to bring this issue to public attention, with disheartening results. Anyone who wishes to be informed on this issue should write:

> Intact Educational Foundation
> 4521 Freemont St.
> Bellingham, WA. 98226

30. Mary Ainsworth's work in bonding (see Bibliography) began in the 1950s and has been largely ignored since what do women (even M.D.s) know about childbirth?

31. See the work of Windle. The problem of delivery-induced brain damage has been complicated by the massive rise in cesarean sectioning, now accounting for about twenty-five percent of all births in America (as high as fifty percent in affluent areas). During a lecture tour of California in 1983 I was handed a report by a school-district official concerning profiles on dysfunctional schoolchildren. Forty percent of the educationally handicapped children of that district had been delivered by cesarean sectioning. In my travels I lost the report and have no idea of its origins or accuracy.

32. In 1979, three years after I had dropped out of the world of affairs, two women searched me out (I was two miles from the nearest road of any sort and not readily available) and told me of their two-year research, under a foundation grant, on child day-care centers in the United States. They painted a disheartening picture and wanted to enlist my support in their inevitable public enlightenment campaign, but I was having none of it, convinced, as I was, that our culture was destroying itself on every hand in an inevitable fashion.

33. The hostile, aggressive child found in day-care and schools has become our norm, and we now consider such hostile aggression as human nature since, after all, it's displayed from earliest childhood.

34. California legislator John Vasconcellos was responsible for this research into the root causes of crime and violence. I am indebted to his office staff, who sent me a copy of the preliminary report.

CHAPTER FOUR

1. I read this account while on my travels and have no record of its source, other than a major magazine. Lytt Gardner (see Bibliography) has reported on the relation between emotional and physical stimuli deprivation and dwarfism. As a postscript I recall that the psychotic father, responsible for isolating the child, committed sui-

cide at her being discovered, and left a note of wonderful understatement: "No one will ever understand."
2. Object-constancy is Piaget's term for this first shift. See Bibliography or any of Piaget's numerous works.

CHAPTER FIVE

1. See Cassirer.
2. See Luria.
3. L. S. Vygotsky (see Bibliography) has some excellent observations on child play as well as the relation between language and memory.
4. See Jensen regarding this "pointing syndrome." Vygotsky thought pointing the result of an incomplete grasping reflex—a strange and mistaken notion.

CHAPTER SIX

1. Miguel Serrano (see Bibliography) wrote that Chile had a well-developed spiritual system long before Europeans arrived. Serrano had a spiritual teacher in his early years, and spent many years in India searching for the origins of Chilean spiritual disciplines. His unique understanding gave him insight into those two fascinating characters, Herman Hesse and Carl Jung. He was ambassador to India for nine years and spent some four additional years in the Himalayas.
2. My friend Lee Sannella first put me onto the trail of separation dreams undergone around age four and five. My audiences all over the world concur that at this age most of us have separation dreams of some sort, often with accompanying anxiety. Consider that in pre-literate societies where natural intelligence is less interfered with by intellect, most mothers nurse their children for two to three years, and most lactating mothers do not conceive. This spaces children at about four-year intervals, at which point some eighty percent of the child's structures of knowledge are complete, the corpus callosum is nearing completion, the locus of awareness shifts into the new brain, and preparations begin for the shift to society as criteria and bonding. Nature's planning is superb and complete.

3. See Propp.

4. I need only mention Beatrix Potter's *Peter Rabbit* series, Thornton Burgess, A. A. Milne (the genius of this genre), the Uncle Remus tales, folk tales and myths in general. In mythology the line of demarcation between animal and human is crossed at liberty; each turns into the other. Australian aborigine mythology is a prime example.

5. See Wickes.

6. The metaphoric and symbolic capacity of mid-brain and right-hemisphere imagery becomes sophisticated and universal, of course, and is as rapid as any brain action. This early play imagery, of direct animal, dream metaphor, remains as the foundation of our creative thought, as I show in Chapter Twelve.

7. Howard Gardner's excellent article, "The Making of a Storyteller" (see Bibliography), is full of insight into the child's mind. He relates how the four- or five-year-old can use almost anything to symbolize almost any agent or object in almost any situation. He points out that children enter into symbolic activity by age two. He refers to "object dependent children" who pay careful attention to the physical attributes of a thing and insist on using only concrete objects in their make-believe. Object independent children, on the other hand, are willing to use just about any block or object to stand for what they want to suggest. The development of imagination undergoes a shift in the third and fourth years, from a need of other people and real world props (what might be called mediators) to sustain their fantasy, to an independence of such props, at which point children carry out their imagination largely through words. Gardner points out that by four or five, narrative language has become the prime medium of play. That is, the child furnishes herself with her own input of words to bring about the corresponding response of internal imagery projected on her external world. (This can happen quite early, as with our child Shakti, whose medium of play by age three was certainly verbal.)

   In the same issue of *Psychology Today* (March 1982), Anthony Brandt, reporting on the work of Dan Graves, says: "Just as children's logical understanding of the world must be constructed, so must their ability to engage in pretense and fantasy."

8. Jerry Mander (see Bibliography) has written an exceptional work on television and the power of imagery.

9. Hu Mon Yu (see Bibliography) points out that mathematical symbols can only be grasped by a young person who has a grasp of symbolic thought in general—one who can represent his own experience symbolically. The child must first get abundant perceptual data before he remodels, reconstructs, builds up concepts, and formulates principles. We must "let them have ample time to mess around, to gain empirical experience and perceptual knowledge" before we subject them to abstract concepts.

CHAPTER SEVEN

1. See Mowatt.

2. I read of this English research into aborigine tracking many years ago and have long since lost the citation. On both my extensive lecture tours of Australia (some six months in all) I heard many personal reports of this particular aboriginal ability.

3. Referring to the mid-brain as our "subtle emotional energy" and the old brain as our "physical system" gives a clear model for our grasp of different functions and is essentially correct. Obviously a rich interplay and overlap of all brain functions takes place, but within the boundaries of this triune nature.

4. Certainly child development seems to follow Epstein's outline. I would be pleased were he to take into cognizance the triune nature of the brain and the obvious shifts of behavior that parallel his work and Piaget's.

5. Piaget; Polansky; Propp; Stallibrass; Vygotsky; B. White; Wickes; Wilson.

CHAPTER EIGHT

1. John Hasted (see Bibliography) is a mathematician and physicist at the University of London. The metal-bending at the Monroe Institute, under Colonel John Alexander's tutelage, was more extreme, the shapes more bizarre, than anything in Hasted's book. Alexander states that twenty-five people create an optimum atmosphere, giving mutual support and a group energy. Laboratory con-

trol eliminates all of these supports, and that Hasted got the results he did is all the more remarkable. The Shakti, or energy involved, is a most conscious energy and is less likely to respond in atmospheres and attitudes of restriction, suspicion, doubt, or seriousness. My own hunch is that all these events are but variations on the old-fashioned poltergeist experiences and that the quixotic, playful, and unpredictable element is an integral part, putting this entire category of phenomena off limits to hard-core physical science for the simple reason it is not a hard-core physical process. We invite our playful spirit to participate and she may, or may not. Knowing how my own creative Shakti responds in meditations, I cannot think of anything less conducive to her performing than a "scientific atmosphere" of skepticism. Shakti does not need to prove anything to anyone. She plays.

2. See Jahn.

3. See Piaget and Inhelder.

4. See Manning.

5. See Feinberg. True to tourism's lure, fire walking is now a regular nightly floor show at a famous hotel on Sri Lanka. Of even more interest, two groups are now touring the United States with programs, one in neurolinguistic procedures, and the other in overcoming fear, both of which conclude with fire walking by the participants. So we are now adding many thousands of Americans to the list of fire walkers yearly, which surely will bring down the delusion of behaviorism.

6. See Donna and Gilbert Grosvenor, "Ceylon," *The National Geographic*, Vol. 129, No. 4, April 1966.

7. See Josephson.

8. French physicist Bernard d'Espagnat (see Bibliography) is one of many leading physicists questioning the dualistic-mechanistic worldview, as a result of Bell's theorem and the general implications of quantum mechanics.

9. The paranormal aspects of concrete operational thinking were a major notion in my book *Magical Child*, and at that naive stage of my undevelopment I felt such powers necessary to a true development. I know better now.

CHAPTER NINE

1. Arthur Koestler (see Bibliography) echoed Paul MacLean's thoughts that a breakdown between intellect and emotion was to be blamed on the sparse neural connections of our new brain to our mid-brain, and attributed this to the "newness" of our new brain and evolution's failure to catch up in connecting it with the limbic system. This is an error of logical typing. As Stephen Jay Gould of Harvard points out (see *The New Scientist*, Volume 1301, 137–141) evolution operates by a "punctuated equilibrium," biological change can take place quickly, and generally does so at the beginning of a species' history—not gradually and piecemeal. Had nature intended our intellect to be subservient to our animal brains, and that emotional limbic structure of the mid-brain, she would long ago have linked our new brain to our mid-brain as she did the two animal brains. The intellect really develops only when integrated into intelligence, the job of post-biological development. Our truncated development is at fault, not evolution. Our fault lies in our belief systems, mechanistic ideologies, and arrogant ignorance.

2. Tim Gallwey reported on this event and showed the movies made of it at the educational conference at the University of California where I also spoke. I have not read his book, *The Inner Game of Tennis*, and so did not list it in my bibliography.

3. See Strauch.

4. I read of this Englishman's movie of the rope trick in an English journal of psychology back in the early 1960s and do not have the source now.

5. Charles Tart (see Bibliography) has described the mutual hypnosis experience.

6. See "Lucid Dream Sharing" (Miscellaneous Articles) for a report by Jean Campbell, Poseidia Institute, Virginia Beach, Va. Since this report's publication, this research has been replicated and expanded.

CHAPTER TEN

1. See Martin. I am indebted to Hugh Martin for many insights into the scientific world, its prejudices and machinations.

2. Hugh Martin reported on the estimates the first atomic scientists made concerning the probable explosive power of an atomic bomb. The highest estimate was 500 tons of TNT equivalency. The actual explosion of the first bomb was the equivalent of at least 20,000 tons of TNT and vaporized half the scientific equipment and nearly vaporized a bunch of the scientists. So much for all the reassurances given us that our scientific predictions are reliable.

3. I am seriously indebted to Minas Kafatos (see Bibliography) for his corrections and help in my trying to grasp the issues of complementarity and the quantum problem. I found the Kafatos-Nadeau theory absorbing, and it opens for us an entirely new metaphor for understanding our own position. Almost all references to physical theory in this chapter come from Kafatos—his paper, correspondence, or personal contact. I trust I have not violated his theory too strenuously.

4. Bell's theorem, or variations thereof, has been proven in a half dozen major tests about the globe, and our major scientific journals have all conceded that quantum mechanics has won the day in physics. This hardly means acceptance of the data, however, since scientists can ignore with marvelous aplomb anything not fitting their own theories. See D'Espagnat; Kafatos.

5. See Muktananda, *Mystery . . .* ; Singh. A great deal of superficial talk about the Self goes on currently, but the yogic psychology of the Self is also a cosmology and a creative principle.

6. For David Bohm's work see Bibliography. Wonderful conversations with him are in Wilber. Bohm's theory gives a frame of reference in which Bell's theorem has meaning and purpose.

7. See Sheldrake. Again, I find no easy way to model Rupert Sheldrake's theory, but by combining Sheldrake and Bohm we come up with a view quite consistent with yogic psychology. Recently Bohm proposed that the universe is composed of light waves. Matter may be, Bohm said, "frozen light." Light photons are long, slow, and weak wave lengths. Matter waves, we have assumed, were very fast waves. That is, we assumed a fast wave field "collapses" to produce energy particles of matter,

whereas light waves are the opposite. The only universe we know, however, or can ever know, is one of imagery, including those images of our instruments whose readings we accept as "reality." All imagery is at base a visual process originating within our brain/mind system, which brain, in turn, is a translating device. Among its many properties, the melanin molecule can transfer or translate sound waves into light waves. Cross-indexing of our sensory system is a common phenomenon. Some people hear *or* feel sounds tactilely, or experience smell along with hearing, as often found in Zuccarelli's new holophonic sound. Seeing flashes of light accompanying sounds, when the eyes are closed, is very common. (I experience this with any sudden loud sound, and often with more subtle sounds.) So again we are left with the fact that the reality we experience, including the awesome universe reaching forever out beyond us, is the result of a dynamic, and defies precise placement. According to yogic psychology, this dynamic is a play between sound and light, and precisely that play is the work of our brain/mind, a game of complementarity. I feel that David Bohm's work will be the intellectual bridge that arcs the gap of paradox involved.

8. Rupert Sheldrake's theory that causal fields, which supersede time and space, underlie our reality is quite evident in the wave-particle complement of physics; explains such intuitive phenomena as aborigine Dream Time; and is clearly manifest in the idiot-savant syndrome. Idiot-savants are people who, while uneducable and with I.Q.s ranging from 40 to 60, are capable of astonishing feats of computation or information retrieval. Mathematical savants are the most publicized. (The British reportedly employed a couple of them as computers during World War II.) These people cannot respond to the written problem of 20 minus 10, but can give, when asked, almost instant answers to extremely involved calculations. In 1931, for instance, Drs. D. C. Rife and L. H. Snyder asked their mental patient savant to double the grains of corn on each checkerboard square, which meant doubling the number 1 (one) 64 times. It took the patient forty-five seconds (quite long actually, in savant terms) to give the quadrillion-fold answer: 18,466,734,709,551,616.

Charles and George, savant twins at Letchworth Village mental hospital in New York State, specialize in calendrical calculations. They can immediately identify the day of the week for dates as far in the future as A.D. 7000, or many centuries in the past. When giving past dates, they automatically compensate for the changeover from the Julian to Gregorian calendar systems made in 1752, though neither is aware that such historical systems existed. Not educable, they had been given a perpetual calendar as children, and taught by their mother how to use the mechanical device. The calendar covered only a two-hundred-year period but it apparently furnished the nucleus, or opened the channel, for their one and only talent. As with all idiot-savants, they could give no explanation of how they came up with their answers. They simply knew. See *Science Digest*, May 1981, p. 12, and *Scientific American*, August 1965, p. 46.

I was recently told of an idiot-savant under study for several years now in a New York City hospital. His specialty is automobiles. He can be taken to a window, shown the busy city street below, and, from a single glance, recount the hundreds of automobiles within sight, and tell the name, model, year, engine type, and so on, of each in turn. His knowledge includes the latest models hot off the Detroit or Tokyo press, though he, too, is illiterate and uneducable. (I have only hearsay for this reference, though the case certainly fits the syndrome.)

Recall from Chapter 7 my five-year-old son giving that theological dissertation. I think he displayed a variation of this same syndrome, as do people like Edgar Cayce and general "psychics." Indications are that the essence of all human experience, like all physical formation as matter, resonates on some implicate energy level, congregating according to categories of endeavor. We are continually setting up, in effect, fields of compatible variables of behavior and possibility. Consider, for instance, that the problem of God has been uppermost in man's history. Or, consider the enormous physical, emotional, financial, intellectual, and even political energy invested in automobiles. Once created, a field of comtible variables (such as thoughts on God or automobiles) tends to express its implications, since that is the nature of implicate energy, and does so according to whatever explicate cues trigger it. The field flows back into a living situation, or physical form, according to the cumulative strength it has taken on, the amount of activity generating the field and, in turn, generated by the field.

Ordinarily we select from available fields according to the models given us that are compatible with those fields. We build conceptual patterns according to the dynamic between the implicate possibility and explicate model. Then we can (supposedly) handle that type of activity in a controlled, logical fashion. The idiot-savant fails to develop through this ordinary dynamic yet, through some childhood experience, opens to a particular field of variables without the usual intellectual filters and control. Because, of logical necessity, a field holds all possible variations of its compatible variables, and the savant's channel is not filtered by ordinary brain function, he can give a near-instantaneous response to any variable selected *for* him by the appropriate stimulus question. He is incapable of learning or development since he cannot voluntarily arrive at a solution; retrace his steps to see how he derived his answer (reversibility thinking); or extract the essence or ability and correlate to other contexts, as can an ordinary restrictive conceptual system.

Sheldrake's suggestion that learning and memory probably do not take place in the brain at all but in fields that translate through the brain can explain the savant syndrome, as surely as behavioristic psychology cannot. In Chapter 12 I show how a variation of this field effect underlies all creative discovery, scientific, artistic, or what-have-you. These functions give strength to my argument that child learning is essentially imprinting if and when model and blueprint *match*. (Which behooves us, it seems to me, to strive to match our models to be learned with the developmental stages of the child, rather than concentrate, as we do, on modifying the child's behavior to fit our mismatched learning models.)

We have within us a subtle-body system critical to development. Explored fully in yogic psychology, it is

yet another variation of this wave-field function of causation. Our individual experience registers in personal
causal fields just as our broad species-wide experience
does in broad generic ways. Our subtle, or dream, body
is the most immediate expression of this personal field
effect and along with it our personal history and awareness we call ego-personality. Since implicate energy is
more powerful than explicate energy, once built up, our
personal implicate field or subtle body and ego-soul would
(and I think does) logically persist after our physical
body dies, precisely as we find phantom limb pain per-
sisting in a person after the limb is gone. But phantom
limb pain eventually dissipates, and an ego-soul must
eventually dissipate as well. Not integrated into the Self,
and denied the continual supportive feedback of its
physical and causal systems, an implicate order system
cannot be sustained.

The issue of complementarity enters here. Just as
wave and particle expressions are complementary, mutually exclusive yet mutually interdependent, so are subtle
and physical systems of personality, as well as ego-self
and the Self. We express, as our conscious awareness,
one state or the other. At night when we dream we
express in our subtle forms (from both archetypal and
personal physical experience), and during the day we
identify with and are subject to physical expressions.
The sensory system itself is subtle energy; remove it
from the physical system and the body becomes inert
protoplasm. Focused on the body we register a physical
world; focused within we can register other states; but
should the gating mechanism separating the two break
down we would experience delirium, hallucination, schizo-
phrenia, and so on.

A cohesive, structured ego cannot be sustained in
its subtle form if detached permanently from its body
(again as we find in phantom limb pain). That is why we
have built into us a developmental system to lead us
beyond this wave-particle complementary function once
it is well established. On disintegration of an ego structure, its various traits, tendencies, compulsions, abilities,
perceptions, and conceptions built up as an integrated

personality would gravitate toward larger aggregates of life tendencies. (We find this explored in the yogic theory of *samskara*.) Thus we reap as we sow both individually and universally, while alive, and, thus, detached from the physical system by death, while not integrated into the Self, that conscious aggregate called ego-personality (that longs so for survival) simply cannot manifest very long.

Ian Stevenson of the University of Virginia has collected many cases of young children suddenly manifesting intricate knowledge of a recently deceased person's life history. Stevenson uses these cases as an argument for reincarnation. A more viable, logical, and likely solution lies in this function of "fields of compatible variables." I doubt that my son's strange oration indicated reincarnation of some top-flight theologian. A child may, like the idiot-savant, suddenly become open to a field aggregate as my son did (through his rapport with me and my passionate concerns). Or she may open to that peculiar field called personality, a specific memory-set of some late-departed still intact within the subtle realm. The child may give full expression to the pool tapped into, and even form a partial identification with it. But no universal mechanism of reincarnation is warranted from such effects. Life is made of the dynamics between wave and particle consciousness, not mechanics. Most of the children manifesting this phenomenon are, as was my son, in the midst of their intuitive period of development.

Thus the death-and-dying movement's assumptions that a bright new world awaits us at the end of death's dark tunnel is questionable. The persistence of an ego-soul detached from its physical inputs might be equivalent to short-term memory in the same way phantom limb pain is. Perhaps by relating with other detached ego-souls one might sustain his ego structure longer, even indefinitely, establishing consensus realities of a sort. But this kind of action could be neither permanent nor developmental. An ego could not develop beyond such an insubstantial dreamlike mode since development beyond one's stage generates only from the Self, not from consensus within that modality, and always only from the concrete to the abstract (and concreteness is missing).

Automatic writing, Ouija board activity, messages from spirit guides, and "discarnate entities" all fall into the same category of phenomena and draw on subtle or implicate energy memory pools. That is why these messages from the "other side" are generally vapid truisms of a vague generality, largely shaped by the person who instigates, receives, and interprets them ("channeling" is the current term). Guidance of this sort cannot lead anywhere except into circles and generally creates a dangerous form of ego-inflation from which little growth or change takes place. Subtle or astral input is numinous and awesome to a physically oriented ego, and to mistake this kind of psychic flatulence for genuine insight, which comes only from the Self, is a major error (though a commonplace and best-selling one). We do well to remember that the realm of insight-intelligence, the Self, has no content, contains no information, and is not available to reportage. (Insight registers in us *only* as conceptual-perceptual change.)

Finally, consider the phenomenon of thought itself, and the common Cartesian error that equates ego awareness with thought. Thought is only one form consciousness can take, and a primitive form at that. Seldom do we use thought in precise, computative, intellectual ways. Thought happens to us in that incessant dialogue of gibberish in our heads called roof-brain chatter. This non-breakable tape-loop (from which only the enlightened saint is free) is, however, a natural dynamic between implicate and explicate orders of energy and has its own role to play. Memory is an implicate order process, subtle, not physical, and every thought throughout our life registers in both our own, personal implicate memory pool as well as to some extent in the larger, species-wide ones. Since all implicate-explicate flows are complementary systems, these pools, in turn, impress back on us, triggering our ongoing thought. This automatic feedback, though random and haphazard, is exactly the same creative phenomenon as the more stable feedback between wave-form energy as blueprint for physical forms, and those explicate expressions of it giving us our stable world.

David Bohm speaks of thoughts as things, as material processes. Indeed, our making real or manifesting our implicate memory fields is a particle energy process, different from physical matter only in the nature of compatible variables involved and the required mode of expression. As a result, so long as we are identified with our physical bodies and world, we are as much subject to this thought flow, over which we have little or no control, as we are subject to our physical universe, and the two prove interconnected. Both are, in fact, simply *samskaras*, repetitive habit forms. The job of the brain/mind, along with supplying us with our world to view, is to think, and it will do its job in this automatic, repetitive way, just as it furnishes us a mechanical, repetitive world, until ego is integrated into insight-intelligence. Only when the ego-self is united with the Self are we free of such automatism.

When our post-biological integration of ego and Self fails to take place, however, we are lodged in this tape-looped feedback between inplicate fields of thought, personal and collective, and individual mind. Spiritual development brings about a "quiet mind," which means a mind free of this implicate-explicate tape-loop. This can happen only through integration into a higher function, the creation itself, at which point mind is used in the service of the more powerful energy. An ego-mind free from identification with those physical foundations from which it arises is literally free from the world. The ability to *be* moved beyond the implicate-causal order, with its archetypal tape-loops and vast evolutionary fields, in order to integrate into the Self, is achieved through grace (power) from a teacher and the modeling afforded by that teacher. And again, the teacher capable of establishing this kind of bonding is one who stands fully *in* that state of the Self, while here among us in flesh and blood.

CHAPTER ELEVEN

1. Robert Monroe's book (see Bibliography) covers only a fraction of his experiences over many years. His ongoing work at his institute in Faber, Virginia, now covers a wide field and has attracted the enthusiastic support of thousands of people who benefit from his "hemi-sync" process. Inquiries can be addressed to:

   Monroe Institute of Applied Science
   P.O. Box 175, Route 1
   Faber, Va. 22938

2. See Muktananda, *Play* . . .
3. Psychologists Joe Kamiya and Charles Tart were among those who discovered the relationship between states of consciousness and brain-wave patterns back in the 1960s. The notion that through biofeedback we can duplicate the wave patterns of high yogic and Zen states and so achieve those states without the years of discipline involved proved an error of logic typical of our time. Currently brain research persons are discovering a whole array of new chemical substances used by the brain and keep attributing various states of consciousness to the translating substances. Now the idea is growing that we will chemically produce an ideal mental state—the same error made earlier but in a new guise.
4. Wilder Penfield (see Bibliography) agreed with Nobel laureates Roger Sperry and Sir John Eccles that mind is a separate entity from brain yet dependent on brain. The cerebellum gives the ideal physical setting for such an objective state. Post-biological development integrates mind into the intelligence of the Self, and this alone utilizes all the new brain and leads to an independence of ego from brain/mind and body.
5. See "Quizzing the Hidden Observer" (Miscellaneous Articles).
6. John Lorber, British neurosurgeon, asked the ridiculous question "Is your brain really necessary?" (see Lewin) for quite sound and serious reasons, since people are found who have virtually no neo-cortex, or new brain, yet are

quite functional. Again, present indications point toward our huge new brain being almost superfluous to our ordinary life, as currently used. Our ordinary life in this physical body can be handled pretty well by our two animal brains. With no other involvement offered us in our current mechanistic-dualistic worldview, very little of the new brain is employed.

7. Monroe has a new book in the works that recounts the adventures of the many people exploring the possibilities of conscious exploration his system holds.

8. Gregory Bateson (see Bibliography) speaks of the *stochastic* process: Nature creates an open field of random possibility with a highly selective purposiveness behind the randomness. Creation takes place through an open-ended profusion. Nature throws out a billion stars (if needed) and chances on a planetary system; throws out a million planetary systems (if needed) and chances on life; throws out billions of lives and finally expresses her end-goal—a life that achieves realization, or unity, of the whole creative process.

9. Rudolph Steiner assumed that modern man, with his super intellect, could now rationally think his way through to his own spiritual evolution (and I suppose immortality), and had no further need of spiritual teachers or gurus. In this Steiner represents the fall of modern man: the arrogance of an inflated intellect divorced from intelligence. The more complex or advanced an intellect might become, the more critically necessary is the spiritual model and guide—not the lesser, as witness our growing nightmare today. Intellect guiding itself sinks to self-encapsulation and dogma (Steiner not exempt). Krishnamurti made roughly the same statement and the same error, and his highly intellectualized form of meditation leads to frustration since it can only be approximated at best, and it leads to dryness. (Krishnamurti's system is intellectual in the last analysis and ignores Kundalini and the play of consciousness which underlies real life.) Ironically, both men railed against Eastern gurus while they themselves clearly functioned as the most classical examples of gurus all their lives.

CHAPTER TWELVE

1. The geometric nature of new brain imagery comes from a synthesis of various sources: personal experience, yogic theory, sleep-dream research, Arthur Deikman's explorations of hypnagogic and anagogic imagery (see Tart, *Altered States...*), and "Universal Forms of Hallucination . . ." (Miscellaneous Articles).
2. See Laski.
3. See Hans Selye, *From Dream to Discovery—On Being a Scientist* (New York: McGraw-Hill, 1964).

CHAPTER THIRTEEN

1. I came across a brief reference to this trial in a 1979 copy of the *Journal of American Psychology*.
2. See Sheldrake, specifically pages 181 and 204. We continually create morphic fields and are then subject to our own creations. This brings about the true "world of Maya," or delusion, a mental creation separate from the truth of The Creation.
3. Both Paul MacLean and William Gray point out that the new brain seems devoted exclusively to the outside world and our survival in it. Other research claims that only five percent or so of the new brain is used. Thus John Lorber could rightfully ask if our brain is really necessary, since we have attributed nearly everything to the neo-cortex, and now find its role possibly diminished. Further, we find that when attending to the outer world our brain requires *less* blood and oxygen than it does when we close our eyes and attend to the inner world of thought. So little of the new brain is needed to attend to that outer system since it is the weakest. Non-localized reality, the reality of creation, is the translating job of the new brain, but this is a spiritual development that seldom happens—or at least only minimally. Were this development to take place, our physical system would be freed from intellectual interference (with all its emotional imbalances which bring disease and disaster on us).
4. David Bohm speaks of our *illusions* (inner plays of mind) which become *delusions* when we believe they apply to our external, shared world; which prompts us to enlist

others in a general *collusion* that our *delusions* about our *illusions* are true. A buildup of the energy investments thus made creates a morphic field of ever-increasing probability, a cultural tendency. This is precisely the yogic theory of *samsakara*, and involves the theory of karma, the actions and reactions of a deluded, self-replicative nature. In the final chapter of this book I discuss the avenue to real action, free of this monumental snare.

CHAPTER FOURTEEN

1. The *Brain/Mind Bulletin* of March 26, 1984, reports "further evidence for the idea that the brain can integrate sophisticated information without cognitive activity." The *Bulletin* of March 5, 1984, reports that "unconscious mind plays a more primary role in mental life than anyone has previously suspected. Stimuli registered outside awareness have a measurable effect on behavior." Emmanuel Donchin, director of the Laboratory for Cognitive Psychophysiology, University of Illinois, reports that "as much as ninety-nine percent of cognitive activity may be nonconscious." Psychologist Robert Zajonc claims the unconscious mind also registers likes and dislikes before the conscious mind even knows what is being responded to: "Feeling can operate separately from cognition." Among many things, these observations lend credence to my theory of imprinting to the vast majority of information rather than "learning" in our behavior-modification terms. All this indicates that the brain shapes its information into meaningful experience of which our ego-intellect is then aware.

2. By now I think I have given grounds for questioning MacLean's (and a general) notion that evolution has lagged in not connecting our intellectual brain tightly into subservience to our limbic structure (which is, after all, an animal emotional system). Intellect *must* be free of emotion if it is to be available to intelligence and creativity. Intelligence operates from the heart of the creation itself, and far surpasses the mid-brain's limited response.

3. The new sports psychology lends credence to theories

such as Ralph Strauch's, that intellect interferes with an optimal physical response for our well-being in this physical world. So even the five or ten percent of new brain usage, locked in on the physical brain as it is, is itself perhaps misplaced. The real direction for us is to use these insights from sports psychology and the martial arts to rediscover the "wisdom of the body." This might help to free our consciousness, that we might move on into the great non-physical realms within, the only adventure that counts for long.

4. Ernst Lehrs (see Bibliography) quotes Werner Heisenberg (p. 33) that science is not a chain of brilliant discoveries opening out, but a narrowing of scope of inquiry into nature. "Understanding diminishes . . . science as a path or progressive self-restriction." Lehrs refers to "the self-restriction of scientific inquiry to one-eyed colour blind observation.

CHAPTER FIFTEEN

1. Irina Tweedie's account (see Bibliography) of her transformation under a Sufi guru in India in the 1960s is one of the great accounts of spiritual growth and must reading for anyone interested in a genuine transcendence. Of particular interest to the present chapter was her account of the piercing of the sexual chakra, one of the most intense accounts in all the literature.

2. I found Elisabeth Haich's book (see Bibliography) an interesting, intelligent, and informative work.

3. John Woodroffe (see Bibliography) is complex, difficult, and oppressively dull, but his huge, exhaustive study of Kundalini indicates the complexity of the issue, and the necessity of severe simplification in a work such as mine here, to make the role of Kundalini meaningful. Kundalini is represented as a snake in many ancient systems. An old Celtic cross exists in Ireland that has the hooded snake entwined about it. The caduceus, the twin snakes wound about the staff of Mercury, was adopted by the medical profession, and Kundalini has always been called a healing power. Richard Katz's study of the Kung (see Bibliography) concentrates on this healing aspect. The

original Masonic Order was based on the movement up the spine by the Kundalini, the thirty-two degrees of Masonry being the thirty-two bones of the spine and skull.

4. See Haich; Pearce, *Bond of Power*; Tweedie. Chagnon relates how the Yanomama prepare for contests of strength through periods of celibacy. In the New Testament Jesus refers to those who make themselves eunuchs for the sake of the Kingdom of Heaven. The word he used referred equally to a self-disciplined celibacy as well as to castration, depending on interpretation, and since the Sufic order, from the same geographical locale, understands the need of sexual energy for Kundalini transcendence, I doubt Jesus meant castration. The Gnostic Gospels speak of the absolute necessity for celibacy.

5. Some of Schwaller de Lubicz's works have been translated into English but my sole source is John Anthony West's superb book, *Serpent in the Sky*.

CHAPTER SIXTEEN

1. For some reason, in *Bond of Power* I attributed this experience to a third party. Perhaps it was a twinge of embarrassment over such a Lolita-type involvement, since my flesh-and-blood paramour was nineteen at the time, and I was forty.

2. See Nambiar.

CHAPTER SEVENTEEN

1. See Herrigel.

2. Krishna Prem (see Bibliography) makes clear that "we get to heaven by using heaven's wings." We get to the Self by surrender to that Self. Intellect is of use only as integrated into intelligence.

3. Bateson's stochastic process bears resemblance to Ilya Prigogine's theory of dissipative structures, with which I am not familiar enough to make use of here, but which early readers of this manuscript say is most relevant. When we refuse to recognize the underlying purpose of our universe, we see only random chaos and dissolution.

4. See Jensen.

5. See Simeon.

CHAPTER EIGHTEEN

1. See Leonard.
2. See Hemigel.
3. Sanskrit names are complex, made of different words. Gurumayi's name, Chidvilasananda, is made of *Chid* (Sanskrit for consciousness, the universal creative energy), *vilas* (play), and *ananda* (love of). So her full name, Chidvilasananda, means "a love of the play of consciousness." Gurumayi itself is from two words, *guru* meaning teacher, and *mayi* meaning mother. (The word guru, as stated, is two words itself, *gu* for darkness and *ru* for light, the guru being the teacher who leads us from darkness to light.) So Gurumayi's full name means "the lover of the play of consciousness who is the mother of all teachers who lead us from darkness to light."
4. See Castaneda, *The Teachings of Don Juan*. In Carlos Castaneda's last book, *The Eagle's Gift*, he discusses the narrow gate issue. Jesus spoke of the broad way that leads to destruction being followed by nearly everyone, while the narrow gate leading to life is found by very few. In the *Bhagavad Gita*, Krishna tells Arjuna very few ever find Him. Nature operates by profusion. The Christian Church (and most other religions) may be seen as an institution designed to sanctify the broad way leading to destruction, an attempt to establish some decency and order to the mass plunging over the cliff. The real followers of the way may be rather naturally driven underground, as true Yoga has always been essentially covert, subversive, in effect. Nevertheless, the Church acts rather as the necessary physical body, with all its frailties and shortcomings, which houses the Spirit, hidden though it may be. The Church has given birth to a steady stream of great beings down through the centuries who seem to be manifested in spite of the institution, and about whom the Church always seems indecisive: Should they be sanctified or burned at the stake?

Bibliography

AINSWORTH, MARY, M.D. "Deprivation of Maternal Care: A Reassessment of Its Effect." *Public Health Papers*, No. 14, 97–165. Geneva: World Health Organization, no date.

AINSWORTH, MARY, M. D. *Infancy in Uganda*. Baltimore: Johns Hopkins University Press, 1967.

AINSWORTH, MARY, M.D. "Patterns of Attachment Behavior Shown by the Infant in Interaction with His Mother." *Merrill-Palmer Quarterly*, No. 10 (1964), 51–58.

ARMS, SUZANNE. *Immaculate Deception: A New Look at Women and Childbirth in America*. Boston: Houghton Mifflin Co., 1975.

BATESON, GREGORY. *Mind and Nature: A Necessary Unity*. New York: E. P. Dutton, 1979.

BELSKY, JAY. "Child Maltreatment: An Ecological Integration." *American Psychologist* 35, No. 4 (April 1980), 320–335.

BERNARD, J., and L. SONTAG. "Fetal Reactions to Sound." *Journal of Genetic Psychology*, No. 70 (1947), 209–210.

BERTALANFFY, LUDWIG VON. *A Systems View of Man*. Ed. Paul LaVoilette. Boulder, Colo.: Westview Press, 1981.

BOHM, DAVID. *Causality and Chance in Modern Physics*. Philadelphia: University of Pennsylvania Press, 1971.

BOHM, DAVID. *Wholeness and the Implicate Order*. London: Routledge & Kegan Paul, 1979.

BOHM, DAVID. "Insight, Knowledge, Science and Human Values." In *Education and Values*, ed. Douglas Sloan. New York: Teachers College Press, Columbia University, 1980.

BOWER, T. G. R. "The Visual World of the Infant." *Scientific American*, December 1966.

BOWLBY, J. "The Child's Tie to His Mother: Attachment Behavior." In *Attachment*. New York: Basic Books, 1969.

BRACKBILL, YVONNE. "Effects of Obstetric Drugs on Human Development." Presented at the conference, Obstetrical Management and Infant Outcome, American Foundation for Maternal and Child Health, November 1979.

BRUNER, JEROME. "Processes of Growth in Infancy." In *Stimulation in Early Infancy*, ed. A. Ambrose. London: Academic Press, 1969.

CARTWRIGHT, ROSALIND D. *Night Life: Explorations in Dreaming*. Englewood Cliffs, N.J.: Prentice-Hall, 1977.

CARTWRIGHT, ROSALIND D. *Primer on Sleep and Dreaming*. Reading, Mass.: Addison-Wesley, 1978.

CASSIRER, ERNST. *Language and Myth*. New York: Harper & Row, 1946.

CASTANEDA, CARLOS. *The Eagle's Gift*. New York: Simon & Schuster, 1980.

CASTANEDA, CARLOS. *The Teachings of Don Juan*. New York: Simon & Schuster, 1970.

CHAGNON, NAPOLEON A. *Yanomama: The Fierce People*. New York: Holt, Rinehart, 1968, p. 52.

CHAMBERLAIN, DAVID. *Consciousness at Birth: A Review of the Empirical Evidence*. Chamberlain Publications, 5164 35th St., San Diego, Ca. 92116.

CHANCE, PAUL. "The Remedial Thinker" (on the work of Reuven Feuerstein). *Psychology Today*, October 1981.

COGHILL, C. E. *Anatomy and the Problem of Behavior*. New York: Harper & Row, 1964.

CONDON, W., and LOUIS SANDER. "Neonate Movement Is Synchronized with Adult Speech: Interactional Participation and Language Acquisition." *Science*, January 1974.

DE BONO, EDWARD. "Teaching Thinking." From a talk to the Fourth World Conference on Gifted and Talented Children, Montreal, 1981.

DE CHATEAU, PETER, and BRITT WIBERG. "Long-Term Effect on Mother-Infant Behavior of Extra Contact During the First Hour Post Partum." *Acta Paediatrix*, 66 (1977), 137–143.

D'SPAGNAT, BERNARD. "The Quantum Theory and Reality." *Scientific American*, November 1979.

DE MAUSE, LLOYD. ed. *The New Psychohistory*. New York: Atcom/The Psychohistory Press, 1975.

DOSSEY, LARRY, M.D. *Space, Time, and Medicine*. Boulder, Colorado: Shambhala, 1982.

DURANT, WILL. *The Story of Civilization*. Part I, *Our Oriental Heritage*. New York: Simon & Schuster, 1935.

EPSTEIN, HERMAN. "Brain Growth Spurts." *On the Beam: New Horizons for Learning*, I, No. 2 (April 1981).

EPSTEIN, HERMAN. "Phrenoblysis: Special Brain and Mind Growth Periods." *Developmental Psychobiology*. New York: John Wiley & Sons, 1974.

FANTZ, ROBERT L. "The Origin of Form Perception." *Scientific American*, May 1961.

FANTZ, ROBERT L. "Pattern Vision in Young Infants." *Psychological Review*, No. 8 (1958), 43–47.

FEINBERG, LEONARD. "Fire Walking in Ceylon." *Atlantic Monthly*, May 1959.

FODOR, J. A. "Speech Discrimination in Infants." *Perception and Psychophysics* 18, No. 2 (1975), 74–78.

FOULKES, DAVID. "Longitudinal Studies of Dreams in Children." *Dream Dynamics*, ed. J. H. Masserman. New York: Grune and Stratton, 1971.

FRENCH, J. D. "The Reticular Formation." *Scientific American*, May 1957.

FRENCH, R. M. (trans.) *The Way of a Pilgrim*. New York: Seabury Press, 1965.

FRYE, NORTHROP. *Fearful Symmetry: A Study of William Blake*. Princeton: Princeton University Press, 1947.

GARDNER, HOWARD. "The Making of a Storyteller." *Psychology Today*, March 1982.

GARDNER, LYTT I. "Deprivation Dwarfism." *Scientific American*, July 1972.

GEBER, MARCELLE. "The Psycho-Motor Development of African Children in the First Year and the Influence of Maternal Behavior." *Journal of Social Psychology*, No. 47 (1958), 185–195.

GRAY, P. H. Imprinting in Infants." *Journal of Psychology*, No. 46 (1958).

GRAY, WILLIAM. "Understanding Creative Thought Processes: An Early Formulation of the Emotional-Cognitive Structure Theory." *Man-Environment Systems*, No. 9 (1979).

GREGORY, R. E. *Eye and Brain: The Psychology of Seeing.* New York: McGraw-Hill, 1966.

GROF, STANISLAV, M.D. *Realms of the Human Unconscious.* New York: E. P. Dutton, 1976.

HAICH, ELISABETH. *Sexual Energy and Yoga.* London: Allen & Unwin, 1971.

HALES, D., B. LOZOF. R. SOSA, and J. KENNELL. "Defining the Limits of the Maternal Sensitive Period." *Developmental Medicine and Child Neurology,* 19, No. 4 (August 1977), 454–461.

HARLOW, HARRY F. "Love in Infant Monkeys." "*Scientific American,* June 1959.

HARLOW, HARRY F., and MARGARET HARLOW. "Social Deprivation in Monkeys." *Scientific American,* November 1962.

HASTED, JOHN. *Metal-Benders.* London: Routledge & Kegan Paul, 1981.

HERRIGEL, EUGEN. *Zen in the Art of Archery.* New York: Pantheon Books, 1953.

HULL, DAVID, MARSHALL KLAUS, and JOHN H. KENNELL. "Parent-to-Infant Attachment." *Recent Advances in Paediatrics,* No. 5 (1976).

JAHN, ROBERT G. "The Persistent Paradox of Psychic Phenomena: An Engineering Perspective." *Proceedings of the IEEE* 70, No. 2 (February 1982).

JENSEN, ADOLF A. *Myth and Cult Among Primitive Peoples.* Chicago: University of Chicago Press, 1963.

JONES, BLURTON N. *Ethological Studies of Child Behavior.* New York: Cambridge University Press, 1972.

JOSEPHSON, BRIAN. "Possible Connections Between Psychic Phenomena and Quantum Mechanics." *The Academy* 14, No. 4 (December 1975).

JOSEPHSON, B. D., and V. S. RAMACHANDRA, eds. *Consciousness and the Physical World.* Elmsford, N.Y.: Pergamon Press, 1980.

KAFATOS, MINAS, and ROBERT NADEAU. "The General Principle of Complementarity." (A paper on the macrocosmic applications of quantum physics currently in preparation for publication.)

KATZ, RICHARD. *Boiling Energy: Community Healing Among the Kalahari Kung.* Cambridge, Mass.: Harvard University Press, 1982.

KAUFMAN, C., and L. ROSENBLOOM. "Depression in Infant Monkeys." *Science*, February 1967.

KENNELL, JOHN H., M.D., and MARSHALL H. KLAUS, M.D. "Early Mother-Infant Contact: Effects on Breastfeeding." *Breastfeeding and Food Policy in a Hungry World*. New York: Academic Press, 1979.

KENNELL, JOHN H., M.D., and MARSHALL H. KLAUS, M.D. "Early Mother-Infant Contact: Effects on the Mother and the Infant." *Bulletin of the Menninger Clinic* 43, No. 1 (1979), 69–78.

KENNELL, JOHN H., M.D., MARY ANNE TRAUSE, and MARSHALL H. KLAUS, M.D. "Evidence for a Sensitive Period in the Human Mother." *Parent-Infant Interaction*. CIBA Foundation Symposium 33, 1975.

KLAUS, MARSHALL, M.D. "Human Maternal Behavior at the First Contact with Her Young." *Pediatrics* 46, No. 2 (1970), 187–192.

KLAUS, MARSHALL, M.D. "Maternal Attachment: Importance of the First Post-Partum Days." *New England Journal of Medicine*, No. 9 (1972), 286.

KOESTLER, ARTHUR. *Janus: A Summing Up*. New York: Random House, 1978.

KRIPKE, D. F. "Ultradian Rhythms in Sleep and Wakefulness." *Advances in Sleep Research*, Vol. 1, ed. E. Weitzman. New York: Spectrum.

KRISHNA, GOPI. *Higher Consciousness*. Bombay: Taraporevala Sons & Co., 1974.

KRISHNA, GOPI. *The Awakening of Kundalini*. Bombay: Taraporevala, 1976.

LASKI, MARGHARITA. *Ecstasy: A Study of Some Secular and Religious Experiences*. Bloomington: Indiana University Press, 1962.

LAVOILETTE, PAUL A. "The Thermodynamics of the 'Aha!' Experience." Presented at the 24th Annual North American Meeting of the Society for General Systems Research, Symposium on Psychotherapy, Mind and Brain. San Francisco, Jan. 10, 1980.

LAVOILETTE, PAUL A. "Thoughts About Thoughts About Thoughts: The Emotional-Perceptive Cycle Theory." *Man-Environment Systems* 9, No. 1 (January 1979).

LEBOYER, FREDERICK. *Birth Without Violence*. New York: Alfred Knopf, 1974.

LEHRS, ERNST. *Man or Matter*. London: Faber & Faber, 1958.

LEONARD, GEORGE. *The Silent Pulse*. New York: E. P. Dutton, 1978.

LERNER, MICHAEL. "The Nutrition–Juvenile Delinquency Connection." *Medical Self-Care*, Summer 1982.

LEVINE, SEYMOUR. "Stimulation in Infancy." *Scientific American*, May 1960.

LEWIN, ROGER. "Is Your Brain Really Necessary?" (on the work of John Lorber). *Science*, December 12, 1980.

LOZOFF, B., M.D. "The Mother-Newborn Relationship: Limits of Adaptability." *Pediatrics* 91, No. 1, 1–12.

LUCE, GAY GAER. *Current Research in Sleep and Dreams*. Public Health Service Publication No. 1389.

LURIA, ALEXANDER R. *The Role of Speech in Normal and Abnormal Behavior*. New York: Liveright, 1961.

MACLEAN, PAUL. *A Triune Concept of the Brain and Behavior*, ed. D. Campbell and T. J. Boag. The Clarence M. Hincks Memorial Lecture Series. Toronto: University of Toronto Press, 1973.

MANDER, JERRY. *Four Arguments for the Elimination of Television*. New York: William Morrow and Co., 1977.

MANNING, MATHEW. *The Link*. London: Van Duren Press, 1975.

MARTIN, HUGH. *Relativity—The Real Story*. (Manuscript in preparation.)

MASSIE, HENRY, M.D. "The Early Natural History of Childhood Psychosis," Mt. Zion Hospital, San Francisco, Calif., 1977. Typescript.

MITCHELL, GARY. "What Monkeys Can Tell Us About Human Violence." *The Futurist*, April 1975.

MONROE, ROBERT. *Journeys Out of the Body*. New York: Doubleday & Co., 1973.

MONTAGU, ASHLEY. *Touching: The Human Significance of the Skin*. New York: Columbia University Press, 1971.

MONTAGU, ASHLEY. *Life Before Birth*. New York: New American Library, 1964.

MONTAGU, ASHLEY. *Prenatal Influences*, Springfield: Charles C. Thomas, 1962.

MOWATT, FARLEY. *Never Cry Wolf*. New York: Bantam, 1984.

MUKTANANDA, SWAMI. *Mystery of the Mind*. South Fallsburg, N.Y.: SYDA, 1981.

MUKTANANDA, SWAMI. *The Perfect Relationship*. South Fallsburg, N.Y.: SYDA, 1980.

MUKTANANDA, SWAMI. *Play of Consciousness*. South Fallsburg,
N.Y.: SYDA, 1980.

MUKTANANDA, SWAMI. *Where Are You Going?* South Fallsburg,
N.Y.: SYDA, 1982.

NAMBIAR, O.K. *Mahayogi Walt Whitman: New Light on Yoga*.
Bangalore, India: Jeevan Publications, 1978.

ODENT, MICHAEL, M.D. "The Evolution of Obstetrics at
Pithiviers." *Birth and the Family Journal* 8, No. 1 (Spring
1981).

PAGELS, ELAINE. *The Gnostic Gospels*. New York: Random
House, 1979.

PAYNE-AYERS, LARRY, and ROBIN LESLIE. *On Underwater Birthing: A Birth Story*. Privately printed; available from the
authors, 150 Calle del Monte, Sonoma, Calif. 95476.

PEARCE, JOSEPH C. *Bond of Power*. New York: E. P. Dutton,
1981.

PEARCE, JOSEPH C. *The Crack in the Cosmic Egg*. New York:
Simon & Schuster, 1971.

PEARCE, JOSEPH C. *Exploring the Crack in the Cosmic Egg*.
New York: Simon & Schuster, 1974.

PEARCE, JOSEPH C. *Magical Child*. New York: E. P. Dutton,
1977.

PEARCE, JOSEPH C. "Nurturing Intelligence: The Other Side
of Nutrition." Address at 1982 Oxford University, World
Health Organization, and MacCarrison Medical Society
Conference on Nutrition and Childbirth. See *Nutrition
and Health* I (1983), 143–152. London: A. B. Academic
Publishers.

PENFIELD, WILDER. *The Mystery of the Mind: A Critical Study
of Consciousness and the Human Brain*. Princeton:
Princeton University Press, 1975.

PETERSON, JAMES. *Some Profiles of Non-Ordinary Perception
of Children*. Unpublished seminar study. University of
California, Berkeley, 1974.

PIAGET, JEAN. *The Child's Conception of the World*. New
York: Humanities Press, 1951.

PIAGET, JEAN. *The Origins of Intelligence in Children*. New
York: International Universities Press, 1952.

PIAGET, JEAN. *Play, Dreams and Imitation in Childhood*. New
York: W. W. Norton, 1962.

PIAGET, JEAN, and B. INHELDER. *The Early Growth of Logic in the Child*. Atlantic Highlands, New Jersey: Humanities Press, 1964.

PINES, MAYA. *The Brain Changers—Scientists and the New Mind Control*. New York: Harcourt Brace Jovanovich, 1973.

POLANSKY, NORMAN. *Profile of Neglect: A Survey of the State of Knowledge of Child Neglect*. U.S. Dept. of Health, Education and Welfare, Community Services Administration, 1975.

PREM, KRISHNA. *Initiation into Yoga: An Introduction to the Spiritual Life*. Bombay: B. I. Publications, 1976.

PREM, KRISHNA. *The Yoga of the Bhagavad Gita*. Baltimore: Penguin Books, 1973.

PREM, KRISHNA. *The Yoga of the Kathopanishad*. London: John M. Watkins, 1955.

PRESCOTT, JAMES. "Body Pleasure and the Origins of Violence." *The Futurist*, April 1975.

PROPP, VLADIMIR. *Morphology of the Folktale*. Austin: University of Texas Press, 1968.

REYMOND, LIZELLE. *To Live Within: The Story of Five Years with a Himalayan Guru*. Baltimore: Penguin Books, 1973.

RIMLAND, BERNARD. *Infantile Autism*. New York: Appleton-Century-Crofts, 1964.

RINGLER, NORMA, MARY TRAUSE, MARSHALL KLAUS, M.D., and JOHN KENNELL, M.D. "The Effects of Extra Post-Partum Contact and Maternal Speech Patterns on Children's IQs, Speech, and Language Comprehension at Five." *Child Development* 49 (1978): 862–65.

ROBINSON, JAMES M., ed. *The Nag Hammid Library (The Gnostic Gospels)*. New York: Harper & Row, 1977.

ROCHLIN, GREGORY. "The Dread of Abandonment: A Contribution to the Etiology of the Loss Complex and to Depression." *The Psychoanalytic Study of the Child*, Vol. 16. New York: International University Press, 1961.

RUSSELL, PETER. *The Global Brain*. Los Angeles: J. P. Tarcher, 1983.

SALLEY, R. "REM Sleep Phenomena During Out-of-the-Body Experiences." *Journal of the American Society for Psychical Research*, April 1982.

SANNELLA, LEE, M.D. *Kundalini—Psychosis or Transcendence?* San Francisco: Dakin, 1976.

SCOTT, MARY. *Kundalini in the Physical World*. London: Routledge & Kegan Paul, 1983.

SCOTT, MARY. *Science and Subtle Bodies: Towards a Clarification of Issues*. London: College of Psychic Studies, 1975.

SERRANO, MIGUEL. *Serpent of Paradise: The Story of an Indian Pilgrimage*. London: Routledge & Kegan Paul, 1983.

SERRANO, MIGUEL. *C. G. Jung and Herman Hesse: A Story of Two Friendships*. London: Schocken Books, 1968.

SHAH, IDRIES. *The Way of the Sufi*. Middlesex, England: Penguin, 1974.

SHELDRAKE, RUPERT. *A New Science of Life: The Hypothesis of Formative Causation*, Los Angeles: J. P. Tarcher, 1981.

SIMEON, SAINT. "Practical and Theological Precepts." *Philokalia, The Complete Text,* compiled by St. Nikodimos of the Holy Mountain and St. Markarios of Corinth. Trans. G. E. Palmer and Philip Sherrard. London: Faber and Faber, 1983.

SINGH, JAIDEVA. *Siva Sutras—The Yoga of Supreme Identity*. Delhi: Motilal Banarsidass, 1979.

SPERRY, ROGER W. "Conscious Phenomena as Direct Emergent Properties of the Brain." *Psychological Review* 77, No. 6 (November 1970).

SPITZ, RENE. *The First Year of Life: A Psychoanalytic Study of Normal and Deviant Development of Object Relations*. New York: International University Press, 1965.

STALLIBRASS, ALISON. "Child Development and Education: The Contribution of the Peckham Experiment." In *Nutrition and Health*, Vol. 1. London: A. B. Academic Publishers, 1982, pp. 45–52.

STALLIBRASS, ALISON. *The Self-Respecting Child: A Study of Children's Play and Development*. Middlesex, England: Penguin Books, 1974.

STRAUCH, RALPH. *The Reality Illusion*. Wheaton, Ill.: Theosophical Publishing House, 1983.

TART, CHARLES. *Altered States of Consciousness*. New York: John Wiley, 1969.

TART, CHARLES. "Psychedelic Experiences Associated with a Novel Hypnotic Procedure: Mutual Hypnosis." *American Journal of Clinical Hypnosis*, No. 10 (1967), 65–78.

TART, CHARLES. *Scientific Studies of the Psychic Realm*. New York: E. P. Dutton, 1977.

TART, CHARLES, HAROLD PUTHOF, and RUSSELL TARG, eds. *Mind at Large*. New York: Praeger, 1980.

TINBERGEN, NIKOS. "Ethology and Stress Disease." *Science*, July 5, 1974.

TOWBIN, ABRAHAM, M.D. "Birth Spinal Injury and Sudden Infant Death." My reference from the Spartanburg, S.C., *Journal*, March 2, 1968.

TURNBULL, COLIN. *The Forest People*. New York: Simon & Schuster, 1961.

TWEEDIE, IRINA. *The Chasm of Fire*. Tisbury, Wiltshire, England: Element Books, 1979.

VERNY, THOMAS, with JOHN KELLY. *The Secret Life of the Unborn Child*. New York: Summit/Simon & Schuster, 1981.

VYGOTSKY, L. S. *Mind in Society: The Development of Higher Psychological Processes*. Cambridge: Harvard University Press, 1978.

WERNTZ, DEBORAH, REGINALD G. BICKFORD, FLOYD BLOOM, and DAVID SHANNAHOFF SINGH KHALSAN. "Selective Cortical Activation by Altering Autonomic Function." Presented at the Western EEG Society, February 1981; *EEG Journal*, forthcoming.

WEST, JOHN ANTHONY. *Serpent in the Sky: The High Wisdom of Ancient Egypt*. New York: Harper & Row, 1979.

WHITE, BURTON L. *The First Three Years of Life*. Englewood Cliffs, N.J.: Prentice-Hall, 1975.

WHITE, LESLIE A. *A Science of Culture; a Study of Man and Civilization*. New York: Noonday Press, 1969.

WHITTLESTONE, W. G. "The Physiology of Early Attachment in Mammals: Implications for Human Obstetric Care." *The Medical Journal of Australia*, Vol. 1 (January 14, 1978), 50–53.

WICKES, FRANCES. *The Inner World of Childhood*. New York: Appleton-Century-Crofts, 1968.

WILBER, KEN, ed. *The Holographic Paradigm—and Other Paradoxes*. Boulder, Colo.: Shambala, 1982.

WILLIAMSON, SCOTT G., and INNES H. PEARSE. *Science, Synthesis and Sanity, an Enquiry into the Nature of Living*. Edinburgh: Scottish Academic Press, 1980.

WILSON, SHERYL C., and THEODORE S. BARBER. "Vivid Fantasy and Hallucinatory Abilities in the Life Histories of Excellent Hypnotic Subjects: Preliminary Report with Female Subjects." Paper presented at the Annual Meeting of the American Association for the Study of Mental Imagery, Minneapolis, June 20, 1980.

WINDLE, W. F. "Brain Damage by Asphyxia." *Scientific American*, October 1969.

WOODROFFE, JOHN. *Serpent Power*. Auromere, India: Ganesh & Co., 1980.

YOGANANDA, PARAMAHANSA. *Autobiography of a Yogi*. Los Angeles: Self-Realization Fellowship, 1946.

YU, HU MON. "Teaching and Learning Elementary Mathematics." *Education Network News* 2, No. 6 (July-August 1983).

ZASLOW, R. W. *Resistance to Human Attachment and Growth: Autism to Retardation*. Los Gatos, Calif.: Nova Press, 1970.

Miscellaneous Articles from the Brain/Mind Bulletin:

1. "Adrenaline Stimulates 'Unconscious Learning'—Brain Integrates Sophisticated Information Without Cognitive Activity," 9, No. 7 (March 26, 1984).

2. "Bilateral 'Synch' Key to Intuition?" Themepack No. 15, Vol. V.

3. "Blindsight Ability Raises Questions About Awareness." Themepack No. 15, Vols. I and II.

4. "Body Clocks: Bonding, Sexuality, Hospitalization," 7, No. 15 (September 13, 1982).

5. "Canadian Study Frames New Right-Left Paradigm," 8, No. 7 (March 28, 1983).

6. "Cognitive Complexity and Emotional Range," 7, No. 6 (March 8, 1982).

7. "Congenitally Blind Use Own Version of Imagery," 8, No. 9 (May 9, 1983).

8. "Conversations Between Heart and Brain." Themepack No. 15, Vol. III

9. "500,000 Papers Published Yearly on Brain/Mind Research." Themepack No. 5, Vols. I and II.

10. "French Research Links Hearing to Body Dynamics," 8, No. 4 (January 24, 1983).

11. "Holophonic Sound Broadcasts Directly to Brain," 8, No. 10 (May 30, 1982).
12. "Lucid Dream Sharing," 7, No. 15 (September 13, 1982).
13. "Melanin as Key Organizing Molecule," 8, Nos. 12–13 (July 11 and August 1, 1983).
14. "Multiple Personalities Proof of Brain's Versatility," 8, No. 16 (October 3, 1983).
15. "Out-of-Body Incidents Calming." Themepack No. 5, Vol. III.
16. "Quizzing the Hidden Observer." Themepack No. 5, Vol. III.
17. "Recent Studies Show Strong Role for Unconscious in Everyday Life," 9, No. 6 (March 5, 1984).
18. "Stressed Female Rats Produce Deviant Males." Themepack No. 15, Vol. V.
19. "Triune Theory Describes Brain Hierarchy." Themepack No. 15, Vols. I and II.
20. "Universal Forms of Hallucination Aid Brain Research." Themepack No. 15, Vol. V.

For further information, write:
>Brain/Mind Bulletin
>P.O. Box 42211
>Los Angeles, Calif. 90042.

Articles on Underwater Birthing:

"Nonviolent Birth Underwater." Los Angeles *Times*, December 11, 1981.
"Underwater Birthing Reduces 'Primal Trauma.' " Los Angeles *Herald Examiner*, March 31, 1982.
"Underwater Delivery." San Diego *Tribune*, January 5, 1982.
"Giving Birth Underwater." *Newsweek*, January 16, 1984.

For further information, write:
>Rainbow Dolphin Centre
>Wharau Road
>Kerikeri, New Zealand

>Attention: Esthelle Myers.

Index

About the Author

JOSEPH CHILTON PEARCE is the author of *The Crack in the Cosmic Egg, Exploring the Crack in the Cosmic Egg, Magical Child,* and *The Bond of Power.* A former humanities teacher, he now lectures frequently throughout the world on the subject of the Magical Child.

BANTAM NEW AGE BOOKS

Bantam New Age Books are for all those interested in reflecting on life today and life as it may be in the future. This important new imprint features stimulating works in fields from biology and psychology to philosophy and the new physics.

☐	25881	**MAGICAL CHILD MATURES** Joseph C. Pearce	$4.50
☐	25388	**DON'T SHOOT THE DOG** Karen Pryor	$3.95
☐	25344	**SUPERMIND: THE ULTIMATE ENERGY** Barbara B. Brown	$4.95
☐	24147	**CREATIVE VISUALIZATION** Shakti Gawain	$3.95
☐	24903	**NEW RULES: SEARCHING FOR SELF-FULFILLMENT** **IN A WORLD TURNED UPSIDE DOWN** Daniel Yankelovich	$4.50
☐	25223	**STRESS AND THE ART OF BIOFEEDBACK** Barbara Brown	$4.95
☐	26076	**MAGICAL CHILD** Joseph Chilton Pearce	$4.50
☐	25748	**ZEN/MOTORCYCLE MAINTENANCE** Robert Pirsig	$4.95
☐	25982	**THE WAY OF THE SHAMAN** Michael Harner	$4.50
☐	25437	**TO HAVE OR TO BE** Fromm	$4.50
☐	24562	**LIVES OF A CELL** Lewis Thomas	$3.95
☐	14912	**KISS SLEEPING BEAUTY GOODBYE** K. Kolbenschlag	$3.95

Prices and availability subject to change without notice.